STRATEGIC
MANAGEMENT

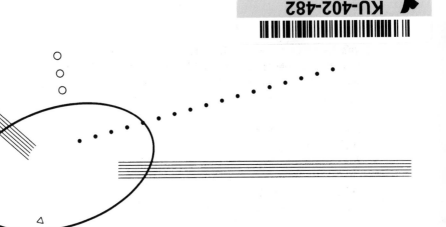

A
Stakeholder
Approach

R. Edward Freeman
University of Minnesota

CAMBRIDGE UNIVERSITY PRESS
Cambridge, New York, Melbourne, Madrid, Cape Town, Singapore,
São Paulo, Delhi, Dubai, Tokyo

Cambridge University Press
The Edinburgh Building, Cambridge CB2 8RU, UK

Published in the United States of America by Cambridge University Press, New York

www.cambridge.org
Information on this title: www.cambridge.org/9780521151740

© Cambridge University Press 2010

First published under the Pitman Publishing imprint in 1984
This digitally printed version by Cambridge University Press 2010

A catalogue record for this publication is available from the British Library

ISBN 978-0-521-15174-0 Paperback

PREFACE TO THE 2010 REISSUE

When I sat down to write *Strategic Management: A Stakeholder Approach* in June of 1982 I had no idea that it would still be relevant to business scholars and practitioners some 25 years later. I was summarizing the work of many business thinkers such as Russell Ackoff, Jim Emshoff, Eric Rhenman, Eric Trist, and others and stating what I took to be obvious and plain, common sense. Managers had to deal with those groups and individuals that could affect or be affected by their company, i.e., stakeholders. That seemed to me, and still does, to be the essence of strategic thinking.

Many people found this idea to be radical. By placing "stakeholder" in the center of strategic thinking, the unit of analysis is changed to a more relational view of business. "Stakeholder management" didn't make the usual distinctions between "economic" and "social", or "business" and "non business". It is ironic that the scholars who have used and developed the idea the most were those in corporate social responsibility. I argued in the book, and continue to believe, that "social responsibility" is one of those ideas that prop up a story about business that is no longer useful. I am most thankful that thousands of managers who have been students in my seminars over the years have found a measure of usefulness in the idea of stakeholder management. It is now "old hat" in many areas of business.

Yet, we still need a new story about business. The recent global financial crisis has made this plain. I believe that the central characters in that story must be companies and their customers, employees, suppliers, communities, and financiers. Other groups such as NGOs, governments, unions, etc. may also be important to particular businesses. The idea that one of these groups (financiers, for instance) always has priority over the others, simply misses the main contribution of business and capitalism. Business works because the interests of all of these stakeholders can be satisfied over time. It is the intersection of these interests which is central to effective and sustainable stakeholder management.

Many people have suggested that dealing with multiple stakeholders leads to trade-offs and conflict. I have come to believe that this is the wrong focus for a "stakeholder theory of business". Where stakeholder interests conflict there is an opportunity for "value creation". Where critics raise issues about products and services and company behaviour, there is yet another opportunity for value creation. In this book I focused too much on the conflicts among multiple stakeholders rather than on finding integrative products, services, and behaviours that dissolve those conflicts. This new narrative about business must also be one of "business in society". It needs to place a concern with ethics, responsibility, and sustainability on a par with profits. All are important and none can be ignored. More than ever, we need a story about "responsible capitalism".

I believe that the stakeholder approach, and the research of the scholars who have developed this idea over the last 25 years is a good place to start. My colleagues and I have summarized this work in Freeman, Jeffrey Harrison, Andrew Wicks, Bidhan Parmar, and Simone de Colle, *Stakeholder Theory: The State of the Art* (Cambridge University Press, 2010). I have received far too much credit for the development of the stakeholder approach to business. It was in the DNA of the Wharton Applied Research Center and the Busch Center at Wharton in the late 1970s and early 1980s. The work of many scholars has begun to put the idea into the DNA of business theory and practice. It is for them that I am thankful to my editor, Paula Parish and the team at Cambridge University Press for re-issuing this book.

R. Edward Freeman
October 2009

'Twas brillig, and the slithy toves
Did gyre and gimble in the wabe:
All mimsy were the borogoves,
    And the mome raths outgrabe.
— From *Through The Looking Glass,*
Lewis Carroll

PREFACE

Managers in today's corporation are under fire. Throughout the world, their ability to manage the affairs of the corporation is being called into question. The emergence of a multitude of government regulations, corporate critics, media attacks, and most importantly, substantial competition from Far Eastern and European firms have put the modern manager in a pressure cooker. He or she finds an increase in the external demands placed on the corporation and a decrease in the internal flexibility of the corporation to respond. Criteria for performance are no longer clear and the notion of "effective management" is increasingly becoming a contradiction in terms.

Meanwhile, the "solutions" to the dilemma of the modern manager dominate the best-seller lists. Lessons from Japanese, U.S. and European companies are drawn; the latest techniques from psychology are touted to solve the "people problem"; ringing cries are issued for less government, givebacks by labor and a new industrial policy; and managers are urged to work harder and longer, take more courses, learn the latest techniques and to focus on rebuilding their companies to be more competitive in global markets.

I believe that these current analyses of the managerial dilemma are only partially correct. And, I believe that the underlying issue is that managers must have new concepts that enable them to see their jobs realistically. These new concepts must help managers view the world as it is *today,* not as it was 30 years ago. The sociologist R.S. Lynd put it quite well in his 1939 book, *Knowledge for What* (Princeton: Princeton University Press, p. 207);

> If praying to the gods for rain does not increase the fertility of our fields, it avails little to redouble our prayers or to make alterations in their wording; we would better turn our energies to the techniques of agriculture.

This book is about a concept which begins to turn managerial energies in the right direction: the concept of "stakeholders." Simply put, a stakeholder is any group or individual who can affect, or is affected by, the achievement of a corporation's purpose. Stakeholders include employees, customers, suppliers, stockholders, banks, environmentalists, government and other groups who can help or hurt the corporation. The stakeholder concept provides a new way of thinking about strategic management — that is, how a corporation can and should set and implement direction. By paying attention to strategic management, executives can begin to put their corporations back on the road to success.

This book is a result of a project begun at The Wharton School in 1977 under the auspices of the Wharton Applied Research Center and continued within the Policy and Strategy Implementation Research Program in the Department of Management at Wharton. I have been extremely fortunate to have a supportive and intellectually stimulating environment in which to work on the ideas expressed here. Also, each unit has provided necessary funds where appropriate. In particular, several Directors and Senior Staff members of the Applied Research Center have been helpful. I must express gratitude to Jim Emshoff, Arthur Finnel, Vinnie Carroll, Bob Banker, Bob Mittlestadt, Bill Hamilton and others who have contributed a great deal to this book during the course of its development. I have been even luckier to come upon a number of outstanding research assistants, "SRAs," and students who have spent countless hours talking with me about the stakeholder approach to strategy. Most of these students are now successful executives in their own right. Of particular note are Emily Susskind, Mark Kramer, Marci Plaskow, Lisa Armstrong, Sally Schreiber, Loretta Murphy, Arthur Cohen, Roberta Wilensky, Ellen West, David Ontko and Jim Sayre, all of whom prepared drafts of cases and briefing papers which serve as a large part of the empirical basis for this book. Marci Plaskow was especially diligent in bringing relevant articles to my attention over a two year span. David Reed collaborated with me on a paper that serves as a basis for Chapter 7, as well as other ideas. David's knowledge of the U.S. business world is phenomenal, and his ability to apply the stakeholder concept to many different problems helped me to see the logic of the concept. Larry Richards worked with me on applying the stakeholder audit concept developed in Chapter 4 in several organizations. Jill Goldman, Joyce Ackerman and Jeff Belanoff volunteered their time to critique a number of papers, cases and ideas. And, a number of undergraduate and graduate students at the University of Pennsylvania have been helpful. Perhaps Gordon Sollars is owed the biggest intellectual debt. Without the benefit of his attention and his lively mind, I would not have written this book, even though he may be appalled by the final content.

My colleagues at the Department of Management have been equally helpful. John Lubin has encouraged me to develop the stakeholder approach into a full-blown method for strategic management. Peter Lorange has been instrumental in my understanding of strategic management processes, and I have borrowed heavily from his work. Paul Browne and Bala Chakravarthy have been a constant source of ideas and help. William Evan has forced me to ask a completely different set of questions with regard to the stakeholder concept than those outlined here. This present work has benefitted greatly from our attempt to work out the notion of "management" as "a fiduciary relationship to stakeholders." William Gomberg has taught me not to be afraid of values, or anything else for that matter, and I am grateful for his advice during a course in managerial philosophy with Gomberg and Andy Van de Ven. Greg Shea deserves special thanks for his support. Others in a large and diverse school have been helpful, especially Graham Astley, Tom Dunfee, Charles Fombrun, Dora Futterman, William Lanen, Paul Tiffany, William Hamilton and Joan Zielinski. Professor Robert Wachbroit of the Philosophy Department at Penn has been invaluable in getting me to think more clearly about organizational issues.

I have also benefitted from much help external to the university. Professors Mel Horwitch of MIT; Fred Sturdivant of Ohio State; Jim Post, Henry Morgan, Ted Murray and John Mahon of Boston University; Dan Fenn of Harvard and the Kennedy Library; Barry Mitnick, William King and Aubrey Mendelow of Pittsburgh; John Rosenblum and Alec Horniman of Virginia and Robert Virgil of Washington University have all contributed valuable comments and insights. Andrew Van de Ven of Minnesota must take the blame for "what do you stand for" as inspiring the discussion on enterprise level strategy. Ned McClennen of Washington University deserves credit for my obsession with Prisoner's Dilemma. This book is far better for the careful reading given it by Ed Epstein. His enthusiasm and support together with his scholarly insight into the nature of the corporation have helped a great deal.

During the course of the stakeholder project many organizations and managers have been helpful and supportive. I have talked, in both formal interviews and informally, to several thousand managers over the past five years, and I am grateful for their views on the problems with the external environment and on the stakeholder approach to these problems. In particular Robert Herson, Clem Huffman, Fred Mitchell and Mac McCarthy have been instrumental in the development of these ideas. Ram Charan has taught me a great deal about business. Edwin Hartman has saved me from a number of mistakes, and warned me of several that remain. Bill Roberts and Michael Weinstein of Pitman Publishing have tried to make the book readable.

From 1976 onwards, Jim Emshoff, Dean Donald Carroll and Professor John Lubin of Wharton have been willing to listen to the crazy ideas of a philosopher. I am deeply grateful to them for taking such a risk, and for teaching me about organizational life. So many have been involved in the development of these ideas that I am tempted to blame all of them for the shortcomings and confusions that remain.

My wife and friend, Maureen Wellen, has given me the necessary support to do this research and to actually write this book. I am lucky that in her professional role as a manager she has also been my harshest critic, and it is, of course, to her that this book is dedicated. My IBM Personal Computer, "Dora", and my Osborne 1, "S.G." should take credit for the typing of the manuscript. Sullivan and Simone have graciously stayed out of the way enough to allow this book to be finished.

Princeton Junction
August 1983

CONTENTS

Part I

THE STAKEHOLDER
APPROACH

The purpose of Part I is to explain how a recently emerging concept, "stakeholders in an organization," can be used to enrich the way that we think about our organizations. We will discuss why U.S. managers need new concepts, tools and techniques, and new theories if they are to be successful in the current business environment.

Chapter One, "Managing in Turbulent Times," explores recent environmental shifts, as well as the corporate responses to such shifts. Current approaches to understanding the business environment fail to take account of a wide range of groups who can affect or are affected by the corporation, its "stakeholders." Changes have occurred which make our present framework of the firm inappropriate. We manage based on our understanding of the past, rather than the future, and in response to the business environment of yesteryear, rather than today. This chapter outlines the problem and calls for change in the way that we think about the business organization.

Chapter Two, "The Stakeholder Concept and Strategic Management," introduces the notion that organizations have stakeholders and traces the history of this idea through several research areas of management thought, most notably corporate planning, organization theory, social responsibility, systems theory and strategic management. It strongly suggests that the stakeholder notion can be used to enrich the current state of the art in strategic management, and summarizes the recent empirical research.

Chapter Two is more "academic" than the other chapters, as it concentrates on the intellectual history of the idea rather than its application.

Chapter Three, "Stakeholder Management: Framework and Philosophy," addresses the need to analyze stakeholder issues on three levels: rational, process and transactional. It argues for a framework which "fits" these three levels of analysis together. Techniques for mapping stakeholders, understanding organizational processes, and analyzing interactions with stakeholders are explained. It closes with some basic propositions for successful stakeholder management.

One

"MANAGING IN TURBULENT TIMES"

INTRODUCTION

Bob Collingwood was President and Chief Executive Officer of the U.S. subsidiary of Woodland International, a large multinational company headquartered in Europe. Bob was responsible for all of Woodland's activities in the U.S. His functional responsibilities included manufacturing as well as public affairs, as Woodland was fully integrated in its U.S. operations. Bob was measured on profitability as well as several other financial criteria. As he checked his appointment calendar for the upcoming two weeks, he could see that the schedule listed appointments with one external group after another, with agendas ranging from traditional labor-management issues to concerns with Woodland's social responsibility.

On Monday a state legislature in the Northeast where Woodland had major manufacturing facilities would open two days of hearings on a bill requiring companies to notify the state government before moving a plant out of state. A test marketing program for a new product line would be launched on Thursday, and he needed to be involved with the marketing people on some last minute decisions. On Saturday, the leaders of a coalition of consumer organizations would arrive to hear his talk about the merits and safety of several of Woodland's products. And, on Sunday an environmental group was going to hold a demonstration to protest air pollution caused by a Woodland plant.

The following week Collingwood was scheduled to go to Washington for a meeting concerning his compliance with the newest set of regulatory guidelines. When he returned, he was to meet with one of the local unions about their upcoming new contract. It was rumored that the union leadership had begun plans to unionize Woodland's large "9 to 5" workforce. Following the meeting with the union, Bob would discuss a summer jobs program for unemployed teenagers with several minority group leaders.

The Comptroller's report was also waiting for him on his desk. Sales were down 15 percent. His profit index was 20 percent short of his first quarter goal.

Bob Collingwood had risen rapidly at Woodland International, and was headed for "stardom" in company headquarters in Europe if he so desired. However, Bob did not feel prepared for the diverse mix of situations which he now faced. The dissimilar problems with the varied pressure groups each demanded an instantaneous solution. One, or all, of them could keep Bob and his best people working even longer hours than usual. While his people were both functionally and operationally competent, there just did not seem to be a way to pull the diverse management tasks together.

While Bob and his people had the skills and abilities to meet each situation and to manage the crises when they arose, these skills were insufficient. Bob knew that he needed a framework and a strategy for managing diversity and turbulence, to get out of the crisis-reaction-crisis cycle.

This book is about Bob and the thousands of managers around the world like him who meet all the criteria for "good managers," yet who do not seem able to manage well in today's fast changing business environment. It explains a framework for management, the stakeholder framework, which offers a method for Bob and his colleagues to begin to understand their environment systematically and to begin to manage it in a positive proactive fashion. This book is theoretical in the sense that it develops a generalizable and testable approach to managerial strategic decision-making. However, it is practical in the sense that any theory of strategic decisions must be applicable in "real-world" organizations. The bridge between theory and practice is a difficult one to build. By speaking to both executives and academics, I shall attempt to build such a bridge, for the problems are too important to ignore either side.[1]

TURBULENT TIMES

Both business and service organizations are experiencing turbulence.[2] Local, national and global issues and groups are having far-reaching impacts on organizations. Gone are the "good old days" of worrying only about taking products and services to market, and gone is the usefulness of management theories which concentrate on efficiency and effectiveness within this product-market framework.[3]

Our "world-view" or "paradigm" or "framework" or "way of looking at the world" does not encompass this turbulence.[4] And, in fact our current theories are inconsistent with both the quantity and kinds of change which are occurring in the business environment of the 1980s. Current approaches emphasize the static nature of organizations, and the predictable and relatively certain parts of an organization's external environment.[5] A new conceptual framework is needed.

Somewhere in the past, organizations were quite simple, and "doing business" consisted of buying raw materials from suppliers, converting it to products, and selling it to customers. Exhibit 1.1 depicts this "Production View" of the firm. For the most part owner-entrepreneurs founded such simple businesses and worked at the business along with members of their families. The family-dominated business still accounts for a large proportion of the new business starts today. The central point is that given the Production View as a conceptual framework, the owner-manager-employee need only worry about satisfying suppliers and customers in order to make the business successful.

A number of factors coalesced to make larger and larger firms more economical. The development of new production processes, such as the assembly line, meant that jobs could be specialized and more work could be accomplished. New technologies and sources of power became readily available. Demographic factors began to favor the concentration of production in urban areas. These and other social and political forces combined to require larger amounts of capital, well beyond the scope of most individual owner-manager-employees. Additionally, "workers" or non-family members began to dominate the firm and were the rule rather than the exception. Ex-

EXHIBIT 1.1   *The Production View of the Firm*

ENVIRONMENT

| Suppliers | Resources | Firm | Products | Customers |

ENVIRONMENT

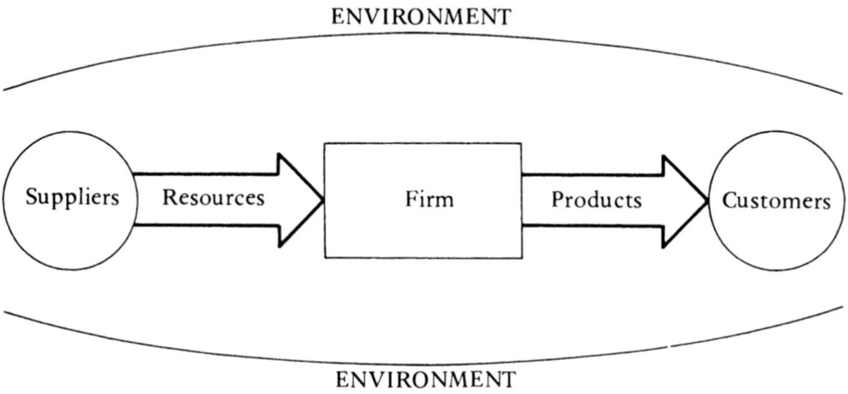

hibit 1.2 depicts the resulting separation of ownership and control, which we might call thė "Managerial View" of the firm. Ownership became more dispersed, as banks, stockholders and other institutions financed the emergence of the modern corporation. In order to be successful, the top managers of the firm had to simultaneously satisfy the owners, the employees and their unions, suppliers and customers.[6]

The conceptual model, depicted by the Managerial View of the firm, is more complicated than the Production View. If a manager only used the Production View to understand the world and managed the business using the concepts and techniques which resulted from it then failure would be the sure result. By paying no attention to owners and employees, each of which now had a stake in the firm, and by having no concepts with which to manage these relationships, managers could guarantee their own demise in the form of new management or debilitating strikes and work stoppages. Success in the "new" environment required a *conceptual shift*. It required

EXHIBIT 1.2   *The Managerial View of the Firm*

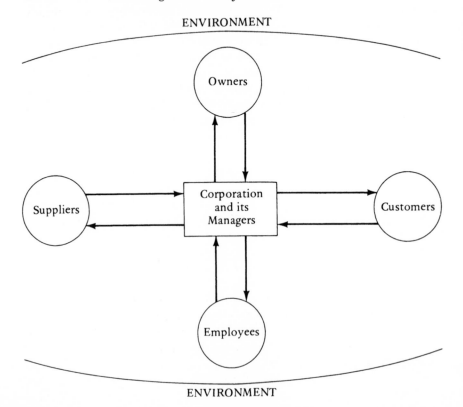

the adoption of new concepts and ideas which dealt with owners and employees as a matter of everyday occurrence rather than as an exception.

An analogy of such a conceptual shift being necessary may help us. Suppose that you make a New Year's resolution to do a better job of cleaning up your office. You buy a file drawer and construct a set of "categories" into which you file all of your important papers, memos and reports. Each file is carefully labeled, and let us suppose that you are religious in your zeal to keep your desk clean and your papers filed. You find that your system works quite well for some time, but you notice that as time passes the file labeled "MISCELLANEOUS" keeps getting larger and larger. You have to add new files with new categories, some of which overlap the old set of categories. Cross-referencing becomes such a nightmare that you and your secretary finally give up.

Furthermore, you find that some of your files are no longer used. You make very few additions or deletions to these old files. If these problems are left unsolved, pretty soon your filing system becomes a mess. You can't find anything "important" anymore. Your files have become an effective way of dealing with the past, but not the present and future. Your desk soon reassumes its cluttered look and you must make another effort to start over at the New Year.[7]

What went wrong in this simple example? Your filing system became obsolete as changes took place in the world around you. Patching up the system by adding new files worked for a while, but eventually the whole file drawer needed to be "rethought," and a newer more appropriate set of files and categories needed to be established. In short you were in need of a conceptual revolution.

Managers in the modern corporation are in a similar position. We are in need of new concepts, new "conceptual filing systems," which reorient our way of looking at the world to encompass present and future changes. Piecemeal solutions such as calls for "increased productivity" using Japanese or European or Theory N techniques are not the answer, for they only add, subtract or refile some of the issues that need addressing. Likewise, calls for business-government-labor cooperation are only part of a solution. Such proposals for "an industrial policy" do not address the underlying conceptual revolution that is necessary.

I believe that Exhibit 1.2 is a picture of the predominant framework for the modern corporation. The corporation is viewed as a resource-conversion entity, taking raw materials and converting them into products, with dollars measuring the transactions. Returns are provided to owners in the forms of dividends or capital appreciation in the marketplace. Wages, benefits, and oftentimes job security, are provided to employees. Clearly, Exhibit 1.2 is inappropriate for the current state of the modern corporation.[8]

There have been varying degrees of recognition of the external environment which surrounds this resource-conversion entity called the modern corporation. Many have argued, from Adam Smith (1759) onward, that business is a social institution, but that its role can only be realized by an external environment which allows "laissez faire capitalism." Such a policy requires that the dominant mode of thought be oriented towards "production," while recognizing, or at least saying, that business is a social institution. On the other hand, there have been calls for the nationalization of business activity on the grounds that the modern corporation is too far removed from its social roots.[9]

Both approaches seem to miss the mark. I believe that we need to more carefully understand the causes of this external turbulence and to construct a framework which allows managers to more effectively handle turbulent external environments. The turbulence that business managers have experienced in recent years can be understood as coming from two main sources. The first, I shall call "internal change," or the changes in the relationships depicted in Exhibit 1.2. The second source of turbulence is "external change," or change in the very nature of the picture in Exhibit 1.2, so that it is no longer an appropriate picture of the external environment of the modern corporation.[10] The changes that I shall catalog have not occurred all at once, nor are some of them even recent. The problem is that our conceptual system that we use to understand and deal with these issues is no longer valid. External turbulence is nothing new to managers in business. What is necessary is the development of a theory, or picture, of the world which allows us to manage these changes more effectively. We need a new filing system.

INTERNAL CHANGE

Change has occurred in each of the relationships in Exhibit 1.2. Such changes are internal to the conceptual system that the Managerial View represents. Internal change requires us to constantly reassess current objectives and policies in light of new demands by groups that we are used to dealing with such as customers, employees and their unions, stockholders and suppliers. Internal change requires action, but it does not directly challenge our conceptual map of the world.[11] Internal change occurs within the current "filing system"; it happens according to well-understood rules; and, difficult as it is, internal change is what we are used to dealing with on a daily basis. Let's see some examples of the internal changes that have occurred over the past few years.

Owners

No longer can management assume that the primary concern of those who own shares of stock is return on investment. The 1960s were a ripe period for owners who wanted not only returns, but control as well. Thus, the Wall Street Rule, "If you don't like the management, sell the stock," was turned on its head to "If you don't like the management, buy enough stock to throw the bums out."[12] The Wall Street Journal is filled with the latest news of mergers, takeovers and white knights. The Chief Executive Officer (CEO) who worries only about paying dividends to stockholders, or increasing the value of their equity by earnings per share and stock price increases, is sure to be a prime candidate for unemployment through takeover. Of course, if the Price/Earnings ratio is high enough, the chances of takeover will be greatly diminished, and we see that some CEOs have emphasized the P/E ratio at the expense of making needed investments for the future. The dilemma is the well-known tradeoff between short-term results and long-term health. By concentrating on the short-term, in the form of managing the P/E ratio, the CEO maintains a margin of safety from takeover. However, by doing so the company becomes vulnerable to competitive attacks, rapid declines, and eventual takeover bids, negating the very margin of safety provided by high P/E ratios.

The relationship with owners has changed in a second way, perhaps even more fundamental. In 1969 Ralph Nader announced the formation of Campaign GM, a group which bought two shares of General Motors stock and intended to wage a proxy fight on social issues including the need for public transportation, and the rights of women and minorities, and on business issues such as product design for safety and emissions control.[13] GM executives were not alone as "shareholder activism" increased to touch most of the Fortune 500. While the direct results are difficult to measure, suffice it to say that the CEO must worry about more than returns and takeovers in managing the owner relationship.[14]

Customers

For many years American businesses were dominant at home and their technology was dominant worldwide. That dominance has ended. Customers have many more choices today, and their view of U.S. products has changed, in both consumer and industrial products. "Made in Japan" has set new standards of quality, and where these standards have been ignored, the customer relationships have changed dramatically.

Hayes and Abernathy (1980) have argued effectively that U.S. managers have concentrated on designing and producing imitative, rather than innovative products. Our flair for technological innovation has been dampened, as U.S. managers have overemphasized the philosophy of being market-driven. The emphasis on trivial differences of product differentiation and packaging has made true innovations such as the laser and transistor almost unable to be managed in our corporations, and have given way to concerns of image and short-term returns from different customer perceptions. Combined with a penchant for making backward integration the major investment program, and a reluctance to invest in new manufacturing processes, Hayes and Abernathy claim that it is no wonder that U.S. managers find themselves coming out second best to foreign competitors in a marketplace that emphasizes quality.[15]

Employees

The United States has experienced an unprecedented drop in productivity over the past few years. While this phenomenon is a complicated one, and not easily understood or reducible to single causes, it should force scholars and managers alike to rethink the "manager-employee" relationship.[16] *Business Week* (1980) talks of the "new industrial relations" and even high productivity companies such as AT&T have begun to experiment, as part of their contracts with their unions, with "quality circles" and "quality of work life." The work force in the U.S. is younger, and its values are changing. Many have argued that authoritarian management styles must be replaced with a more "human" approach, or that the concept of "participation" must be explored in practice. In particular, Peters and Waterman (1982) have argued that managing the "culture" or "shared values" of employees is more important than understanding strategy and structure. Their study of companies with "excellent performance" is remarkable in the finding of a managerial style that emphasizes the importance of employees to the company.

The changing nature of the employee relationship must be understood for each business, and we must act, for low productivity is a warning signal of decline that cannot be ignored. However, the issue is not so simple as understanding the needs of employees qua employees. Employees are oftentimes customers, stockholders, and members of special interest groups. The internal change in this relationship, therefore, must be analyzed in conjunction with the external changes surrounding the organization.[17]

Suppliers

OPEC is one of many symbols of the changing nature of the business-supplier relationship.[18] Raw materials come from around the world, and no longer can a country such as the U.S. depend solely on its abundance within its shores. The transnational corporation has evolved to deal with the world-wide markets in raw materials.[19] Yet the issue is not one of "where is the market," for as OPEC so expensively illustrates, there is much more at issue than the price and quality of commodities. Political issues and the politics of control are as important in managing supplier relationships as are price-quality relationships. Even though OPEC has lost some of its effectiveness recently, as markets have adjusted to higher prices by a decrease in the rate of growth, and as alternative energy sources have become more cost-effective, from a managerial standpoint the locus of control has shifted from the oil companies to the OPEC nations.

Where are the OPECs of 1990, today? After all, OPEC was formed in 1960 and for 13 years gradually usurped power and control from the major oil companies until the "crisis" of 1973. These strategic surprises are not confined to the exciting world of international politics and finance. In the fast growing "silicon chip" industry managers must also cope with "managing with scarcity." Public organization executives feel the same pressure when budgets are drastically reduced. How can service levels be maintained with scarce resources?

Thus, changes have occurred within the comfortable framework of the firm. Owners, customers, employees and suppliers are not what they once were, and the implications for management theory and practice are for change to accommodate these shifts.

EXTERNAL CHANGE

We can no longer assume that each of the groups depicted in Exhibit 1.2 continues to want the traditional outputs of the corporation and expects the same kinds of decisions from management. However, the more difficult assignment is understanding external change—change that affects the very nature of Exhibit 1.2—change that originates in that murky area labeled "environment" and affects our ability to cope with internal changes. *When external change is added to internal change, a redrawing of Exhibit 1.2 will be needed.* But first, let us examine these external changes more closely.

External change is the emergence of new groups, events and issues which cannot be readily understood within the framework of an existing model or theory. It represents the need for new file folders in our conceptual system, and eventually for a whole new filing system. It is that dark and dangerous area known as "the environment," which serves as a convenient label for our ignorance, and which is as likely to serve up an OPEC as a Republican President. It is that abstruse area of the corporate plan that forecasts regulatory changes, increases in inflation and interest rates and changes in demographics.

External change produces uncertainty. It makes us uncomfortable

EXHIBIT 1.3   *Internal and External Change*

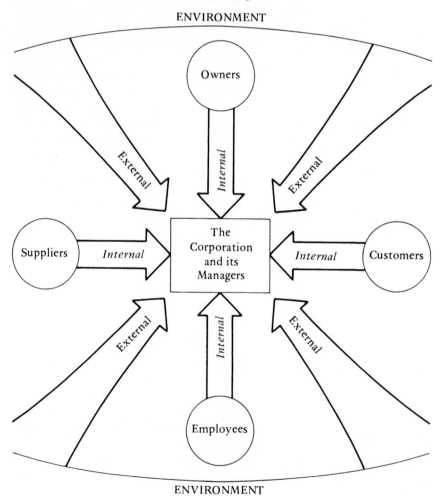

because it cannot be readily assimilated into the relatively more comfortable relationships with suppliers, owners, customers and employees. Exhibit 1.3 depicts the difference between internal and external change. It is important to note that the distinction between internal and external change is relative to a particular framework or theory. Using the Production View of Exhibit 1.1 we simply cannot understand the emergence of owners and employees without adding to, or changing, our theory. When enough external changes have occurred so that our current theory no longer gives us valid answers then we must abandon the theory and turn to a new set of concepts which explains both external and internal change. In short, what we need is a theory or set of concepts which can turn external change into internal change, thereby reducing uncertainty and discomfort. Such an "intellectual" or "conceptual" move serves as a legitimizing force so that such changes can be positively managed. It also allows our scanning systems to look for broader newer kinds of external change. External change is depicted as a set of arrows from the environment that affect our comfortable relationships with suppliers, owners, customers and employees. External change can be understood in terms of the emergence of several new groups and the restructuring of old relationships of lesser importance, who have come to have a stake in the actions or inactions of the corporation. Many of these changes have been around for some time, yet we have been quite slow to incorporate them into our framework for managing the firm. So, events and pressure groups with which we should be familiar become crises because we have not incorporated the idea of their existence into our day-to-day routine.

Governments

The recent past has seen an increase in the awareness of the role of government in the business enterprise. So much so, that public officials have been elected on the promise of curtailing this role, and seeking a return to "free enterprise." The business-government relationship in the U.S. has been founded on the principles of the "watch-dog," i.e., it is the legitimate role of government to regulate business in the public interest, and to enforce strict anti-trust laws to insure adherence to market principles. In addition the Congress and the Courts have always played a major role, at least indirectly, in shaping the strategies and policies of the modern corporation. Epstein (1969), Lindbloom (1977), McQuaid (1982) and many others have debunked the myth of the separation of the business and political arenas.[20]

While business has always had to contend with government in some form or other, current perceptions of its pervasive influence require a closer examination. It used to be sufficient to have a couple of lawyers or lobbyists or even public relations people whose role was to insure compliance with regulations, or respond to legal challenges, or represent the firm before Congress and state legislatures. However, the explosion in the scope of government in the post World War II economy of the U.S. has made this method of coping ineffective. No longer do most firms rely solely on the abilities of several trade organizations and lobbying groups such as the U.S. Chamber of Commerce and the National Association of Manufacturers to manage their relationship with multiple actors in the government.

Critics of "big government" such as Weidenbaum (1980) have estimated the cost of regulation to business at over $100 billion, and a recent study of the incremental costs of six agencies, EPA, EEO, OSHA, DOE, ERISA and the FTC has been estimated at $2.6 billion.[21]

Of course, these numbers are easily disputed and bitter exchanges among a number of interested parties have taken place regarding how to measure the costs and benefits of government. Critics of "laissez faire capitalism" have claimed that business attacks on the ills of government are misfounded, and that if we look closely we will see that regulatory agencies often benefit and protect the industries that are regulated. Furthermore, some critics argue that government intervention in the marketplace has real social benefits that would not have occurred without government action. Thus, cleaner air and water, safer automobiles and a general increase in the standard of living are attributed in part to government action.

The issues here are far from settled and political scientists and policy makers continue to debate cause and effect. I believe that from the managerial standpoint these repartees miss the major issue: how to manage in a world where there are multiple influences from various levels of government, or more properly from governments, and where the corporation and its managers can in turn affect the direction of public policy and government action? A necessary condition for answering this question is that we understand the interactions that are possible among business and various government actors. Government is not a monolithic entity, and it does not exist in a vacuum. Agencies, Congressional Committees, Presidential Commissions, Staff Members are all susceptible to multiple influences. (Each must be responsive to those groups and individuals who can affect it.) Exhibit 1.4 is a partial and enormously simplified diagram of some of the key government actors and their stakes in business.[22]

Most of the talk of reform centers on the so-called "harassment" agencies of the Business Roundtable study. Yet the U.S. federal bureaucracy is a large and fragmented "entity." The common boss of many agencies is the President, and conflicts among competing agencies simply cannot be resolved by the standard business practice of escalation, because the decision-making

EXHIBIT 1.4 *The U.S. Business-Government Relationship:
A Simplified Picture*

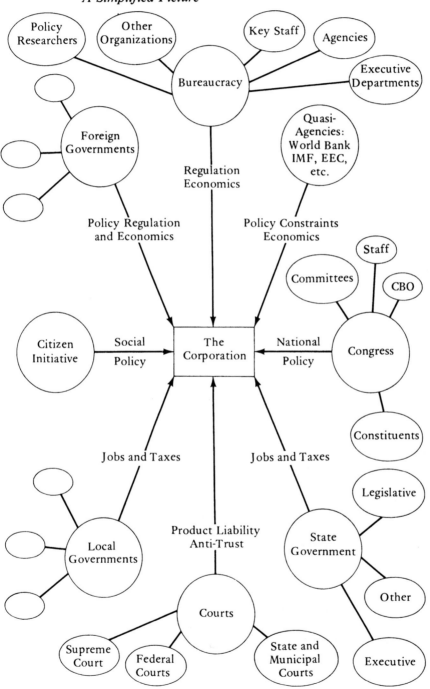

system would be paralyzed. So, many contradictory regulations are written, and it seems as if the bureaucracy has a life of its own.

Additionally there are many "quasi-agencies" which affect business such as the World Bank, the IMF, the U.N., the O.A.S., etc. These organizations are not entirely U.S. dominated, and they sometimes propose policy constraints, for example, by de facto determining the amount of credit available to some countries to purchase goods and services.

Foreign governments are structures in themselves which we must understand if we are to be successful in other countries. The most often heard complaint is that other governments don't "play fair," meaning that there are different sets of rules for home companies and for foreign companies. "How can we compete with Japan, Inc. when we must spend resources overcoming government obstacles, and Japanese companies not only have no obstacles, but have protection and assistance in access to markets, capital and basic research and development?"

The Congress considers several thousand pieces of legislation every session, some of which can have drastic effects on businesses. In addition, national policy changes, such as tax and depreciation schedules, capital formation incentives, and the creation of new forms of regulation affect the business community as a whole, even if the marginal effect on a single firm is slight. Hence, today's CEO must spend a good deal of time and resources worrying about proposed public policy legislation from Congress.

State governments offer a different set of issues for management, and these issues vary from region to region. Companies who operate on a national scale often find themselves with numerous sets of regulations. Most national breweries, for example, ship to multiple states from large regional breweries, yet tax and packaging requirements vary from state to state, even to the kind of packaging which is permissible. State legislatures consider several hundred thousand pieces of legislation every session, and the resources expended just to stay informed, much less to try to actively participate, are enormous. Concerns with jobs and taxes permeate the Northeast, while concerns with how to manage the enormous recent growth permeate the Southwest. Laws which encourage plant location and penalize plant closings are proposed in each legislative session, making it difficult to formulate and implement policy in the traditional piecemeal legislative fashion.

The courts offer yet another source of government influence on business. The old model learned from the grammar school civics books of the separation of executive, legislative and judicial branches of government simply does not apply in today's world; and no amount of tears will bring about that pristine Jeffersonian world.[23] From historic products liability decisions and equal opportunity cases, to anti-trust issues, the courts, at the state and federal levels can affect the nature of business.

Local government also gets into the act, as it depends more than other governments directly on the revenue generated by business for its lifeblood. One need only visit the decaying urban areas in the Northeast to see this point. Not only does the tax base erode when business no longer operates, but more importantly, revenue producing jobs are gone and the local economy takes a nosedive.

Finally, there is the matter of direct government through citizen initiative. There have been initiatives on the ballots in a number of states which would directly affect business. These range from bottle deposit bills passed in several states to bills to curtail smoking in public. An amendment to the Constitution of the U.S. has even been proposed for a system of national referenda, similar to the system used in several European countries. Needless to say the effect on an individual business can be considerable.

The point of Exhibit 1.4 is not merely to reaffirm that any one government or piece of government can affect a firm but rather, when taken in conjunction, we see that the cumulative effect is enormous. Management simply must undertake an organized effort to deal with governments in a strategic fashion, and if the model of the firm is that of Exhibit 1.2, then it is almost impossible to do so. They will react to events and crises in the short term and will not play their necessary role in the public policy process.[24]

Competitors

Competition has been the cornerstone of our system of managerial capitalism and perhaps the change in the nature of competition which has taken place in recent years should more properly be understood as an internal change. However, the major factor has been an external one, that U.S. business has not had to deal with in the past: foreign competition. Hence, the denotation as external change. In the 1950s "Made in Japan" meant "junk" or "cheap" or some such derogatory term, while in the 1980s it is perceived to be the hallmark of quality. The effect on the automobile industry has been debilitating. The real competition for GM is hardly the traditional new model from Ford or Chrysler, but rather the market leading behavior of Honda, Nissan, Toyota and Volkswagen. Nor, is this phenomenon specific to automobiles. There is competition from abroad in almost every "U.S. dominant" industry. The most difficult issue with foreign competition is that they do not play by the same rules, in terms of government, culture and other factors. Hence, to know the competition is a gargantuan task which requires an ability to understand other cultures from the ground up, from language to other ways of life.

In part, it is the emergence of foreign competition which makes the necessity to abandon the Managerial View of the firm so urgent. As long as all significant competition is domestic, everyone must play by the same rules. Each competitor bears the burden and shares the benefits of government, a fickle consumer population, environmentalists, etc. There is an "umbrella effect" by which firms in an industry can implicitly or explicitly coordinate their response to various issues. No one is at a competitive disadvantage, hence everyone can afford to proceed as if the Managerial View were still appropriate. When foreign competitors figure out how to satisfy customers and government with high quality products that are less expensive and meet all requirements, then the umbrella folds. This scenario has already taken place in several businesses.

Consumer Advocates

Much has happened since the early 1960s when President Kennedy announced the "Consumer Bill of Rights" beginning the modern "consumer movement." Consumer advocates today affect almost every industry involved in consumer goods marketing. Most executives are familiar with the story of Ralph Nader and General Motors' Corvair, which resulted in national prominence for Nader and the end of a product line for GM. Other activists have taken on other industries from pharmaceuticals and infant formula to utilities, many perhaps spurred by Nader's original success.[25] Even with today's "New Right" approach to public policy that has been favored in many quarters, we still find the voice of the consumer advocate — though the ability to get swift action via government agencies such as the FTC has waned.[26]

However, the problem is really much deeper. The consumer movement can be viewed on the one hand as merely a means to publicity and national prominence for aspiring politicians, following Nader's example. These consumer advocates constantly seek attention and media coverage; they will have to find issues which appeal to both media and the majority of the public. No doubt there are some consumer advocates who fit this mold.

An alternative view of the consumer movement is perhaps better understood using Hirschman's (1970) model of exit, voice and loyalty.[27] Hirschman argues that social phenomena can be understood in terms of people who can choose one of three possible strategies in most situations. Let us consider the customer of a firm, and suppose that for whatever reason, the customer is unhappy with the product. He or she can exit, simply take the business elsewhere and buy from another producer, given that there is a reasonable number of competing firms. Exit is the paradigm of the "economic" strategy. When enough customers exit, the firm gets the message that its product is no longer viable, that it is not producing at the "efficient frontier." Feedback to managers who rely solely on the exit strategies of their customers is "poor, nasty, brutish and short."

Alternatively, the customer can exercise "voice," that is, complain and try to get the firm to change or give redress. "Voice" is the paradigm of the political strategy, or using the political process to achieve change. It comes in multiple forms. Voters exercise voice at the ballot box. Interest groups try to exercise voice by pressuring government or business to act. Consumer groups may bring suit against a manufacturer, or they may use the political process to initiate change via intervention with regulatory agencies, initiatives, Congressional lobbying, etc. Feedback to the manager when customers use the voice strategy is more immediate (and in fact could conceivably be too immediate if the customer has not given the product time to work, or gotten accustomed to its side effects, or whatever quirk it may have).

Hirschman argues that the degree of organizational loyalty will determine the mix of exit and voice that is used. He argues that both exit and voice are necessary for the efficient functioning of the marketplace, for the costs of exit alone may well be too high, because the firm never has a chance to recover. Voice becomes the signal for management that change may be in order. Of course, voice, too, has a cost. The information that voice provides does not come free to the managers who need it. Voice mechanisms must be assessed in part in terms of whether they are cost effective, and in terms of the available alternatives.

Hirschman's model yields an interesting analysis of the consumer movement. We should not view it as adversarial, or to be avoided, but as a rational response. Voice should be encouraged and complaints welcomed with open arms. By announcing to management that some actions or particular policies or products are unacceptable, consumer advocates force management to continually be responsive to changing marketplace needs.

Many successful companies recognize the importance of the consumer movement. Proctor and Gamble expends a great deal of resources handling consumer complaints, and AT&T has formed Consumer Advisory Panels (CAPs) to assist them in diagnosing consumer reactions to possible changes in rate structures and new products and services. These companies have not had an easy time in dealing with consumer leaders, but they now know that the alternatives are not pleasant. A recent session with several Japanese managers elicited a list of those groups who could affect the company in

Japan. Further discussion revealed that "consumer advocates" were considered to be most important. When questioned as to why, the response of the Japanese managers was simple and revealing, "we want to listen so that we can fix what is wrong with the product."

Many consumer leaders want change in the marketplace. They know that, if necessary, government can be brought into the picture. However, the cost ultimately would be borne by the consumer, either through higher taxes or higher product costs. Therefore, they are amenable to real voluntarism, and to negotiation outside the formal arena of government. The predominant response of business leaders to consumer advocates has been adversarial, which in turn heightens the wariness of consumer leaders, which in turn. . . . conflict escalates, and both sides lose. If we believe that the consumer movement is here to stay, and given Hirschman's analysis it is rational to hope that it is here to stay, then it becomes a major managerial challenge to take advantage of the opportunities presented by the consumer movement.

Environmentalists

Yet another outgrowth of the turbulent 1960s is the concern with environmental quality: clean air, water and land, as well as conservation of natural resources. The "environmental movement" has roots that are as old as the pioneers. Several prominent organizations such as the Sierra Club and the Audubon Society have been around for some time. Several events of the 1960s heightened the consciousness of many members of the public, and gave rise to the environmental advocates which many executives now face.

Throughout the early part of our history, and spurred more recently by Sputnik and its aftermath, technology was seen as unalterably good. The possibility of unintended consequences occurring simply was not taken into account. Few questioned the costs of polluting water and air supplies for it seemed as if nature was infinitely self-renewable. Rachel Carson's *The Silent Spring,* published in 1962, questioned whether or not our society was in for trouble due to pollution and its aftereffects. The "culprits" naturally enough, were "Big Businesses," and the answer to the problem was government regulation.

During this period the U.S. was proceeding with plans to land someone on the moon and to build a colossal supersonic transport (SST) aircraft which was an order of magnitude more sophisticated technologically than the British-French Concorde (Horwitch, 1982). Activists attacked this latter effort as wasteful and harmful to the environment. Controversial issues such as the sonic boom, and harm to the ozone layer and oceans were raised. Government departments sponsored studies which tried to prove the critics wrong, thereby intensifying the debate. The important issue about the SST controversy was that for the first time there was a national debate over the costs and benefits of a particular technology, and over these costs and benefits in environmental terms. This debate was followed by the Clean Air Act of 1970 and the Clean Water Act of 1972. The Environmental Protection Agency was formed and environmental concerns were institutionalized.

Executives complained of onerous regulations. Automobile manufacturers were again hurt, and the cost of automobiles climbed. Foreign competitors could meet the new standards much more effectively than U.S. manufacturers, in part because their product lines did not depend on the large "gas guzzler," making the industry vulnerable to competition from Germany and Japan. Some companies tried to respond to environmental demands, yet the cleanup costs of generations of neglect were staggering.

There are no easy answers to the questions and issues raised by environmentalists. The need to take this external change into account is still with us, despite recent political shifts to the right. The Managerial View of the firm, depicted by Exhibit 1.2, becomes overloaded again when the cumulative effect of these changes is considered.

Special Interest Groups

There is a more general phenomenon that underlies the shifts in the business environment engendered by government, foreign competition, consumer advocates and environmentalists, that is the concern with "special interest groups" (SIGs) or "social interest groups" or "single issue politics." The idea behind SIGs is that a group or individual can use the political process to further a position on a particular issue such as gun control, abortion, women's rights, prayer in schools, or Congressional veto of the FTC, or any of hundreds of other issues. The problem which SIGs represent for the manager is that one can never be sure that an ad hoc group will not form to oppose the company on any particular issue.

Special interest politics is not a new phenomenon.[28] However, changes in modern communications technology and the financing of elections makes it especially important for managers to be aware of the agendas of interest groups. Epstein (1980) has analyzed the emergence and impact of Political Action Committees (PACs) who by their very nature can get the ear of legislators. Organized protest groups can attract media attention nationwide, and can use the political process to their advantage. Thus, the ability of business managers to respond to a variety of issues and events is crucial to success in industries that are vulnerable to special interest groups.

Today's managers need theories and realistic help in dealing with special interest groups as they affect their businesses. In particular they need to take this external change into account when setting their business strategy.

Media

Little stirs the anger in an executive more than an "unfair" story in the press. When one's company or products, or even one's character has been attacked in a forum where there is little chance of reply, the feeling of anger quickly turns to helplessness. More and more post-Watergate investigative reporters have turned their attention to the private sector. There, spurred onward by such films as *The China Syndrome,* new seminars on "how to handle the press" have emerged. It is quite easy to wake up in a cold sweat from the nightmare of the "60 Minutes" crew showing up unannounced at corporate headquarters to investigate the latest consumer or employee complaint.

Mass communications technology has indeed changed the role of the media with regard to business. More than ever, large organizations live in a fishbowl with their every action open to some form of public scrutiny. The media represents another form of external change for the executive who wishes to succeed in today's environment.

THE NEED FOR A FRAMEWORK

As managers like Bob Collingwood try to formulate coherent strategic plans and to implement these plans in some semblance of their original form, all too often they run afoul of the external environment. The Managerial View of the firm simply provides no cohesive way of understanding the changes that have and will occur. Managers have a difficult time separating real from trivial changes, and in deciding where a response is called for, and where preventive measures need to be taken.

The external events, furthermore, have not merely happened and then gone away, but rather, they have had a lasting effect on business-as-usual. The differing effects of external change are of intensity, and not of kind. For example, the environmentalist concerns affect industries that are involved directly in "exploiting" the environment, such as the forest products and petroleum industries who use products of those industries. But most businesses are dependent on transportation systems to some extent, where environmental concerns have altered both product design and other strategic variables.

The temptation is for executives and theorists to engage in a version of the more popular TV game shows, that I like to call, "Blame the Stakeholder." In "Blame the Stakeholder," contestants who must be managers in companies that have experienced some of the changes cited above, are asked to pick a stakeholder group and to blame the position of the company on that stakeholder group. Of course "Government" is a favorite, as is "Special Interest Groups." "Blame the Stakeholder" makes little progress, however good it makes us feel, and we must take a more careful look at the kinds of responses that are open to us.

Freud (1933) has cautioned us about the false comforts of denial and projection. Denial occurs when we refuse to admit that the external world is the way that it is. In our case, it is a refusal to admit that external groups really do have a stake in the firm, and that they can affect the firm. Denial involves not considering stakeholders to be legitimate in the very weak sense of the term: it is legitimate for us to spend time worrying about our strategy for stakeholders because they can affect the accomplishment of our goals and plans. Projection occurs when we blame someone else, or some external event for our own shortcomings. It is easy to project our inability to satisfy stakeholders' concerns and demands on the group itself, and to call it "unreasonable" or "irrational."

Another response pattern is available and it was summarized best in the comic strip "Pogo": we have met the enemy and he is us. It is the role of the manager to accept and own the problems which result from the failure of the organization to meet stakeholder needs. Not all needs can or should be met, and we cannot avoid horrible mistakes at times, yet our own fallibility is little excuse for failing to acknowledge the inadequacy of continually playing "Blame the Stakeholder."

The response of organizations to these changes in the environment has been as varied as the changes themselves. Ackoff (1974) and Post (1978) have argued that organizations have four basic modes for coping with a changing external environment. The first mode, *inactivity,* involves ignoring the changes and continuing business as usual. The second mode, *reactivity,* involves waiting for something to occur and responding to that change; however, response must be stimulated by an external force. The third mode, *proactivity,* involves trying to predict the external changes that will occur and positioning the organization towards those changes before the fact. The proactive mode is anticipatory. The fourth mode for coping with external forces is the *interactive* mode, that is, active involvement with the external forces and pressures that seeks to create the future for all concerned. While each of these response modes is appropriate for certain sets of circumstances, they all presume the existence of a set of ideas for dealing with any external change, even in the inactive mode. *In short, a necessary condition for adopting one or another of these response modes is to be able to understand the changes that have occurred.*

The very foundation of our ability to respond to change is in need of repair, and the magnitude of change outlined above requires new ideas and practices before we can formulate meaningful responses, regardless of the mode. (Imagine someone adopting an inactive mode, and because of the lack of the proper conceptual apparatus, the inactive mode turned out to yield proactive responses!)

If the dominant conceptual model of the modern business firm is that depicted by Exhibit 1.2, we cannot possibly assimilate the strategic shifts that have occurred, either for the business community as a whole, or for a particular set of businesses. *Major strategic shifts in the business environment require conceptual shifts in the minds of managers* (Emshoff, 1978; McCaskey, 1982). Just as the separation of the owner-manager-employee required a rethinking of the concept of control and private property as analyzed by Berle and Means (1932), so does the emergence of numerous stakeholder groups and new strategic issues require a rethinking of our traditional picture of the firm.

Thus, the environmental shifts that have occurred have given rise to a dilemma. On the one hand it is necessary to understand each of these shifts individually in order to adjust the position of the firm as it now stands relative to the individual shift. However, on the other hand, if enough of these small changes take place, piecemeal responses will not be adequate. The changes, both internal and external, that have taken place yield a need for a radical rethinking of our model of the firm. This rethinking, or conceptual revolution, is a subtle point. Like the dilemma it is intended to dissolve, it must redraw the boundaries of the manager's job in terms that he or she can understand, while taking into account the sum of all the changes that have occurred. The concepts that we need to employ must help us to understand the changes in the individual relationships of groups that affect the corporation, and they must assist in putting the pieces together again. The ship must stay afloat even while it is being repaired.

THE STAKEHOLDER CONCEPT

One possible approach to this conceptual problem of dealing with the external environment of the firm is to redraw our picture of the firm, Exhibit 1.2, in a way that accounts for the changes described in this chapter.

Exhibit 1.5 is a map of the firm which takes into account all of those groups and individuals that can affect, or are affected by, the accomplishment of organizational purpose. Each of these groups plays a vital role in the success of the business enterprise in today's environment. Each of these groups has a stake in the modern corporation, hence, the term, "stakeholder," and "the stakeholder model or framework" or "stakeholder management." The Stakeholder View depicted in Exhibit 1.5 is enormously oversimplified, for each category of stakeholder groups can be broken down into several useful smaller categories. All employees are not alike, just as all government is not alike. We shall see more of the complications of Exhibit 1.5 in chapter 3.

If we explore the logic of this concept in practical terms, i.e., in terms of how organizations can succeed in the current and future business environment, we are on the proper road to understanding and managing in turbulent times. However, the road is not an easy one. Cherished myths die

EXHIBIT 1.5   *Stakeholder* View of Firm*

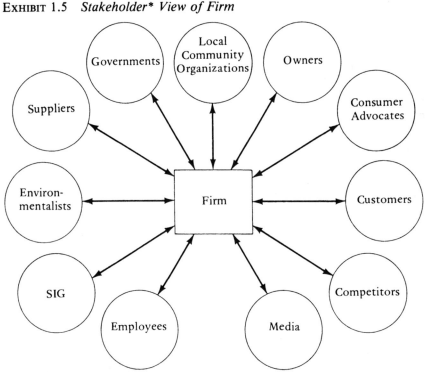

*Stakeholder = Any group or individual who can affect or is affected by
 the achievement of the firm's objectives. The groups listed here are
 examples of categories of stakeholders.

hard, and for good reason: they have served us well in the past. The cost of error, given the current situation, is quite high. No longer will U.S. business merely see the results of using the old model in a new environment in terms of law suits and regulations, but also in terms of foreign competition with better products and services who can satisfy a variety of stakeholder needs.

Two issues immediately come to mind from Exhibit 1.5. The first is the need for new theories and models about certain non-traditional groups, and the need for organizational processes to put these conceptual models to work. Thus, managers must understand how government really works, as opposed to the "7th Grade Civics Book" model that most of us have (Fenn, 1979; Horwitch, 1982). We must understand how new issues arise and get on the agenda of Congresspersons and other government officials, and we must understand what organizational mechanisms are necessary for helping to shape the agenda. Tradition, in terms of "lobbying" or "voting Republican" or more recently "organizing PACs" need not be thrown away, but unless we are satisfied with the state of current business-government relations the need to rethink these strategies in other terms is critical.

A similar argument can be constructed for each stakeholder group. The point is that we must understand our strategy for each group and must assess the strategy in real terms. Just as in the Managerial View where we have well defined management concepts for each group, so must we develop expertise in new areas to deal with consumer advocates, environmentalists, the media, SIGs, etc. We must understand how stakeholder groups and the issues of each are started, the importance of key issues and the willingness of groups to expend resources either helping or hurting the corporation on these issues.

The second major area for analysis is the need for integration. We can no more manage in isolation than Alfred Sloan could manage GM in isolation given the turbulence caused by the managerial revolution and the need for the concepts expressed in Exhibit 1.2. Thus, we need concepts and processes which give integrated approaches for dealing with multiple stakeholders on multiple issues. For each major strategic issue we must think through the effects on a number of stakeholders, and therefore, we need processes which help take into account the concerns of many groups. For each major stakeholder, those managers responsible for that stakeholder relationship must identify the strategic issues that affect that stakeholder and must understand how to formulate, implement and monitor strategies for dealing with that stakeholder group. Many organizations do this well with one stakeholder group, viz., IBM with customers, AT&T with regulators, Campbell Soup with suppliers, etc. Integrative metaphors are necessary which take into account the tried and true wisdom of "Customer Service," "Employee Participation," "Return to Owners," etc. However, these metaphors or organizational values must seek to integrate a number of stakeholder concerns.

SUMMARY AND PROLOGUE

This chapter has shown that changes have occurred in the external environment of business which necessitate changes in the way that executives think about their organizations and their jobs. In particular, I have suggested that shifts in traditional relationships with external groups such as suppliers, customers, owners and employees, as well as the emergence and renewed importance of government, foreign competition, environmentalists, consumer advocates, special interest groups, media and others, mean that a new conceptual approach is needed.

This book is to explore the new approach, called "the stakeholder approach," *in practical terms.* My focus is on how executives can use the concept, framework, philosophy and processes of the stakeholder approach to manage their organizations more effectively. It is, however, a beginning rather than a panacea. I shall draw on the work of many others and seek to use their insights to begin the construction of a stakeholder model of the firm. I shall pay particular attention to the problems identified above: the need for theories and strategies for dealing with particular groups and issues, and the need for processes for integration across issues and groups.

The remaining chapters in Part I are a further description of the building blocks of the stakeholder model. Chapter 2 sets forth the conceptual history of the stakeholder approach and related concepts. Chapter 3 describes the stakeholder framework and philosophy in more detail. Part II focuses on the managerial processes necessary to use the stakeholder concept. Chapter 4 explicates "direction-setting" processes. Chapter 5 describes a process for formulating strategic programs for specific stakeholders. Chapter 6 focuses on implementation and control and describes the experiences of one large organization which has begun to implement the stakeholder approach. The chapters in Part III explore the implications for management practice and theory, if we move the stakeholder concept from the periphery to the center. Chapter 7 examines the work of the board of directors. Chapter 8 looks at the issue of the functional disciplines of management. Chapter 9 explicates the need for a new concept of the role of the executive, given the stakeholder approach. It also contains a brief summing up and a discussion of future research.

NOTES

1. The profile of Bob Collingwood is a composite taken from the executives who have participated in the research on which this book is based. During the past five years I have had the opportunity to talk with several thousand managers in a number of industries. These talks have taken various forms, from structured interviews on which I have files of data to informal conversations during executive education programs. I have tried to wander around a number of organizations to try and get a conceptual handle on the kinds of external problems which their managers deal with on a day to day basis. My goal is to begin to construct a theory, so I have been trying to understand the entities which the theory is about. For a more sophisticated view of theory construction with which I am in general agreement, even though the present effort must fall short of its criteria, see Goodman (1955), Quine (1960) and Rudner (1966). I have tried to differentiate between theory construction and theory validation in Freeman (1977). Quine (1960) using Neurath's metaphor, has put the point elegantly by likening theory change to rebuilding a ship while it remains afloat: "The ship may owe its structure partly to blundering predecessors who missed scuttling it only by fools' luck. But we are not in a position to jettison any part of it, except as we have substitute devices ready to hand that will serve the same essential purpose" (Quine, 1960, p. 124).

2. While what I have to say applies to both business and non business organizations I shall concentrate on the applications of the stakeholder concept to corporations, and in particular, for profit corporations. It should be equally clear that government agencies have stakeholders, as do not-for-profit organizations and volunteer organizations. For an example of applying this methodology to hospitals see Freeman, Banker and Lee (1981).

3. Of course, this is a tremendous oversimplification of the issues. Business has always dealt with non-marketplace stakeholders. Joseph Wharton, himself, was heavily involved in lobbying the government for import protection laws (Sass, 1982). For an even earlier view of the essentially social nature of capitalism see Braudel (1981).

4. "Paradigm" is a completely overused and misunderstood term, especially in the social sciences. For a discussion of why "paradigms" are not the tidy little animals they are often supposed to be see Kuhn (1970), Lakatos and Musgrave (1970), Feyerabend (1975) and Gutting (1980). Alternatively see Barnes (1982) and Mohr (1982) for more direct applications to social science. McCaskey (1982) uses the notion of "conceptual maps" which may be more applicable to the argument being developed here.

5. There are relatively few studies of organization-environment relationships over time, for the obvious reasons that longitudinal studies are quite difficult and expensive. See Van de Ven and Joyce (1981) for reviews of several longitudinal research programs. Emery and Trist (1965) analyzed the underlying reasons for environmental turbulence and proposed a framework for understanding the relationships in the environment which did not directly affect the organization,

but which could determine how turbulent the organization's environment happened to be. The contributions of organization theorists in general are discussed in chapter two.

6. The literature on the emergence of the modern corporation is extensive. Chandler (1962; 1977) provides a readable account with a guide to many other sources contained in the footnotes.

7. I am grateful to Professor Mariann Jellinek of McGill University for the file drawer analogy.

8. My argument here is a conceptual one. I know of no logical guarantee which could be issued to support the claim that a "weltanschauung" was of a certain sort. Quine (1960) discusses the resulting "translation problem" among persons who have different world-views or, in his case, speak different languages. There is weaker evidence that Exhibit 1.2 does depict the intended world-view of managers from the viewpoint of writers of textbooks on business. I only claim that if Exhibit 1.2 is the predominant world-view, then the organization-environment turbulence which we see today for most corporations is a logical consequence.

9. It is often overlooked that Renault, owned by the French government, owns 51% of American Motors, Inc., and that British Petroleum, owned by the British government, owns a majority position in SOHIO. There are other cases of this phenomenon.

10. My distinction between internal and external change is directly indebted to Watzlawick, Weakland and Fisch (1974). However, the two kinds of change are quite ancient relating to Aristotle's distinction between differences in degree (internal) and differences in kind (external).

11. See McCaskey (1982) for a discussion of conceptual maps.

12. See chapter seven, below, for a "stakeholder" approach to stockholders. I am grateful to David Reed for helping me to understand that the stakeholder concept can be used to analyze the business-owner relationship.

13. For an account of the Nader episode see Nader (1972) and Hay, Gray and Gates (1976).

14. For an account of stockholder activism see Vogel (1978).

15. The argument is quite complicated here. A number of criticisms of U.S. management practices have surfaced in recent years. For a sample see Hayes and Abernathy (1980), Charan and Freeman (1980), Ouchi (1981), Pascale and Athos (1981) and Peters (1981). In reality these critiques go back to fundamentals enunciated by Barnard (1938).

16. Recent commentators include Lasch (1978) and Yankelovich (1981) as well as the economic argument by Calleo (1982).

17. This point applies equally well to all stakeholders.

18. The formation of OPEC has been well documented. See, for example, Stobaugh and Yergin (1979).

19. One account of the rise of the multinationals is Vernon (1977).

20. It is really quite difficult to imagine how "business" and "politics" could be anything but inherently bound. Nonetheless, there are countless executives, whom I have spoken with in the past few years, who insist that business and

government have (should have) nothing in common. "Markets are markets and politics is politics!"

21. The study of regulation that was sponsored by the Business Roundtable, was conducted by Arthur Andersen and Co., an accounting firm. It relied on the reports of managers in the affected industries, and aggregated the costs across industries. The study is available from the Business Roundtable and Arthur Andersen and Co.

22. I wish to thank Professor Dan Fenn, Professor Ed Epstein and Professor Paul Tiffany for helping me to understand the business-government relationship.

23. See Fenn (1979).

24. See Epstein (1969) for an analysis of the role of the corporation in the public policy process.

25. For an account of the rise of the consumer movement which goes well beyond the popular belief that it started in the 1960s with Ralph Nader, see the collections of essays edited by Kelley (1973) and Aaker and Day (1974). I am grateful to Professor Currin Shields of Arizona University and past president of the Conference of Consumer Organizations, and to Ms. Esther Shapiro, Consumer Advocate for the City of Detroit, for many helpful discussions of the consumer movement.

26. See Pertschuck (1982) for an analysis of the current state of the consumer movement.

27. I believe that Hirschman's analysis is applicable to a number of stakeholder groups. There has been a great deal of discussion of his ideas in the economics and sociology literature. See Hirschman (1981) for a collection of essays that expand on Hirschman (1970). Evan (1975) applies Hirschman's analysis to a model of organizational constitutionalism.

28. For an account of special interests in the U.S. see Wilson (1981).

Two

THE STAKEHOLDER CONCEPT AND STRATEGIC MANAGEMENT

The changes catalogued in the previous chapter have spawned conceptual chaos in the management discipline. From the canned packages developed by management consulting firms to the theoretical treatises of academics, there has been an explosion in available advice to the practicing manager. Sorting out what is real from what is ephemeral is not an easy task, given that the fundamental assumptions on which theories of management and organization are based are undergoing radical shifts. Therefore, in setting out a brief history of the concept of stakeholder, I will cover a number of uses of the concept in the academic and non-academic literature, as well as relate the development of the concept to the strategic planning and strategic management literature. I shall try to help Bob Collingwood and the managers like him through the maze of academic literature and practical jargon.

HISTORY OF "STAKEHOLDER"

The actual word "stakeholder" first appeared in the management literature in an internal memorandum at the Stanford Research Institute (now SRI International, Inc.), in 1963.[1] The term was meant to generalize the notion of stockholder as the only group to whom management need be responsive. Thus, the stakeholder concept was originally defined as "those groups without whose support the organization would cease to exist." The list of stakeholders originally included shareowners, employees, customers, suppliers, lenders and society. Stemming from the work of Igor Ansoff and Robert Stewart in the planning department at Lockheed, and later Marion Doscher and Stewart at SRI, the original approach served an important information function in the SRI corporate planning process.[2] The SRI researchers argued that unless executives understood the needs and concerns of these stakeholder groups, they could not formulate corporate objectives which would receive the necessary support for the continued survival of the firm.

EXHIBIT 2.1   *A History of the Stakeholder Concept*

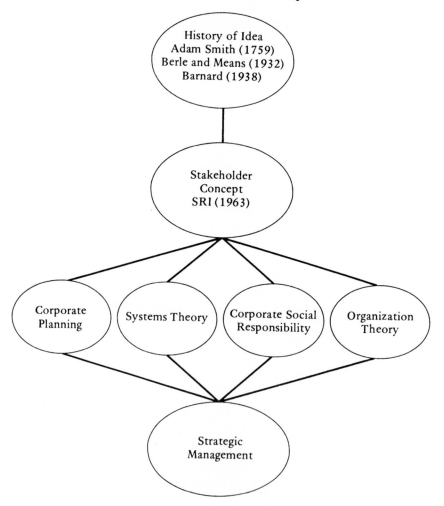

From the original work at SRI, the historical trail diverges in a number of directions, as depicted in Exhibit 2.1: (1) the corporate planning literature; (2) the work of Russell Ackoff, C. West Churchman and systems theorists; (3) the literature on corporate social responsibility; and (4) the work of Eric Rhenman and other organization theorists.

The Corporate Planning Literature

In his now classic book, *Corporate Strategy* (1965), Ansoff argued for a rejection of the stakeholder theory, which he explicated in the following passage:

> While as we shall see later, "responsibilities" and "objectives" are not synonymous, they have been made one in a "stakeholder theory" of objectives. This theory maintains that the objectives of the firm should be derived balancing the conflicting claims of the various "stakeholders" in the firm: managers, workers, stockholders, suppliers, vendors.

Ansoff credited Abrams (1954) and Cyert and March (1963) with a similar view, but went on to reject the theory in favor of a view which separated objectives into "economic" and "social" with the latter being a "secondary modifying and constraining influence" on the former.[3] The passage quoted above, clearly indicates that Ansoff has the "dominant coalition" view of organizations in mind when he explicates the stakeholder view. The point of the SRI definition is however, a bit different. The issue is pure and simple: survival. Without the support of these key groups the firm does not survive, by definition of what we mean by "stakeholder." Of course whether SRI has the right groups is a different issue. Are lenders necessary for the survival of a debt-free firm? Is "society" (however that loose term may be defined) necessary for the survival of a privately owned specialty steel firm? Conversely, isn't government necessary for the survival of public utilities?[4]

The thrust of Ansoff's criticism is to point out that the stakeholders whose support is necessary for survival is a contingent phenomenon, dependent on a number of situational variables. Ansoff, wrongly I believe, rejected such a theory in favor of one which searches for a universal objective function, where stakeholders serve as constraints on the level of the objective which is obtainable at a point in time. Such a search for the real objective of the firm was to occupy a substantial part of the corporate planning literature during the subsequent years.[5]

By the 1970s the stakeholder concept began to surface in a number of places in the strategic planning literature. In a review article on the state of the art of corporate strategy, Bernard Taylor (1971) claimed that the importance of stockholders would diminish. He wrote, "In practice it is clear that in the 1970s business will be run for the benefit of other stakeholders, too" (Taylor, 1971). Haselhoff (1976) explored the implications for the formulation of organizational goals. King and Cleland (1978) in their text, *Strategic Planning and Policy*, gave a method for analyzing "clientele groups," "claimants" or "stakeholders" which grew out of their earlier work on project management. Taylor (1977) summarized the latest SRI approach. Rothschild (1976) used the concept to explain a planning process developed at General Electric. Hussey and Langham (1978) presented a model of the organization and its environment with stakeholders being differentiated from the firm and consumers, and used it to analyze the role that management plays in effective corporate planning processes. Derkinderen and Crum (1979) used the stakeholder notion in their analysis of project set strategies, and the idea plays a central role in Heenan and Perlmutter's (1979) analysis of organization development for multinational corporations. Specific applications of the concept in managerial processes in the strategic planning literature include Davis and Freeman's (1978) method for technology assessment and Mitroff and Emshoff's (1979) method for strategy formulation called "Strategic Assumptions Analysis" and later developed by Emshoff (1980) and Mason and Mitroff (1982), and Rowe, Mason and Dickel's (1982) formulation of techniques for strategy analysis.

Although there are many definitions of "strategy," "policy," "planning" and the variants of each, the basic idea is that planning and policy are concerned with the configuration of an organization's resources in relationship to its external environment. The concept of strategic planning is inherently connected with setting some direction for the organization, based on an analysis of organizational capabilities and environmental opportunities and threats. Thus, adequate information about the environment, past and future changes and emerging strategic issues and problems is vital to an effective corporate planning or policy-making process. As planning moved from reactive policy making to proactive strategy formulation the need for "environmental scanning" increased.[6]

SRI's original use of stakeholder analysis was precisely in this area. By developing "measures of satisfaction" of those groups whose support is necessary for the continued survival of the organization, an important input into the corporate planning process was made. Information systems can then be developed to scan and track the responses of key stakeholder groups to changes in corporate strategy. Adjustments can be made if stakeholder expectations get far enough out of line to warrant withdrawal of their support. Stakeholder behavior is taken as given, or as a constraint on strategy, in Ansoff's terms. Strategy is formulated against this static environment, which is forecastable in the long run. This use of the stakeholder concept is as an intelligence gathering mechanism to more accurately predict environmental opportunities and threats.

A second feature of this "corporate planning" use of "stakeholder" is that stakeholders are identified at a generic level as customers, suppliers, owners, public, society, etc., and analysis is performed at that level of generality. Hence, public attitude surveys, stockholder interviews and the like are the available analytical techniques. Since the major concern is with forecasting the future environment and not with changing specific stakeholder behavior, there is no need to go beyond this generic stakeholder analysis.

The concern with future forecasts of stakeholder behavior so that the corporation can plan its "best reply," assumes that there will be no radical shifts in a stakeholder's actions. Because the stakeholder environment is taken as static, and because only generic analysis is necessary, adversarial groups are not considered as stakeholders. Particular "special interest groups" interested in negotiation have no place. One negotiates with Ralph Nader not with "special interest groups" as a generic entity. Therefore, the corporate planning model is really another way of analyzing Exhibit 1.2, and of getting more useable information on those "friendly" groups to adapt to internal change. The use of the stakeholder concept is to provide information to strategists at a generic level about traditional "relatives" of stockholders such as employees, managers, suppliers, consumers and the public. As long as the environment is stable, few strategic surprises occur making this interpretation of the stakeholder concept sufficient.

The mainstream of research in strategic planning followed quite different lines, with uses of the stakeholder concept being the exception rather than the rule. Researchers in the tradition of the Harvard Business School's Business Policy curriculum, begun in the 1920s, started to formalize the techniques of situational analysis into processes such as SWOT analysis (Strengths-Weaknesses-Opportunities-Threats). Andrews (1980) and others proposed methods for determining the "distinctive competence" of organizations, and matching these competences with opportunities via generic strategies such as "vertical integration," "find a new use for a product," "find a new market for a product," etc. Christenson, Andrews and Bower (1980) stands even today in its fourth edition as a classic textbook in situational analysis and the case method. Chandler's (1962) groundbreaking study of General Motors, Dupont and Sears linked strategy and structure and generated hypotheses about the proper relationship between these two variables. Aguilar (1967) proposed a framework for understanding environmental scanning and studied how managers obtain and use external information.

In line with Ansoff's original charge of optimizing economic objectives, research emerged on the appropriate business strategies. Bruce Henderson and the Boston Consulting Group formulated a theory about business-level strategy (as opposed to corporate-level strategy) which rested on an analysis of the experience curve, the phenomenon of decreasing costs per unit as volume increases. Henderson's (1979) theory argued that only two variables need be considered when formulating strategy: market attractiveness measured by the growth rate of the market, and business strength measured by market share. It led to the so-called "portfolio approach" to strategy, and the well-known grid where products are characterized as "stars," "problem children," "cash cows" and "dogs." Variants on this approach are summarized by Rothschild (1976).

Another main stream of research in strategic planning emerged as concerned with the planning or administrative process. That is, how can managers decide what the correct strategy is? What kinds of planning systems are needed? Lorange (1980) has summarized the three phases of this concern with administrative systems. The research on administrative systems naturally gave rise to concern with "environmental scanning" systems. However, the primary focus of these early systems was with the identification of macro-economic indicators to be watched if accurate business level strategies were to be formulated. As econometric models became more sophisticated, planning processes began more and more to use computer-based simulations.

Thus, the mainstream of research was quite far removed from understanding the concrete actions of external stakeholder groups.[7] In the 1950s, 1960s and early 1970s the business environment of most U.S. firms was quite stable. Planning processes which relied on methods of forecasting and prediction were, therefore, appropriate. Much progress was made on understanding strategy formulation, both its process and content. However, the concern with the external environment was generic and seen solely in economic terms. The use of the stakeholder concept was limited in scope and pertained primarily to gathering rather general information about traditional external groups.

The Systems Theory Literature

In the mid-1970s researchers in systems theory, led by Russell Ackoff and C. West Churchman "rediscovered" stakeholder analysis, or at least took Ansoff's admonition more seriously.[8] Stemming from their joint work in applying Jungian psychology to develop a personality theory that could be useful for business problem solving (Ackoff and Churchman, 1947), they were instrumental in developing systems theory into a powerful tool for addressing a number of issues in social science (Churchman, 1968; Ackoff, 1970). Ackoff (1974) rehashed Ansoff's argument and defined a method for stakeholder analysis of organizational systems. Propounding essentially an "open systems" view of organizations (Barnard, 1938), Ackoff argued that many societal problems could be solved by the redesign of fundamental institutions with the support and interaction of the stakeholders in the system. This notion of "stakeholders in a system" differs from the use of the concept in the strategy literature. To be concerned with the organizational level of analysis is a mistake. Problems should not be defined by focusing or analysis, but by enlarging or synthesis. For example, a problem of low earnings, which affects stockholders, would first of all be understood in terms of the entire stakeholder system, which forms the context of the problem. The concerns of other stakeholders as they relate to the problem of low earnings would first be explicated. Ackoff argues that system design can only be accomplished by stakeholder participation, and thereby argues for the inclusion of stakeholder groups in solving system-wide problems. Ackoff (1974) contains case studies of how to use this methodology in designing large scale projects. Davis and Freeman (1978) propose a specific method using stakeholder participation for technology assessment.

The concept of corporate strategy or organizational strategy, on this systems view, seems to give way to that of collective strategy, a now popular concept in organization theory.[9] It would be a mistake, in systems terms, to take the point of view of planning for one organization in the system for such a plan might optimize a sub-system, and destroy larger system goals and objectives. Organizational planning should be done only so far as it is relevant to system goals.

There are two important variants of this position which are important to consider. The first might be called "the co-optation" view where an organization and its stakeholders plan together for the future of the organization. Larger system goals are ignored or postponed, as the organization and its stakeholders try to reach agreements (hopefully mutually beneficial ones, as "co-optation" may imply "cooperation") on how the organization is to proceed. The second variant involves the collaboration of a subset of stakeholders planning for the future of each. This idea is best exemplified by labor-management planning of quality of work life experiments, and Trist's (1981) work on socio-technical systems.

Each of these variants tries to overcome the general problem with the systems view that there is not a starting point, or entry point, for how collaboration towards "the systems viewpoint," which is necessarily "God-like," is to proceed. Thus, a utility might sit down with its "consumer advocate" stakeholder and try to plan how it should proceed with a rate increase proposal. But, to create the future of the stakeholder system which includes the utility, consumer group and other stakeholders is a much more difficult, if not impossible task. The systems model of stakeholders, by emphasizing participation, is a far reaching view of the nature of organizations and society. It has been quite useful in problem formulation, and represents an ongoing stream of research using the stakeholder concept. It is not, however, focused on solving strategic management problems which are narrower than total system design.

The Corporate Social Responsibility Literature

Another trail from the original work on the stakeholder concept at SRI was the concern of a number of researchers with the social responsibility of business organizations. The corporate social responsibility literature is too diverse to catalogue here.[10] It has spawned many ideas, concepts and techniques and brought about both real and ephemeral change in organizations. Post (1981) has categorized the main lines of research in the area, and several anthologies (Sethi, 1971; Votaw and Sethi, 1974; Preston 1979, 1980, 1981, 1982) show the breadth and depth of the research issues. Suffice it to say that the social movements of the sixties and seventies in civil rights, anti-war, consumerism, environmentalism and women's rights served as a catalyst for rethinking the role of the business enterprise in society. From Milton Friedman to John Kenneth Galbraith, there are a diversity of arguments.[11]

The distinguishing feature of the literature on corporate social responsibility is that it can be viewed as applying the stakeholder concept to non-traditional stakeholder groups who are usually thought of as having adversarial relationships with the firm. In particular, less emphasis is put on satisfying owners and comparatively more emphasis is put on the public or the community or the employees. Dill (1975) argued:

> For a long time, we have assumed that the views and initiative of stakeholders could be dealt with as externalities to the strategic planning and management process: as data to help management shape decisions, or as legal and social constraints to limit them. We have been reluctant, though to admit the idea that some of these outside stakeholders might seek and earn active participation with management to make decisions. The move today is from stakeholder influence towards stakeholder participation.

Dill went on to set out a role for strategic managers as communicators with stakeholders, and considers the role of adversary groups such as

Nader's Raiders in the strategic process. For the most part, until Dill's paper, and the concern with social responsibility, stakeholders had been assumed to be non-adversarial or adversarial to the extent of "labor-management" negotiations, which has a long history. By broadening the notion of stakeholder to "people outside . . . who have ideas about what the economic and social performance of the enterprise should include," Dill set the stage for the use of the stakeholder concept as an umbrella for strategic management.

During this period two major groups of researchers emerged to form a subdiscipline in management variously called "Business and Society," "Social Issues in Management," etc. In the School of Management at Berkeley a number of scholars began to address a broad range of issues. Votaw (1964) studied corporate power in Europe. Epstein (1969) conducted a classic study of business and the political arena in the U.S. Sethi (1970) analyzed the role of minorities in the firm, by studying the Kodak-FIGHT confrontation. During roughly the same period, the Harvard Business School undertook a project on corporate social responsibility. The output of the project was voluminous, and of particular importance was the development of a pragmatic model of social responsibility called "the corporate social responsiveness model." Essentially it addressed Dill's challenge with respect to social issues; namely, how can the corporation respond proactively to the increased pressure for positive social change? By concentrating on "responsiveness" instead of "responsibility" the Harvard researchers were able to link the analysis of social issues with the traditional areas of strategy and organization (Ackerman, 1975; Ackerman and Bauer, 1976; and Murray, 1976).

For the most part stakeholders were analysed at a generic level, even though Ackerman and Bauer analysed how to integrate social objectives with traditional business objectives, and thus return to Ansoff's orginal argument. Hargreaves and Dauman (1975) coined the phrase "stakeholder audit" as a part of the more generic "corporate social audit" (Bauer and Fenn, 1972).[12] The purpose of the social audit and the resulting literature on social performance was to rethink the traditional scorecard for business. The social audit attempted to construct a social "balance sheet," and to analyze the actions of a firm in terms of social costs and benefits. Methodological problems, however, have made the search for the social analog of the balance sheet and income statement an elusive search.

In addition to these concepts that seek to look at the social responsibility of business, there is a much older body of literature on which scholars in business and society have drawn. Historians, political scientists, economists (especially the more recent public choice economists) and political philosophers have been concerned with the relationship between the corporation and government. Epstein (1969) has analyzed the literature on the role of the corporation in American politics and concluded that "at the present time, corporations should not be subject to special restrictions limiting the nature or extent of their political involvement." He goes on to argue that all "associational political participants" should be governed by requirements on disclosure and lobbying. The rich history of political science and an analysis of the concepts and justice of power can, of course be traced to Plato's *Republic* and Aristotle's *Politics*. Yet as Epstein (1969, 1980) points out there is an amazing scarcity of scholarship on corporate political activity. While kindred concepts in the political science literature such as "constituency" (see Mitnick, 1980, for a review), "interest group," "publics," and "the public interest" have been around for some time, there is little besides the "institutional economists" such as John R. Commons which recognizes and deals with the complexity in which the modern corporation finds itself.

While there have been many criticisms of the research in corporate social responsibility, perhaps the most troubling issue is the very nature of "corporate social responsibility" as if the concept were needed to augment the study of business policy.[13] Corporate social responsibility is often looked at as an "add on" to "business as usual," and the phrase often heard from executives is "corporate social responsibility is fine, if you can afford it." This conceptual split between the "profit-making" piece of business and the "profit-spending" or "socially responsible" part is mirrored in the academic world where the Academy of Management has a division concerned with "Social Issues in Management" and a division concerned with "Business Policy and Strategy."[14]

Given the turbulence that business organizations are currently facing and the very nature of the external environment, as consisting of economic and socio-political forces, there is a need for conceptual schemata which analyze these forces in an integrative fashion. We need to understand the complex interconnections between economic and social forces. Isolating "social issues" as separate from the economic impact which they have, and conversely isolating economic issues as if they had no social effect, misses the mark both managerially and intellectually. Actions aimed at one side will not address the concerns of the other. Processes, techniques and theories which do not consider all of these forces will fail to describe and predict the business world as it really is.

While the corporate social responsibility literature has been important in bringing to the foreground in organizational research a concern with social and political issues, it has failed to indicate ways of integrating these concerns into the strategic systems of the corporation in a non-ad hoc fashion.

The Organization Theory Literature

For the most part, the development of the stakeholder concept was dormant during the 1960s. The exception was the work of several organization theorists who tried to understand the organization-environment relationship. While most of the these theorists did not specifically use "stakeholder," their work remains a constant source of insight. Eric Rhenman (1968) in Sweden explicitly used the stakeholder concept in his work on industrial democracy.[15] Rhenman argued:

> We shall be using the term stakeholders to designate the individuals or groups which depend on the company for the realization of their personal goals and on whom the company is dependent. In that sense employees, owners, customers, suppliers, creditors as well as many other groups can all be regarded as stakeholders in the company.

While similar to the SRI concept, Rhenman's definition was narrower, including any group who places demands on the company and on whom the company has claims, rather than any group whose support is necessary for the survival of the firm. Rhenman goes on to argue that a "stakeholders" conception of the firm can lead to a theory of industrial democracy.[16] Rhenman's use of the stakeholder concept parallels the use at SRI. Again, he is interested in stakeholders at the generic level or as categories of particular groups. His narrow construal of the concept using "and" to denote the fact that the company and stakeholder must have mutual claims could rule out important groups, most notably government and adversarial groups, who are dependent on the firm, but on whom the firm does not depend.[17]

During the same period several other organization theorists were concerned with exploring the relationship between organization and environment, because organizational analysis which depended solely on looking within an organization did not seem to have enough explanatory power. In the early 1960s William Evan began to develop the concept of "organization-set" which analyzes the interactions of an organization with "the network of organizations in its environment." Evan (1966) postulated several concepts and hypotheses which could be used to study interorganizational phenomena, arguing that the majority of organizational research had concentrated instead on intraorganizational relationships. Evan's work led to a host of subsequent research on interorganizational relationships, both conceptual and empirical, which I shall not summarize.[18]

During roughly the same period important conceptual models were developed by Katz and Kahn (1966) calling for an "open-systems" approach to the study of organizations which focused on defining the organization relative to the larger system of which it is a part, and by Emery and Trist (1965) exploring the second order environments of organizations, the connections which occur among environmental elements which affect the organization. James Thompson's (1967) classic study of organizations resurrected the notion of "clientele" as a way to designate outside groups, and used Dill's (1958) notion of the "task environment" of the organization. Thompson puts the notion quite simply as: "We are now working with those organizations in the environment which make a difference to the organization in question . . ."

It is precisely this notion of "those groups which make a difference" which underlies the stakeholder concept, especially from the standpoint of strategic management, since the concern for managers in the business environment described in the previous chapter should be the management of the relationships of those groups which "make a difference." Mahon (1982) has argued explicitly that Thompson anticipates the stakeholder notion, when his views on the social responsibilities of organizations are taken into account. Lawrence and Lorsch (1967) proposed a model of "differentiation and integration" whereby organizations segment themselves into smaller units to deal with specific parts of the external environment, and the attitudes and beliefs that arise from such differentiation and the task of integration or "the quality of the state of collaboration that exists among departments that are required to achieve unity of effort by the demands of the environment."[19] Van de Ven, Emmett, and Koenig (1979) reviewed the organization-environment literature and proposed several meta-conceptual schemes for understanding the burgeoning research.

More recently Pfeffer and Salancik (1978) have reviewed the literature and constructed a model of organization-environment interaction which depends on an analysis of the resources of the organization and the relative dependence of the organization on environmental actors to provide those resources. While they do not explicitly define "stakeholders" they do claim:

> Our position is that organizations survive to the extent that they are effective. Their effectiveness derives from the management of demands, particularly the demands of interest groups upon which the organizations depend for resources and support.[20]

They go on to argue for a "radical" external view of organizations where theorists look to the environment for most of the explanatory force of organization theory. They argue that for the most part, while many have claimed the need to look at the external environment, few theorists have developed concepts which allow the environment to enter into the organizational equation. Their definition of interest groups in terms of dependence and resources, is again quite similar to the SRI concept of stakeholders.

More recently still, two volumes of essays edited by Nystrom and Starbuck (1981) contain essays which assess the state of the art in understanding the organization-environment relationship. Of particular importance is the work of Aldrich and Whetten (1981) on the concept of "populations" of organizations and their evolution, and network analysis which is claimed to "go beyond" the concept of the "organization set" and the attention to stakeholders. Pennings (1981) analyzes the concept of "strategically interdependent organizations" and proposes a set of strategies which organizations can use to cope with the uncertainty that comes with interdependence. Other essays in these volumes, as well as in two additional volumes of essays by Katz, Kahn and Adams (1980) and Van de Ven and Joyce (1981), are rich sources of ideas for the development of the stakeholder concept as it applies to strategic management. However, my purpose is not to review the literature, but to show the intellectual roots of the stakeholder concept.

The literature in organization theory stops short, for the most part, of producing a framework for setting and implementing direction in organizations. For the most part it attempts to be purely descriptive. There is little explicit "fit" between the organization theory literature and the strategic planning literature, as well as the systems theory and corporate social responsibility literature.[21] Each of these streams of research is relevant to the construction of a stakeholder approach to strategic management, and I will build on the research and the insights of others in developing such an approach. However, the results must be applicable to the problem discussed in chapter one; namely, how can executives in corporations begin to understand and manage in the external environment which they currently face? My approach is inherently "managerial." It is a "theory," or more properly, a "framework," about managerial behavior, first, and organizational behavior, second.

A STAKEHOLDER APPROACH TO STRATEGIC MANAGEMENT

While the history of the stakeholder concept, in all of its disguises is a relatively brief one, the concept can be used to tie together a rich body of literature. The major concerns of each main area of research are not mutually exclusive. The concerns with formulating plans and systems of plans for business level entities, with understanding the role of the corporation in social systems, with the social responsibility of business and the need for integrative theories to explain the behavior of a large population of organizations and their environments are of vital importance to managers and organizational researchers. The stakeholder concept can be useful in integrating some of these issues around the concept of organizational strategy, that is around the issues of how organizations can configure themselves and take actions to align themselves with the external environment.

Any strategic management model must deal with a number of key questions. The questions listed below are some which can be understood partially in stakeholder terms.

- What is the direction or mission of the organization? (Strategic Direction)
- What paths or strategies will achieve such a mission? (Strategic Program Formulation)
- What resource allocations or budgets must be made for the strategies to be implemented? (Budgeting)
- How can we be sure the strategies are on track or in control? (Control)
- What are the macro-systems and structures necessary for implementation? (Structure and Systems)

Subsequent chapters will discuss each of these questions in turn. Exhibit 2.2 is a schematic of strategic management processes which can be used to describe a number of actual processes in use in major corporations. Lorange (1980) has explained each of these strategic tasks in detail. Schendel and Hofer (1979) have cataloged the research in strategic management according to these tasks and explicated the strategic management "paradigm," while Freeman and Lorange (1983) have offered a heuristic for understanding and developing new research questions with respect to the strategic management process.

The conceptual shift from "strategic planning" to "strategic management" connotes an important move towards an action orientation. Planning for stakeholder concerns is simply not enough. Programs and policies which can be implemented and controlled, must be the results of these plans. Also, the managers in a firm must do their jobs in a "strategic fashion," i.e., under the umbrella of the direction of the firm. The stakeholder concept can be used to enrich our understanding of each of these strategic tasks in light of the internal and external changes in the business environment, by giving managers and researchers a framework for understanding how these strategic questions can be answered in the turbulent environment of most U.S. corporations.

With all of the research cited above, it might legitimately be asked whether organization theorists and managers need a "new" concept such as "stakeholder." While this criticism is well taken, I can reply that words

EXHIBIT 2.2 *Typical Strategic Management Process (Lorange, 1980)*

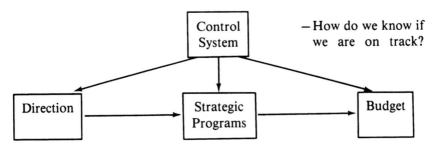

- Where are we going?
- What business(es) are we in?
- What business(es) should we be in?

- How do we get to where we want to go?
- What are the cross-functional programs needed?

- What is our blueprint for action?
- How do we allocate resources for this year?
- What is our operating budget? Strategic budget?

make a difference in how we see the world. By using "stakeholder," managers and theorists alike will come to see these groups as having a "stake." "Stakeholder" connotes "legitimacy," and while managers may not think that certain groups are "legitimate" in the sense that their demands on the firm are inappropriate, they had better give "legitimacy" to these groups in terms of their ability to affect the direction of the firm. Hence, "legitimacy" can be understood in a managerial sense implying that it is "legitimate to spend time and resources" on stakeholders, regardless of the appropriateness of their demands.

There is, of course, a broader notion of legitimacy which is at issue here. Do all stakeholders have an equally "legitimate" claim to the resources of the corporation? Is the problem of the distribution of the goods and services of the corporation to be left up to the marketplace? Or, is it to be solved in virtue of the political "clout" of various stakeholder groups? For the present time I shall put these questions aside, not because they do not bear fruitful research, but rather, I believe that first we must understand the weaker sense of "stakeholder legitimacy": if you want to be an effective manager, then you must take stakeholders into account. If we can integrate the concerns with multiple groups, from government to owners to customers, we will be in a better position to answer the important policy questions which the stakeholder notion raises.[22]

In line with Thompson's (1967) claim, "stakeholder" should denote "those groups which make a difference," or more formally:

> A stakeholder in an organization is (by definition) any group or individual who can affect or is affected by the achievement of the organization's objectives.

It is obvious from my argument in chapter one why those groups who can affect the corporation should be "stakeholders." The point of strategic management is in some sense to chart a direction for the firm. Groups which can affect that direction and its implementation must be considered in the strategic management process. However, it is less obvious why "those groups who are affected by the corporation" are stakeholders as well, for not all groups who can affect the corporation are themselves affected by the firm. I make the definition symmetric because of the changes which the firm has undergone in the past few years. Groups which 20 years ago had no effect on the actions of the firm, can affect it today, largely because of the actions of the firm which ignored the effects on these groups. Thus, by calling those affected groups "stakeholders," the ensuing strategic management model will be sensitive to future change, and able to turn new "external changes" into internal changes. One way to understand the definition is to think of the stakeholder concept as an umbrella for the problems in business strategy and corporate social responsiveness. To be an effective strategist you must deal with those groups that can affect you, while to be responsive (and effective in the long run) you must deal with those groups that you can affect.

Some research already exists which explicitly uses the stakeholder concept in this form, and I shall briefly summarize it here, returning to its claims in subsequent chapters.

Sturdivant (1979) investigated the question of whether the values of senior management and certain stakeholders in the firm were different. He used a previously tested instrument, the Sturdivant-Ginter questionnaire, and surveyed a wide sample of activist groups. Sturdivant found that there were fundamental differences in the values of executives and activists as measured by this instrument.

Sonnenfeld (1981) surveyed the forest products industry in an attempt to define the whole array of public issues and responses to these issues. He measured the amount of interaction time that each relevant functional department had with stakeholders, and surveyed stakeholders to determine their perceptions of the companies' responsiveness to public issues. Sonnenfeld's study was the first in-depth analysis of an industry using systematic surveys and interviews as data. The findings of his study will go a long way towards understanding the ability of strategic management models to respond to public issues.

Chakravarthy (1981) studied the ability of several companies in the coal industry to respond to environmental change. The issues which he studied were more far-reaching than previous studies, since he developed a model for adaptation using in part the stakeholder concept, for both business and public issues. Miles (1982) conducted an in-depth analysis of the tobacco industry and tried to merge the concepts to corporate strategy, "constituencies," and business-government relations. Tiffany (1982) analyzed the evolution of the steel industry since the turn of the century showing the complex interactions and the conscious strategies which were put in place to manage stakeholder groups.

Emshoff and Freeman (1979) reported the results of a specific intervention with New England Telephone on a more traditional "business" issue, which was surrounded by a number of stakeholder concerns, and began to develop several prescriptive propositions for management. Emshoff and Freeman (1981) applied a specific managerial process in a clinical study of the U.S. Brewer's Association and the problem of beverage container legislation. Emshoff and Finnel (1979) used the concept in an analysis of strategy formulation in another clinical study, and Mitroff and Emshoff (1979) and Mason and Mitroff (1982) have used the concept in a number of ways in their formulation and testing of "strategic assumptions analysis." Emshoff (1980) combines stakeholder analysis and strategic assumptions analysis into a general strategy formulation model. Freeman and Reed (1983) argue that the stakeholder concept can be used to understand the corporate governance debate, and Freeman (1983) uses the stakeholder concept as an umbrella for strategic management.

In the following chapters I shall continue within the stream of this research, enriching it by drawing on the literature mentioned above, and expanding it by developing the stakeholder concept into an approach to strategic management. To do so necessitates an analysis of a broad range of strategic tasks, from strategy formulation to organization structure, and a number of additional concepts. My emphasis throughout will be on strategic management, that is, how can the stakeholder concept be used to enrich our understanding of how organizations do, and should, set and implement direction.

A NOTE ON MANAGEMENT THEORY

I believe that management theory is inherently prescriptive, though not in the sense that prescriptions are ungrounded and bear no relationship to descriptions of real organizations. The stakeholder model developed here is prescriptive in the sense that it prescribes action for organizational managers in a rational sense. "If you want to manage effectively, then you must take your stakeholders into account in a systematic fashion," is a prescription, but, it is fundamentally different from "You ought to communicate with critics."[23] I am more certain about the relevance of the first kind of prescription than of the latter. I do believe however, that managers must understand those value statements which the second prescription illustrates. And indeed, the point of formulating enterprise level strategy is to understand those value statements.

Good theories of management are practical, that is, they are relevant to practising managers. Not only do they predict what may happen and allow managers to adjust to those predictions, but they explain the existence of certain phenomena (which the theory is about) and the relationships which these phenomena bear to other phenomena. The stakeholder approach is about groups and individuals who can affect the organization, and is about managerial behavior taken in response to those groups and individuals. I hope that the attention to such detail in the following chapters will be properly construed as an attempt to be clear about the practical implications and the limitations of the stakeholder approach. Because good theories are practical, it is often said that such relevance comes at the expense of "rigor." I believe however that this argument misses a logical point. Any theory or model which is not logically or conceptually rigorous will not be practical. It simply will not guarantee that the conclusions which managers may draw from it are valid. It is not necessary for the theory to be empirically tested for it to be true. However, the more empirical evidence there is for the propositions of the theory, the more confidence we have in it. The role of empirical support for a theory is important both in constructing and in validating a theory, however, conceptual rigor outweighs empirical support. My purpose is to develop a rigorous statement of a stakeholder approach to strategic management. However, I shall concentrate on constructing the approach rather than on the empirical research which can be adduced to validate it. I believe that there is too little theory in strategic management, and I hope to add a modest number of theoretical propositions using the stakeholder concept.

SUMMARY

The stakeholder concept has developed in a number of disciplines over the course of its history. The literature in strategic planning, systems theory, corporate social responsibility and organization theory can be used to develop an approach to strategic management. I have claimed that there is a need for an inclusive definition of stakeholder including as stakeholders, those groups who can affect or are affected by the achievement of an organization's purpose. And, I have speculated that approaches to strategic management, such as the one developed in subsequent chapters, must be prescriptive of effective managerial actions as well as conceptually rigorous.

NOTES

1. The precise origins of "stakeholder" were surprisingly difficult to track down. Ackoff (1974) credits Ansoff (1965) and quotes the references in Ansoff's book to Abrams (1954) and Cyert and March (1963). Mason and Mitroff (1982) attribute the term to Rhenman (1968). An anonymous referee for *Applications of Management Science* pointed out to me that the concept had originated at SRI, which I duly acknowledged in Emshoff and Freeman (1981). Soon thereafter Dr. William Royce, of SRI International, in private correspondence, recounted the story of Ansoff, Robert Stewart and Marion Doscher at Lockheed and SRI in the early 1960s. Professor Kirk Hanson of Stanford then pointed out to me that Rhenman was visiting at Stanford while he was writing *Industrial Democracy in the Workplace*. A trip to SRI International in the summer of 1980 and a talk with Dr. Royce and Dr. Arnold Mitchell clarified a number of historical issues. They were gracious enough to share some original files from that period of time, and to them and to SRI, International, I am grateful.
2. William Royce, private correspondence.
3. The necessity of analyzing social and political issues together with economic and technological ones is argued in Ansoff (1979), Hayes and Abernathy (1980) and Charan and Freeman (1980) as well as numerous other places. The split between "economic" and "social" analysis has always been conceptually arbitrary, or at least since the beginnings of modern utility theory as a foundation for economics (von Neumann and Morgenstern (1946)). Rational agents have preferences over many kinds of things, only some of which are measured in dollar terms. The concept of rationality is much broader than some business theorists pretend. See for instance Schelling (1960, 1978), Buchanan and Tullock (1965) as well as the work of many other "decision theorists."
4. A word of caution about the role that definitions play in theories is appropriate here. Quine (1960) claims that "sentences do not confront the tribunal of experience alone." Austin (1961), Wisdom (1953) and Wittgenstein (1953) and the resulting literature in philosophy of language give quite complex and sophisticated analyses of the role that definitions play in languages.
5. For a brief history of the business policy "paradigm" see Ansoff (1977), Hofer, Murray, Charan and Pitts (1980) and Schendel and Hofer (1979, 1979a).
6. See Utterback (1979) for an analysis of environmental scanning as a strategic task.
7. For a sample of the strategic planning and management literature from multiple

points of view see Abell (1980), Ansoff (1979a), Ansoff, Declerk and Hayes (1976), Grant and King (1979), Hofer and Schendel (1978), Lorange (1979, 1980), Porter (1980), Schendel and Hofer (1979) and Vancil (1979).

8. The precise origins of systems theory are hard to determine. Certainly Barnard (1938) is a candidate for founder. However, the systems perspective on problem-solving goes much further back. Descartes (c. 1628) argued that both analysis (breaking things down into its component parts) and synthesis (building things up by seeing what they were a part of) went together in his oft-derided "rational method." See Churchman (1971) for an attempt to relate the systems approach to traditional philosophy.

9. See Astley (1981) for a recent attempt to work out this notion of collective strategy.

10. The literature is too enormous to document fully here. See Carroll and Beiler (1977), Sturdivant (1977) and Post (1978, 1981) for reviews of the literature.

11. For a commentary on this period of time in the U.S. see Broder (1981), Calleo (1982), Halberstam (1969), Schlesinger (1965) and White (1982) for a sample of views.

12. For a different use of the "stakeholder audit" concept see Freeman, Banker and Lee (1981) and chapter Four below.

13. An interesting argument which turns on the theory of public goods is Keim (1978, 1978a).

14. While too much cannot be made of the way in which professional organizations choose to organize themselves, it should be noted that such an organizational principle could tend to reinforce the split between "business" and "social" issues from an intellectual standpoint.

15. Mason and Mitroff (1982) mistakenly give Rhenman credit for developing the stakeholder concept. Professor Kirk Hanson's help in tracking down the influence of Rhenman on the development of the stakeholder concept is gratefully acknowledged.

16. Curiously enough, the stakeholder concept does not play a role in Rhenman (1973).

17. If we replace "and" with "or" in Rhenman's definition we get a concept similar to the one developed throughout this monograph.

18. See for instance Hirsch (1972), Terreberry (1968), and Evan (1972) for a few of the many applications of this concept.

19. Page 11 of Lawrence and Lorsch (1967). I shall address the implications of the stakeholder approach to the functional disciplines of management in chapter eight below.

20. Page 2 of Pfeffer and Salancik (1978).

21. Rhenman (1973) is an exception.

22. The broader question of stakeholder legitimacy, and ultimately the justification of the modern corporation is beyond the scope of the present book, and is the subject of a joint research project with W.M. Evan. Evan (1975) raises these questions in essentially a stakeholder framework.

23. Kant (1787) distinguished between hypothetical and categorical imperatives.

Modern conceptions of rationality have to do with hypothetical imperatives, such as "if you want to maximize market share, then you must deal with consumer advocates." While such statements are normative, they are not absolute. The means-ends relationship and the linkage between what is rational and what is moral is often misunderstood. See for instance Sen and Williams (1982) for a set of recent essays on the connection.

Three

STAKEHOLDER MANAGEMENT: FRAMEWORK AND PHILOSOPHY

INTRODUCTION

Organizations have stakeholders. That is, there are groups and individuals who can affect, or are affected by, the achievement of an organization's mission. I have shown that if business organizations are to be successful in the current and future environment then executives must take multiple stakeholder groups into account. The purpose of this chapter is to discuss how the stakeholder management framework can be used to better understand and manage both internal and external change, and how the management philosophy which accompanies this framework fits into our more customary way of thinking about organizations.[1]

THE STAKEHOLDER FRAMEWORK

The literature discussed in chapter Two yields a broad range of definitions of the stakeholder concept. From the standpoint of strategic management, or the achievement of organizational purpose, we need an inclusive definition. We must not leave out any group or individual who can affect or is affected by organizational purpose, because that group may prevent our accomplishments. Theoretically, therefore, "stakeholder" must be able to capture a broad range of groups and individuals, even though when we put the concept to practical tests we must be willing to ignore certain groups who will have little or no impact on the corporation at this point in time. Such a broad notion of "stakeholders" will include a number of groups who may not be "legitimate" in the sense that they will have vastly different values and agendas for action from our own. Some groups may have as an objective simply to interfere with the smooth operations of our business. For instance, some corporations must count "terrorist groups" as stakeholders. As unsavory as it is to admit that such "illegitimate" groups have a stake in our business, from the standpoint of strategic management, it must be done. Strategies must be put in place to deal with terrorists if they can substantially affect the operations of the business.

The stakeholder concept must capture specific groups and individuals as "stakeholders." As we move from a theory of strategic planning to a theory of strategic management, we must adopt an action orientation.[2] Therefore, if the stakeholder concept is to have practical significance, it must be capable of yielding concrete actions with specific groups and individuals. "Stakeholder Management" as a concept, refers to the necessity for an organization to manage the relationships with its specific stakeholder groups in an action-oriented way.

The very definition of "stakeholder" as "any group or individual who can affect or is affected by the achievement of an organization's purpose" gives rise to the need for processes and techniques to enhance the strategic management capability of the organization. There are at least three levels at which we must understand the processes which an organization uses to manage the relationships with its stakeholders.[3]

First of all, we must understand from a rational perspective, who are the stakeholders in the organization and what are the perceived stakes. Second, we must understand the organizational processes used to either implicitly or explicitly manage the organization's relationships with its stakeholders, and whether these processes "fit" with the rational "stakeholder map" of the organization. Finally, we must understand the set of transactions or bargains among the organization and its stakeholders and deduce whether these negotiations "fit" with the stakeholder map and the organizational processes for stakeholders.

We might define an organization's "Stakeholder Management Capability" in terms of its ability to put these three levels of analysis together.[4] For instance, an organization which understands its stakeholder map and the stakes of each group, which has organizational processes to take these groups and their stakes into account routinely as part of the standard operating procedures of the organization and which implements a set of transactions or bargains to balance the interests of these stakeholders to achieve the organization's purpose, would be said to have high (or superior) stakeholder management capability. On the other hand, an organization which does not understand who its stakeholders are, has no processes for dealing with their concerns and has no set of transactions for negotiating with stakeholders would be said to have low (or inferior) stakeholder management capability. Each of these levels of analysis needs to be discussed in more detail, if the stakeholder management framework is to become a useful managerial tool.

THE "RATIONAL" LEVEL: STAKEHOLDER MAPS

Any framework which seeks to enhance an organization's stakeholder management capability must begin with an application of the basic definition. Who are those groups and individuals who can affect and are affected by the achievement of an organization's purpose? How can we construct a "stakeholder map" of an organization? What are the problems in constructing such a map?

In chapter One we saw that the traditional picture of the firm consisting of customers, suppliers, employees and owners had to change to encompass the emergence of environmentalists, consumer advocates, media, governments, global competitors, etc. I based this argument on an analysis of the changes in the business environment of the last twenty years. The resulting generic stakeholder map (Exhibit 1.5) can serve as a starting point for the construction of a stakeholder map of a typical firm. Ideally the starting point for constructing a map for a particular business is an historical analysis of the environment of that particular firm.[5] In the absence of such an historical document, Exhibit 1.5 can serve as a checkpoint for an initial generic stakeholder map.

Exhibit 3.1 depicts a stakeholder map around one major strategic issue for one very large organization, the XYZ Company, based primarily in the U.S. The executives in this organization, however, believed that Exhibit 3.1 could be used as a starting point for almost any issue of importance to the company. Unfortunately, most attempts at "stakeholder analysis" end with the construction of Exhibit 3.1. As the literature of the last chapter suggests, the primary use of the stakeholder concept has been as a tool for gathering information about generic stakeholders. "Generic stakeholders" refers to "those categories of groups who can affect. . . ." While "Government" is a category, it is EPA, OSHA, FTC, Congress, etc. who can take actions to affect the achievement of an organization's purpose. Therefore, for stakeholder analysis to be meaningful Exhibit 3.1 must be taken one step further. Specific stakeholder groups must be identified. Exhibit 3.2 is a chart of specific stakeholders to accompany Exhibit 3.1 for the XYZ Company. Even in Exhibit 3.2 some groups are aggregated, in order to disguise

EXHIBIT 3.1   *Stakeholder Map of a Very Large Organization*

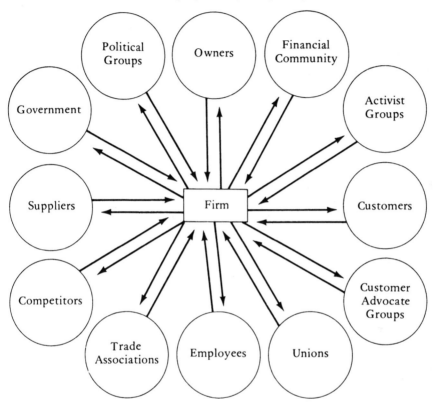

the identity of the company. Thus, "Investment Banks" would be replaced by the names of those investment banks actually used by XYZ.

Most very large organizations have a stakeholder map and accompanying stakeholder chart which is relatively similar to the above exhibits. There will be variations among industries, companies, and geographies at the specific stakeholder level, but the two exhibits can be used as a checklist of stakeholder groups. In the several industries analyzed in subsequent chapters there is little variation at the generic level.

Exhibit 3.3 is an analysis of the stakes of some of those specific stakeholder groups listed in the stakeholder chart (Exhibit 3.2). Thus the stake of Political Parties #1 and #2 is as a heavy user of XYZ's product, as being able to influence the regulatory process to mandate change in XYZ's operations and as being able to elevate XYZ to national attention via the political process. The stake of XYZ's owners varied among specific

EXHIBIT 3.2   *Specific Stakeholders in a Very Large Organization**

Owners	Financial Community	Activist Groups
Shareowners	Analysts	Safety and Health
Bondholders	Investment Banks	Groups
Employees	Commercial Banks	Environmental
	Federal Reserve	Groups
		"Big Business" Groups
		Single Issue Groups

Suppliers	Government	Political Groups
Firm #1	Congress	Political Party #1
Firm #2	Courts	Political Party #2
Firm #3	Cabinet Departments	National League
etc.	Agency #1	of Cities
	Agency #2	National Council
		of Mayors
		etc.

Customers	Customer Advocate Groups	Unions
Customer Segment #1	Consumer Federation	Union of Workers #1
Customer Segment #2	of America	Union of Workers #2
etc.	Consumer's Union	etc.
	Council of Consumers	Political Action Com-
	etc.	mittees of Unions

Employees	Trade Associations	Competitors
Employee Segment #1	Business Roundtable	Domestic Competitor
Employee Segment #2	NAM	#1
etc.	Customer Trade	Domestic Competitor
	Org. #1	#2
	Customer Trade	etc.
	Org. #2	Foreign Competitor #1
	etc.	etc.

*The actual names of most stakeholder groups are disguised.

stakeholder groups. Those employees of XYZ, and the pension funds of XYZ's unions are concerned with long term growth of XYZ's stock, as their retirement income will depend on the ability of XYZ to earn returns during their retirement years. Other shareowner groups want current income, as XYZ has been known for steady though modest growth over time.

EXHIBIT 3.3   *"Stakes" of Selected Stakeholders in XYZ Company*

Customer Segment #1

High Users of Product
Improvement of Product

Customer Segment #2

Low Users of Product
No Available Substitute

Employees

Jobs and Job Security
Pension Benefits

Owners

Growth and Income
Stability of Stock Price and
  Dividend

Political Parties #1 and #2

High Users of Product
Able to Influence Regulatory
  Process
Able to get Media Attention on a
  National Scale

Consumer Advocate #1

Effects of XYZ on the Elderly

Consumer Advocate #2

Safety of XYZ's Products

Customer Segment #1 used a lot of XYZ's product and was interested in how the product could be improved over time for a small incremental cost. Customer Segment #2 used only a small amount of XYZ's product, but that small amount was a critical ingredient for Customer Segment #2, and there were no readily available substitutes. Thus, the stakes of the different customer segment stakeholders differed. One consumer advocate group was concerned about the effects of XYZ's product decisions on the elderly, who were for the most part highly dependent on XYZ's products. Another consumer advocate group was worried about other XYZ products in terms of safety.

As these three exhibits from the XYZ company show, the construction of a rational "stakeholder map" is not an easy task in terms of identifying specific groups and the stakes of each. The exhibits are enormously oversimplified, for they depict the stakeholders of XYZ as static, whereas in reality, they change over time, and their stakes change depending on the strategic issue under consideration. Similarly, the construction of an accurate portfolio is no easy task as the problems with measuring market share have shown.[6] The task becomes even harder when we consider several implications of these three exhibits.

The first implication is that just as Merton (1957) identified the role set for individuals in society, and Evan (1966) generalized this notion for organizations to the organization set, we might combine these notions into a "stakeholder role set," or the set of roles which an individual or group may play qua being a stakeholder in an organization. For example, an employee may be a customer for XYZ's products, may belong to a Union of XYZ, may be an owner of XYZ, may be a member of Political Party #1 and may even be a member of a consumer advocate group. Many members of certain stakeholder groups are also members of other stakeholder groups, and *qua stakeholder in an organization* may have to balance (or not balance) conflicting and competing roles. Conflict within each person and among group members may result. The role set of a particular stakeholder may well generate different and conflicting expectations of corporate action. For certain organizations and stakeholder groups, a "stakeholder role set" analysis may be appropriate. Exhibit 3.4 is an example of the stakeholder role set of employees and a government official.

The second implication of Exhibits 3.1–3.3 is the interconnection of stakeholder groups, or the interorganizational relationships which exist, a phenomenon well studied in organization theory.[7] XYZ Company found that one of their Unions was also a large contributor to an adversarial consumer advocate group who was pressuring a key government agency to more closely regulate XYZ. Networks of stakeholder groups easily emerge on a particular issue and endure over time. Coalitions of groups form to help or oppose a company on a particular issue. Also, some firms are quite adept at working indirectly, i.e. at influencing Stakeholder A to influence Stakeholder B, to influence Stakeholder C.[8]

More traditional examples include the emergence of the courts as a key stakeholder in takeover bids. Marathon Oil successfully used the courts and the agencies involved in anti-trust to fend off a takeover bid from Mobil, while finding U.S. Steel to come to the rescue. AT&T recently marshalled the support of employees and stockholders to try and influence the Congress through a letter writing campaign. While there is some research on power and influence networks, little is known in the way of formulating strategies for utilizing such networks in a positive and proactive fashion. Little is known, prescriptively, about what range of alternatives is open to managers who want to utilize such an indirect approach to dealing with stakeholders. Exhibit 3.5 depicts several networks, and illustrates the necessity of thinking through the possible networks that can emerge or be created to accomplish organizational purposes. We will return to the question of how to analyze networks and coalitions in chapter Five.

The courts and some government agencies play a special role as part of the process by which groups interact. They have a special kind of "stake," one of formal power. While they usually do not initiate action, they can

EXHIBIT 3.4   *Possible Stakeholder Role Set of Employees and Government Officials*

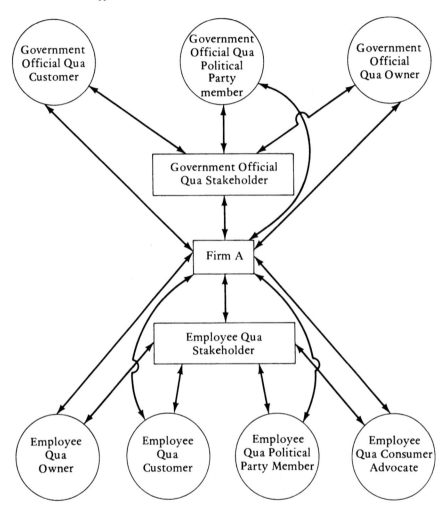

serve as resolver of conflicts, or as guarantor of due process. If we generalize this notion we see that another implication of Exhibits 3.1–3.3 is the phenomenon of the differing kinds of stakes and the differing perceptions of stakes that various groups have. "Stake" is obviously multi-dimensional, and not measured solely in dollar terms. However, exactly what the dimensions are of "stake" is a more difficult question. Exhibit 3.3 ranges across a broad spectrum of phenomena from more traditional dollar returns to

EXHIBIT 3.5   *Typical Indirect or Coalition Strategies*

Example #1: Marathon-U. S. Steel Merger

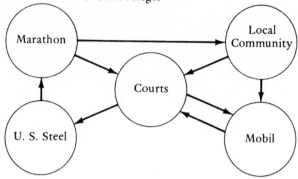

Example #2: AT&T and House Bill 5158

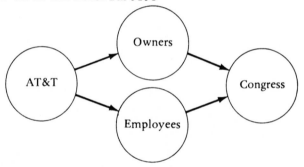

stockholders to a call for "voice" in running the affairs of XYZ (Hirschman, 1970). Clearly we need to understand "stake" in more detail.

One analytical device depicts an organization's stakeholders on a two dimensional grid.[9] The first dimension categorizes stakeholders by "interest" or "stake." The idea is to look at the range of perceived stakes of multiple stakeholders. While there are no hard and fast criteria to apply here, one typical categorization is to classify "stake" from "having an equity interest in the firm" to "being an influencer" or in Dill's (1975) terms, "being a kibbitzer, or someone who has an interest in what the firm does because it affects them in some way, even if not directly in marketplace terms." We might place a middle category between equity and kibbitzer and call it having a "market" stake. These three catagories of a continuum are meant to represent the more traditional theory of the firm's differing stakes of owners (equity stake), customers and suppliers (market stake) and government (kibbitzer).

The second dimension of this classificatory grid can be understood in terms of power, or loosely speaking, the ability to use resources to make an event actually happen.[10] The three points of interest on this continuum are voting power, economic power and political power. Owners can expend resources in terms of voting power, by voting for directors or voting to support management, or even "voting" their shares in the marketplace in a takeover battle. Customers and suppliers can expend resources in terms of economic power, measured by dollars invested in R&D, switching to another firm, raising price or withholding supply. Government can expend resources in terms of political power by passing legislation, writing new regulations or bringing suit in the courts.

Exhibit 3.6 represents this two dimensional grid, with owners being the textbook case of an equity stake and voting power; customers and suppliers having a market stake and economic power; and government having an influencer stake and political power. The diagonal of Exhibit 3.6 represents the development of classical management thought, and the prevailing "world-view" of the modern business firm. Management concepts and principles have evolved to treat the stakeholders along this diagonal. Managers learn how to handle stockholders and boards of directors via their ability to vote on certain key decisions, and conflicts are resolved by the procedures and processes written into the corporate charter or by methods which involve formal legal parameters. Strategic planners, marketing managers, financial analysts and operations executives base their decisions on marketplace variables and a long tradition of wisdom and research based on an economic analysis of marketplace forces. Public relations and public affairs managers and lobbyists learn to deal in the political arena, to curry the favor of politicians and to learn to strategically use PACs, "perks" and the regulatory process.

As long as the "real world" approximately fits this diagonal case of Exhibit 3.6, there are few problems. Each set of managerial problems and issues has an established body of knowledge upon which to draw in times of change. Another way of further supporting the argument of chapter one is to say that the world can no longer be seen in terms of the diagonal of Exhibit 3.6.

For instance, in the auto industry one part of government has acquired formal power, the Chrysler Loan Guarantee Board, while in the steel industry some agencies have acquired economic power in terms of the imposition of import quotas or the trigger-price mechanism. The SEC might be viewed as a kibbitzer with formal power in terms of disclosure and accounting rules. Outside directors, now, do not necessarily have an equity stake. This is especially true of women, minority group members and academics who are becoming more normal for the boards of large corporations, even though it is far from certain that such directors are really effective and not merely

EXHIBIT 3.6   *Classical Stakeholder Grid*

POWER / STAKE	Formal or Voting	Economic	Political
Equity	Stockholders Directors Minority Interests		
Economic		Customers Competitors Suppliers Debt Holders Unions	Foreign Governments
Influencers			Consumer Advocates Government Nader's Raiders Sierra Club Trade Association

symbolic. Some traditional kibbitzer groups are buying stock and acquiring an equity stake. While they also acquire formal power, the yearly demonstration at the stockholders meeting or the proxy fight over social issues is built on their political power base. Witness the marshalling of the political process by church groups in bringing up issues such as selling infant formula in the third world or investing in South Africa at the annual stockholders meeting. Unions are using political power as well as their equity stake in terms of pension fund investing, to influence management decisions. Customers are being organized by consumer advocates to exercise the voice option and to politicize the marketplace.

In short the nice neat orderly world of Exhibit 3.6 is no longer realistic. The real world looks more like Exhibit 3.7 which catalogs some of the differing stakes mentioned above. Of course, each individual organization will have its own separate grid, and given the complexity of the stakeholder role set, there may be groups which fall into more than one box on the grid. The "messiness" of Exhibit 3.7 lends credence to the search for alternative ap-

EXHIBIT 3.7   *"Real World" Stakeholder Grid*

POWER STAKE	Formal or Voting	Economic	Political
Equity	Stockholders Directors Minority Interests		Dissident Stockholders
Economic		Suppliers Debt Holders Customers Unions	Local Governments Foreign Governments Consumer Groups Unions
Influencers	Government SEC Outside Directors	EPA OSHA	Nader's Raiders Government Trade Associations

plications of more traditional management knowledge and processes. Getting the last two degrees of knowledge out of the diagonal of Exhibit 3.6 is simply no longer good enough. We must find innovative ways of understanding both the power and stakes of a variety of influential and interconnecting stakeholder groups. Thus, MacMillan (1978) has argued that elements of strategic planning, traditionally reserved for market stakeholders with economic power, can be applied to the pure political case. While there is a long tradition of applying economic analysis to public policy questions, we are beginning to see the application of political concepts to economic questions, via recent discussions of co-determination and quality of work life.[11]

The second issue which a "power and stakes" analysis surfaces is the issue of congruent perceptions among organization and its stakeholders. There may be differing perceptions of both power and stake depending on one's point of view. An organization may not understand that a particular union has political power, and may treat the union as a "purely economic entity," only to be surprised when the union gets a bill introduced in the legislature to prevent a proposed plant closing. The ABC Company completely misread the power and stake of a group of realtors who were upset over a proposed change in ABC's product. The legislature in the state where ABC operates was composed of a number of realtors, who easily introduced a bill to prevent the proposed product changes. It was only by some tough eleventh hour negotiations that ABC escaped some completely devastating legislation. The DEF Utility could not understand why a consumer advocate group was opposing them on a certain issue which had no economic effect on the group. Finally they spoke to a consumer leader who told them that the only reason that the group was opposing them was that they had not informed the group of the proposed rate change before the case was filed. In short the consumer group perceived that they had a different stake than that perceived by the management of DEF. DEF managers naturally believed that so long as the proposed rate change was in the economic interest of the consumer group and its constituency there would be no problem. The consumer group perceived things differently, that they had a vital role to play as influencer or kibbitzer.

Analyzing stakeholders in terms of the organization's perceptions of their power and stake is not enough. When these perceptions are out of line with the perceptions of the stakeholders, all the brilliant strategic thinking in the world will not work. The congruence problem is a real one in most companies for there are few organizational processes to check the assumptions that managers make every day about their stakeholders. The rational analysis proposed here in terms of stakeholder maps must be tempered by a thorough understanding of the workings of the organization through an analysis of its strategic and operational processes.

THE "PROCESS" LEVEL: ENVIRONMENTAL SCANNING AND THE LIKE

Large complex organizations have many processes for accomplishing tasks. From routine applications of procedures and policies to the use of more sophisticated analytical tools, managers invent processes to accomplish routine tasks and to routinize complex tasks. To understand organizations and how they manage stakeholder relationships it is necessary to look at the "Standard Operating Procedures," "the way we do things around here," or the organizational processes that are used to achieve some kind of "fit" with the external environment. While there are many such processes, I shall concentrate on three well known and often used ones which purport to assist managers in the strategic management of corporations: Portfolio Analysis Processes, Strategic Review Processes and Environmental Scanning Processes. Variations of each of these strategic management processes are used in many large complex organizations. Each is usually inadequate in terms of taking complex stakeholder relationships into account and can be enriched by the stakeholder concept.

As mentioned in chapter Two, a good deal of research during the past twenty years has gone into understanding how a corporation can be seen as a set or portfolio of businesses.[12] Discrete business units are easier to manage and factors for success may well be easier to discern at the business level, than at the aggregated level of the corporation as a whole. The idea is to look at this set of businesses as stocks in a portfolio, with selection and nourishment given to winners and the door given to losers. Corporate planners and division managers (or Strategic Business Unit managers) plot the firm's set of businesses on a matrix which arrays an external against an internal dimension. The external dimension is usually labeled "Industry Attractiveness" and is usually measured by the growth rate of the industry under consideration. The internal dimension is usually labeled "Business Strengths" and is usually measured by market share. The corporate managers, after plotting the portfolio of businesses, seek to arrive at a balanced portfolio which maximizes returns (measured by Return on Equity or Earnings per Share or Return on Investment, etc.) and minimizes risks. Managers of particular businesses are then given a strategic mission based on their place in the portfolio and the potential of the business in question.

As an analytical tool and a management process, Portfolio Analysis can easily be out of touch with the stakeholder maps of most firms, as depicted in earlier exhibits. It simply looks at too narrow a range of stakeholders, and measures business performance on too narrow a dimension. While industry growth rate may be influenced by a number of non-marketplace stakeholders, to rely on it solely is to forego opportunities to influence stakeholders which may determine the future growth rate of the industry. For example, in the auto industry foreign competitors and governments, U.S. government agencies, the Congress, the courts, Ralph Nader and the Center for Auto Safety, environmental groups, the United Auto Workers, etc. all have an influence on future growth rates in the industry. However, if market share is relied upon as the sole criterion to measure competitive strength, we will not necessarily invest resources to deal with all of the groups who can influence future market position. Market share is too broad a measure and an overreliance on it can be detrimental.

To illustrate, consider the fate of JKL Company after spending several million dollars in R&D to develop a new product which would serve as a substitute to a large established market. JKL believed that the product offered high growth potential, and in accordance with accepted theory, introduced the new product before getting approval from a key government agency which closely regulates the industry in which JKL would be competing. The product was later found to be carcinogenic and JKL took a large loss. Market share was not the sole indicator of success for JKL.

Or, consider Proctor and Gamble's experience with Rely tampons. P&G had entered a mature market with a new product and spent heavily to gain market share. When reports linking Rely with toxic shock syndrome surfaced, P&G voluntarily removed Rely from the market rather than jeopardize future products and its corporate reputation. Industry attractiveness was not the sole criterion for the success of Rely. The future attractiveness of the market together with the possibility of tarnishing P&G's excellent reputation, caused them to make a decision that was quite expensive. Even though it cannot be shown that use of Rely caused the disease, the mere possibility of a linkage was enough for P&G to recall the product.

Similarly, Johnson and Johnson acted quickly to recall the entire stock of Extra-Strength Tylenol after several deaths were reported as a result of criminal tampering with bottles of the product. Someone allegedly put cyanide capsules in bottles of the product after it was on retail store shelves. Johnson and Johnson's actions were lauded on "60 Minutes," a show sometimes critical of the actions of large corporations. They have reintroduced the product in "tamper proof" packages, and advertised heavily. Portfolio analysis simply cannot prepare the corporation to deal with issues such as those faced by these companies. Industry or market attractiveness analysis is not sophisticated enough to yield practical conclusions in areas where economics, social and political forces and new technologies combine.

The point of this critique of portfolio analysis is not that managers must be certain of success before taking action, nor that since market share and industry attractiveness do not yield certainty they must be rejected. But, rather, that *the strategic processes that we use must, as a minimum, raise the right questions.* Portfolio analysis processes are enormously useful in helping managers understand some of the factors for success in a business, yet for the most part they ignore non-marketplace stakeholders who can often, though not always, determine the success or failure of a business.

A related issue is that to view the corporation as a portfolio of businesses to be managed like stocks in an investment portfolio runs the risk that managerial processes will become overly concerned with the financial performance of the corporation.[13] While financial performance is vital to the health of a business, it is but one criterion used by external stakeholders to judge the viability of the corporation over time. When interpreted too narrowly, portfolio processes are asking for more regulation of "externalities," more social critics and ultimately less productive work.

A second strategic management process, made famous by Harold Geneen at ITT is the strategic review process (Pascale and Athos, 1981; Charan, 1982). The idea of this process is for the top executives in a corporation to periodically meet with division or Strategic Business Unit (SBU) managers in a formal review session. Progress towards the planned goal is reviewed and new strategies are sometimes formulated. Top executives are usually accompanied by staff experts who have unearthed hard questions for the reviewee to answer. These reviews are usually built into the strategic planning cycle and are used as methods of communicating expectations and evaluating both personal and business performance.

The major problem with strategic reviews, in terms of being in synch with the stakeholder map of an organization, is that they do not encourage and reward an external orientation or stakeholder thinking. The emphasis from the point of view of the divisional manager under review is to "look good" to the senior executives who are reviewing performance. The formality of most strategic review processes and the mixing of personal and business evaluation make it difficult for the division manager to pay attention to multiple stakeholder concerns, which may contradict established corporate wisdom about the factors for success in a particular business. The nature of the organizational beast is such that it doesn't like and doesn't reward bad news and can hardly tolerate innovation. (How else can we explain the state of U.S. business?) It is much easier to play "Blame the Stakeholder" after the fact. "What senior executive in his right mind can hold a division manager accountable for a regulation which accounts for lost profits?" While responsibility for profits has been decentralized in most large multi-business firms, the responsibility for managing non-marketplace stakeholders (and some marketplace stakeholders) has not. Corporate Public Relations and Public Affairs are for the most part responsible for insuring a stable business climate for all the corporation's businesses. Division managers naturally perceive that they have a lack of control over critical stakeholder variables. During one seminar on stakeholder analysis with division managers the predominant response was "Great stuff, too bad my boss isn't here to hear it." Upon giving the same seminar to the top levels in the corporation the predominant response was "Great stuff, too bad our people (the division managers) weren't here to hear it." While too much should not be made of an isolated case, processes like the strategic review process can exacerbate the inability of the organization to ask the right questions.

A third strategic management process which explicitly tries to focus the organization externally is Environmental Scanning.[14] Adopting a metaphor of the radar technology, the idea is for corporate managers to "put up their antennae" and to scan the business horizon for key events, trends, etc. which will affect the business in the future. There are several versions of environmental scanning, each of which has strengths and weakness. Scenario building, whereby several key events and trends are linked together to form a possible future for the organization, is a favorite technique of some corporate planners and a product of several consulting firms. Another technique is trend analysis, whereby key variables, usually demographic and economic are monitored for change. And, futures research, which predicts the future, is yet another technique for helping managers scan the external environment.

While all of these processes are useful, most of them do not yield concrete action steps. It is hard to see how a 10 year forecast can help the SBU manager worried about how to overcome the latest regulation. Consequently, most corporate plans have an environmental scan in the front section of the plan, which states the environmental assumptions on which the plan is based. These assumptions are usually stated in terms of an econometric forecast of macro-economic variables such as inflation, unemployment, interest rates, etc. If the assumptions have not been forgotten by the time the plan produces concrete strategic programs, they surely will be by the time the results are reviewed. Then, no one is held accountable for using the wrong assumptions.

Focusing the strategic management processes in a corporation is a necessary condition for success in the current business environment. However, this external focus must be pervasive, from "front-end" analysis to control processes. Our portfolio analysis, strategic review and environmental scanning processes must get better and more sophisticated, yet this is not the whole story.

Organizational processes serve multiple purposes. One purpose is as a vehicle for communication, and as symbols for what the corporation stands for.[15,16] "The way we do things around here" depicts what activities are necessary for success in the organization. And, the activities necessary for success inside the organization must bear some relationship to the tasks that the external environment requires of the organization if it is to be a successful and ongoing concern. Therefore, if the external environment is a rich multi-stakeholder one, the strategic processes of the organization must reflect this complexity. These processes need not be baroque 25-step rigid analytical devices, but rather existing strategic processes which work reasonably well must be enriched with a concern for multiple stakeholders.

For instance, strategic management processes such as Exhibit 2.2 can easily be enriched by adding "who are our stakeholders" to a concern with corporate mission; "how do stakeholders affect each division, business and function, and its plans" to the formulation of strategic programs; "have we allocated resources to deal with our stakeholders" in the budget cycle; and "what are our critical assumptions about key stakeholders" to the control process. Exhibit 3.8 depicts a revised version of Lorange's schema for strategic management processes. Each of these questions which are added will be discussed in more detail in subsequent chapters. The point is that relatively simple ideas can be used to encourage managers to think through

EXHIBIT 3.8   *Typical Strategic Planning Process Schematic (Lorange, 1980)*

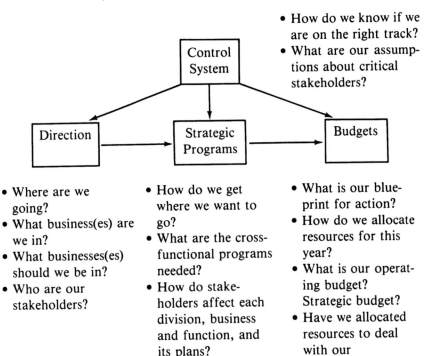

- How do we know if we are on the right track?
- What are our assumptions about critical stakeholders?

Control System

Direction → Strategic Programs → Budgets

Direction
- Where are we going?
- What business(es) are we in?
- What businesses(es) should we be in?
- Who are our stakeholders?

Strategic Programs
- How do we get where we want to go?
- What are the cross-functional programs needed?
- How do stakeholders affect each division, business and function, and its plans?

Budgets
- What is our blueprint for action?
- How do we allocate resources for this year?
- What is our operating budget? Strategic budget?
- Have we allocated resources to deal with our stakeholders?

the external environments of their businesses, and that such ideas must be added to organizational processes if they are to continue to be useful and to "fit" the stakeholder picture of the firm that is emerging.

THE "TRANSACTIONAL" LEVEL: INTERACTING WITH STAKEHOLDERS

The bottom line for stakeholder management has to be the set of transactions that managers in organizations have with stakeholders. How do the organization and its managers interact with stakeholders? What resources are allocated to interact with which groups? There has been a lot of research in social psychology about the so called "transactional environment" of individuals and organizations, and I shall not attempt to recapitulate that research here.[17] Suffice it to say that the nature of the behavior of organizational members and the nature of the goods and services being exchanged are key ingredients in successful organizational transactions with stakeholders.

Corporations have many daily transactions with stakeholder groups, such as selling things to customers and buying things from suppliers. Other transactions are also fairly ordinary and unexciting, such as paying dividends to stockholders or negotiating a new contract with the union. Yet when we move from this relatively comfortable zone of transactions to dealing with some of the changes that have occurred in traditional marketplace stakeholders and the emergence of new stakeholder groups there is little wonder that transactions break down. The lack of "fit" of an organization's transactions with its processes and its processes with its stakeholder map becomes a real source of discontent.

The XAB Company is an interesting study in how this lack of fit can be dysfunctional. XAB understood its stakeholder map and had some organizational processes to formulate and implement strategies with important non-traditional stakeholder groups. However, XAB sent some top executives out to talk with several of these groups who had little empathy with the causes of these groups. Needless to say the company has made little progress with them. Perhaps the strategy and the processes are inappropriate given the objectives of the company. However, another interpretation is that the transactions between company and stakeholders have not given the strategy and processes a fair test.

New England Telephone adopted a stakeholder approach to implementing a plan for charging for Directory Assistance in Massachusetts (Emshoff and Freeman, 1979). The rational analysis of the stakeholder environment was sound and the planning process used to chart out an implementation scenario was successful. However, its transactions with several key stakeholders, most notably and ironically, its own union, as well as the State Legislature, were not successful. The union got a piece of legislation prohibiting the company's plan passed in the state legislature, and even though the company was successful in persuading the Governor of Massachusetts to veto the legislation, as there was no public support, the state legislature overrode the Governor's veto, at the cost of $20 million to the customers of New England Telephone.

Consumer complaints are an area where there is usually a noticeable breakdown in the organization's Stakeholder Management Capability. Many large corporations simply ignore consumer complaints and dismiss them as that 5 percent of the market which they had rather someone else serve. Not only are there few successful processes for dealing with consumer complaints, but the transactions involved are material for every stand-up comic who ever walked. Nothing is more frustrating to the consumer than being told "sorry, I wish I could help you, but it's company policy to do things this way." One consumer leader commented that being told it was company policy may well finish the incident for the manager, but it begins the incident for the consumer advocate.[18] Several successful companies seem to "overspend" on handling consumer complaints. IBM's commitment to service, P&G's consumer complaint department and the Sears philosophy of taking merchandise back with no questions asked, yield valuable lessons in understanding the nature of transactions with customers. These companies act as if consumer complaints yield an opportunity for understanding customer needs which ultimately translates into a good bottom line and satisfied stakeholders.

Other sets of transactions, which often get out of line with process and rational analysis, include the firm's relationships with the media, shareholder meetings, meetings with financial analysts, encounters with government officials and day to day interactions with employees and unions.

Many managers actively perspire during "60 Minutes" in fear of being before the sharp tongues of the reporters and the skillful editing of the news show producers. Some organizations have become proactive and given their senior executives special training on "How to Meet the Press."

Shareholder meetings have become rituals for most corporations, except for the occasional meaningful proxy fight à la Rockwell-SCM. Rather than carry out meaningful transactions with shareholders in accordance with a clearly thought out strategy and process, executives now treat stockholders to lunch and speeches (with the stockholders' money) and a round of abuse from corporate critics who have bought one share of stock in order to be heard.

Meetings with financial analysts are another opportunity for transactions which can be made consistent with a firm's strategy and processes. Many executives understand that U.S. firms have underinvested in modern plant and equipment relative to foreign competition, and that they have lost sight of the marketing prowess of some of their competitors. How U.S. corporations can regain their competitive edge is a source of much debate in managerial and academic circles. Yet to regain competitive position will be neither easy nor inexpensive. Many U.S. firms will have to "take a hit on earnings" for several years in a row to be truly competitive. Most financial analysts are by their nature short-term focused. If executives use meetings with analysts to tout earnings per share, which may be inflated in real terms, then analysts will continue to expect short-term results. Talk of an investment strategy to regain competitive edge will be just talk. The transactions which executives make with analysts must square with the strategy of the organization regardless of the pain. By taking a leadership position in this area perhaps the thoughtful company can change the expectations of financial analysts. Of course, there is a vicious "chicken-egg" cycle here, that illustrates the dilemma of attempting to change stakeholder expectations. If we are measured on short-term performance results, and such a system is reinforced by expectations from the financial community, then to break the cycle involves additional pain. If strategic investments really are necessary then we must bite the bullet, and work to change the expectations of analysts, stockholders, and even board members, even at substantial personal risk.

Transactions with government officials often take place under adversarial conditions. Because government is a source of trouble for many companies, their transactions with government show their discontent. One company is reported to have rented a truck and dumped the requested documentation on the doorstep of the government agency which requested it. When stakeholder relationships are viewed on both sides as adversarial it is a small wonder that anyone ever changes. The Business Roundtable, as a transactional organization for large businesses with the government, published a study decrying the cost of regulation and calling for regulatory reform. While it is clear that the regulatory process has gotten out of control in some areas, a more helpful transaction would have been to try and gain some formal input into the regulatory process. To gain such input would mean that a firm's transactions with the government could be made congruent with its organizational processes, and the firm could formulate strategies for influencing government in a positive way, breaking down the adversarial barriers of so many years and so many hard-fought battles.

Perhaps the most fruitful area for transactional analysis is with the employee stakeholder group. One large company announced that it was committing to "Quality of Work Life," and set up national and local committees to form a partnership with its employees for the long term. However, shortly thereafter the company announced that many employees were in fact "surplus," and offered incentive programs for early retirement. Its transactions were simply inconsistent with its stated future direction for this stakeholder group. Much has been written lately about Japan and Theory Z (Ouchi, 1981), and co-determination in Europe. However, before U.S. managers launch into different directions with employees, perhaps we should understand whether our current managerial principles can work. When processes are set up to treat employees one way, no matter how well-meaning or "humanistic" they may be, and day-to-day transactions treat them another, it is not lack of theory that is the problem. The real importance of the suggestion box in Japan, and Quality Circles that work, is the consistent message that they send to employees, that their ideas have some impact on the firm.

If corporate managers ignore certain stakeholder groups at the rational and process level, then there is little to be done at the transactional level. Encounters between corporation and stakeholder will be on the one hand brief, episodic and hostile, and on the other hand non-existent, if another firm can supply their needs. Successful transactions with stakeholders are built on understanding the "legitimacy" of the stakeholder and having processes to routinely surface their concerns. However the transactions themselves, must be executed by managers who understand the "currencies" in which the stakeholders are paid. There is simply no substitute for thinking through how a particular individual can "win" and how the organization can "win" at the same time.

Clearly, there must be some "fit" among the elements of an organization's Stakeholder Management Capability — defined as its understanding or conceptual map of its stakeholders, the processes for dealing with these stakeholders, and the transactions which it uses to carry out the achievement of organization purpose with stakeholders. Exhibit 3.9 illustrates how some criteria might be used to measure the Stakeholder Management

EXHIBIT 3.9   *Stakeholder Management Capability = f (Stakeholder Map, Organizational Process, Stakeholder Transactions)*

(A) Understands Correct Stakeholder Map

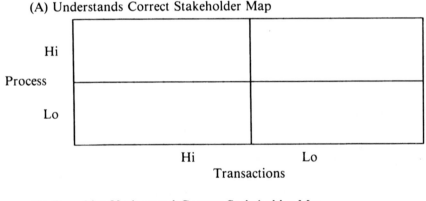

(B) Does Not Understand Correct Stakeholder Map

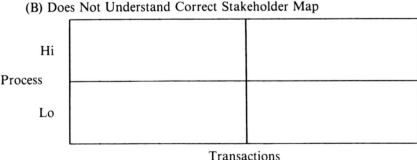

Capability of an organization. Whether an organization falls into the "Understands Correct Stakeholder Map" or "Does Not Understand Correct Stakeholder Map" is a relatively easy test. If, over time, an organization is continually surprised and continually plays "Blame the Stakeholder" then something is amiss. Whether an organization's processes and transactions are in line with that stakeholder map is a more difficult problem, for as I have shown, we do not have an adequate understanding as to what processes are appropriate for the multitude of stakeholders which firms now have. I shall return to the issue of defining a firm's Stakeholder Management Capability in Part II, chapters Four to Six, by way of suggesting several processes to be used to understand and manage stakeholder relationships. However, before attempting such a task it is necessary to be more explicit about the underlying philosophy which accompanies the Stakeholder Management model. How can the multitude of charts, graphs, and maps be integrated into the current managerial wisdom of running a successful business?

THE STAKEHOLDER PHILOSOPHY: A PLEA FOR VOLUNTARISM

While the temptation to play "Blame the Stakeholder" is a strong one, the major problem facing U.S. managers is really not an external one, but an internal one. Pogo's saying is once again applicable, "we have met the enemy, and he is us." The challenge for us is to reorient our thinking and our managerial processes externally, in order to be responsive to stakeholders. There are three levels of analysis which must be consistent, rational, process and transactional. However, there are several common themes, or philosophical propositions, which can serve as "intellectual glue" to hold these ideas together. Such a philosophy of management is necessary if we are to undertake the rather considerable task of regaining managerial competence in the new business environment, without losing even more of our competitive position in the marketplace. We must learn to use our current knowledge and skill-base to respond quickly to the "stakeholder challenge" and to create some initial "win-win" situations, if meaningful change is to occur.

Such a philosophy of management must be based on the idea of voluntarism, if it is to be implemented in U.S. based companies. Not only is voluntarism the only philosophy which is consistent with our social fabric, but the costs of other approaches are simply too high. Voluntarism means that an organization must on its own will undertake to satisfy its key stakeholders. A situation where a solution to a stakeholder problem is imposed by a government agency or the courts must be seen as a managerial failure. Similarly, a situation where Firm A satisfies the needs of consumer advocates, government agency, etc. better than Firm B, must be seen as a competitive loss by Firm B. The driving force of an organization becomes, under a voluntarism philosophy of management, to satisfy the needs of as many stakeholders as possible.

Consider the current "Stakeholder Dilemma" in which many firms find themselves. The following story is a simplified illustration based on several real situations.

An Activist Group (AG) is worried about some aspect of the ABC Company's Product Y. AG believes that if ABC is allowed to continue to produce and sell the product as it now exists, harm will be done to the public and to some of AG's constituents. AG is a credible group in some circles, especially with a key government agency and the national media. While it has not always been successful in getting large corporations to be responsive to its claims, it has had some successes. AG does not have a large reservoir of resources, nevertheless, it can devote adequate resources to the pursual of this current case. ABC believes that there is nothing wrong with its product, and that they should be allowed to continue to sell it. ABC is a veteran of several campaigns against its products, and it has won some and lost some in the past, but each has been expensive to wage.

Let us assume that ABC has two major strategic responses. It can *Negotiate* with AG to reach a mutually agreeable solution with respect to Product Y by listening to the concerns of the leaders of AG, explaining the position of ABC on Product Y, exploring solutions to AG's concerns, voluntarily agreeing how AG and ABC are to proceed on this and future areas of mutual concern, involving other interested parties in the discussions, etc. Or, it can *Play Hard Ball,* by ignoring AG's concern, perhaps disparaging AG and the cause that it stands for, respond when AG files a formal complaint, try to delay AG through countersuits, etc.

Of course, AG also has two very similar strategies. It can *Negotiate* with ABC by attending meetings with ABC managers and presenting the concerns of AG, attempting to understand the needs of other interested parties in Product Y, working with ABC to find a mutually acceptable solution, or a mutually acceptable process for finding a solution to the issue in a timely fashion, etc. AG can also *Play Hard Ball* by trying to make a splash in the media, bringing formal action in the Courts against ABC, complaining to government agencies which regulate ABC, tying ABC up on other issues unrelated to Product Y, introducing legislation prohibiting the sale of Product Y, etc.

Clearly if both parties negotiate, then an agreement which both find mutually satisfactory is the result.[19] Both parties may have to compromise, or at least be willing to compromise, if negotiation is to proceed in good faith, else Negotiate is an identical strategy to Play Hard Ball. If ABC negotiates and AG decides to play hard ball (perhaps after the first session, AG decides to double cross ABC), then ABC will be embarrassed and vulnerable to AG's formal challenges by having admitted that there may be some legitimacy to AG's claims about Product Y. AG members will have the feeling of having "beaten" ABC and may well be successful in their challenge to Product Y. Managers in ABC will not trust AG, and will respond in a "win-lose" way to AG's initiatives. On the other hand if AG tries to negotiate and ABC responds by playing hard ball, the same sorts of feelings arise for AG members as in the case where AG double-crossed ABC. If both parties Play Hard Ball, then the outcome is a long drawn out process with a solution imposed by the courts, government agencies and legislation—plus the cost of doing battle.

The most preferred outcome for ABC, in a cold and calculating sense, is for AG to negotiate and for ABC to double cross, since ABC then "beats" AG. The most preferred outcome for AG is for ABC to negotiate and for AG to double cross, thereby "beating" ABC. Yet when each plays its preferred strategy, Play Hard Ball, the result is far inferior to the result of playing the Negotiate strategy. In a real sense, by following the dictates of self-interest, both lose.

Exhibit 3.10 sets out the form of this stakeholder problem. Of course, it is identical in form with the so called "Prisoners' Dilemma Game" which illustrates the difficulty of achieving cooperative solutions under communication constraints.[20] In the classical form of the game, two suspects to a crime (which they actually committed) are caught, and interrogated separately. Each is told that if they confess a light sentence will be passed depending on whether or not the other confesses. If one prisoner turns state's evidence and the other does not, the book is thrown at the non-confessing prisoner. If both confess, then each gets a medium-length sentence, while if neither confess they are convicted of a much lesser charge. Neither confessing yields a preferred outcome to both confessing, but self-interest dictates confessing. The payoff structure is identical to Exhibit 3.10 with "Negotiate" replacing "Don't Confess" and "Play Hard Ball" replacing "Confess." If the prisoners could communicate they would form an agreement not to confess, or agree to get revenge if the other double-crossed. The lack of communication and the ability to form binding agreements dooms the prisoners to a heavy sentence.

The striking fact about the Stakeholder Dilemma version of this game is that there are absolutely no such communication constraints upon ABC and AG, and there are no constraints which prevent binding agreements. The managerial processes of both groups simply do not include considering communication and responsiveness as normal managerial activities. The

EXHIBIT 3.10   *The "Stakeholder Dilemma" Game*

outcomes	ABC's Strategies	
	Negotiate	Hardball
Negotiate	Mutually acceptable solution	ABC "wins", does not give in
AG's Strategies	Each must compromise	AG "loses"
Hard-Ball	AG "wins", does not give in	ABC & AG have solution imposed from outside
	ABC Loses	Cost of Adversarial proceedings

Payoff Table

		ABC	
		N	HB
AG	N	(2,2)	(4,1)
	HB	(1,4)	(3,3)

1 = Most Preferred Outcome

4 = Least Preferred Outcome

status quo imposes similar Prisoners' Dilemma-like constraints on ABC and AG.

The "Stakeholder Dilemma" game is one which is played out in some form in many organizations.[21] The only way out is to *voluntarily* adopt a posture of negotiation with stakeholder groups. Why negotiate voluntarily? Because, there is no other way to keep from having a solution imposed upon the organization from outside. And, to accept such an imposition of a solution to a problem is to give up the managerial role. Additionally, there seems to be no reason to pay the enforcement costs of adversarial proceedings. How many managers, lawyers and other professionals in large organizations spend most of their time in some sort of adversarial proceedings with stakeholders? Could not these resources be put to work more productively?

Our managerial processes must make managers "Free to Cooperate," rather than forcing them to play the Stakeholder Dilemma Game. Negotiation must become accepted practice, rather than conflict escalation through formal channels. The "try it, fix it, do it" mentality (Peters and Waterman,

1982) which many companies have used successfully with customers, must be applied to other stakeholder groups. This implies that voluntarism as a basic managerial value must permeate the organization which is successful in managing its relationships with multiple stakeholders.

This philosophy of voluntarism can be summarized in several prescriptive propositions which build on successful managerial theories and techniques. These propositions should be taken as tentative statements of a theory which needs much more elaboration, but which are hopefully practical suggestions.

> *Organizations with high Stakeholder Management Capability design and implement communication processes with multiple stakeholders.*

An example of a communication process is the recent formation by some utilities, of Consumer Advisory Panels, whereby the company brings issues which are usually settled in the formal regulatory process to the attention of leaders of consumer advocate groups well in advance of actually filing the rate case. Company executives and consumer leaders can negotiate on issues of mutual concern and avoid the costly adversarial proceedings of the rate case on a number of issues.

> *Organizations with high Stakeholder Management Capability explicitly negotiate with stakeholders on critical issues and seek voluntary agreements.*

An example of explicit negotiation is AT&T's convening an industry-wide conference of telecommunications executives, academics and consumer leaders over the issue of how to reprice local telephone service to bring it in line with its true costs. The outcomes of such a meeting are multiple and not all have been successful. However, the tenor of negotiation was set, and at least some of the local telephone companies have begun to explicitly follow up and negotiate on issues before the rate case proceedings.

> *Organizations with high Stakeholder Management Capability generalize the marketing approach to serve multiple stakeholders. Specifically, they overspend on understanding stakeholder needs, use marketing techniques to segment stakeholders to provide a better understanding of their individual needs and use marketing research tools to understand, viz., the multi-attribute nature of most stakeholder groups.*

We might define "overspending" as paying extra attention, beyond that warranted by considerations of efficiency, to those groups who are critical for the long term success of the firm. Overspending on stakeholders without whose support the company would fail can make sense in a number of instances. For instance P&G overspends on customers, interviewing several thousand customers a year. AT&T overspends on the attention it pays to the regulatory process, which was for a long time, its major source of revenue. Oil companies should, likewise, consider adopting a conscious policy of overspending on OPEC and government and stakeholders who can convey a positive image to the public. Chemical companies have not overspent on environmentalists, for the most part, with the results being onerous regulations and reputations as "spoilers of the environment."

> *Organizations with high Stakeholder Management Capability integrate boundary spanners into the strategy formulation processes in the organization.*

Many organizations have public relations and public affairs managers who have a good working knowledge of stakeholder concerns, and marketing and production managers who have expertise in the needs of customers and suppliers. However, these managers are not always a part of the strategic planning process. Hence, their expertise is lost. The assumption is that those managers who are rewarded to be sensitive to stakeholder needs are in the best position to represent their interests inside the organization. For this representation to occur successfully, those boundary spanners must have some credibility and some meaningful role to play in the organizational processes.

> *Organizations with high Stakeholder Management Capability are proactive. They anticipate stakeholder concerns and try to influence the stakeholder environment.*

The micro-computer industry is full of firms who practice anticipation as a way of life. These firms, some of them quite small, spend resources trying to "guess" what will best serve the customer in the future and where the market will be. Similarly, larger computer manufacturers, should be "guessing" that issues such as "privacy" and "individual freedom" and "computer literacy" will be major concerns as we move to technologies where "1984" is a distinct possibility. Several utilities try to anticipate the concerns of intervenors in their rate cases, and actively seek out those groups which will be critical to try and influence their views.

Organizations with high Stakeholder Management Capability allocate resources in a manner consistent with stakeholder concerns.

Emshoff (1980) tells of analyzing the stakeholders in a large international firm and ranking the stakeholders in order of importance. A rough check was also made of how the firm's resources were allocated to deal with those groups who would be most important in the future. The results of his investigation were that almost no resources were being allocated to deal with those groups felt to be absolutely critical to the future success of the company. Many executives are not reticent to play "Blame the Stakeholder," yet are not willing to devote resources to changing a particular stakeholder's point of view.

Managers in organizations with high Stakeholder Management Capability think in "stakeholder-serving" terms.

Just as many successful companies think in terms of "how to serve the customer" or "how to serve the employees," it is possible to generalize this philosophy to "how to serve my stakeholders." The "reason for being" for most organizations is that they serve some need in their external environment. When an organization loses its sense of purpose and mission, when it focuses itself internally on the needs of its managers, it is in danger of becoming irrelevant. Someone else (if competition is possible) will serve the environmental need better. The more we can begin to think in terms of how to better serve stakeholders, the more likely we will be to survive and prosper over time.

SUMMARY

The purpose of this chapter has been to explicate the stakeholder management framework and philosophy in general terms. I have shown that the three levels of analysis, rational, process and transactional must be consistent if the stakeholder concept is to make a difference in the way that organizations are managed. I have offered a brief sketch of the principles of voluntarism which I believe must go hand in hand with the application of the stakeholder concept to strategic management processes. In the following section I shall try to elaborate on how this is to be accomplished.

NOTES

1. The ideas presented in this chapter form part of a paper, "Managing Stakeholders: One Key to Successful Adaptation" presented to the Academy of Management National Meeting in August 1982. I wish to thank the participants in the symposium on managing adaptation, and its chairperson, Professor Bala Chakravarthy, for many helpful comments. In addition, several Faculty members at the University of Pittsburgh's Graduate School of Management and Rutgers University's Department of Management have made helpful comments. In particular Barry Mitnick and Aubrey Mendelow have been encouraging over the past year.

2. See Schendel and Hofer (1979) for a collection of essays that catalog the development of strategic management. Freeman (1983) is an overview of how the stakeholder concept fits into the development of strategic management theory, as well as a conceptual history of the term, "stakeholder."

3. My use of "rational," "process" and "transactional" parallels Graham Allison's (1971) three levels of organizational analysis. However, the three levels are not mutually exclusive as is often interpreted from Allison's account. Each level of analysis offers a different "lens" for viewing the organization and offers different kinds of explanation for some underlying phenomena broadly called "organization behavior." While the explanations at each level need not be identical, they do need to be consistent. Hence, the concept of "fit" among the three levels. The application of this three-leveled conceptual scheme is not unique to the stakeholder concept, as it is conceivable that we could define the process and transactional levels to complement a "portfolio approach" to strategic management.

4. Chakravarthy (1981) defines a similar concept of the adaptive capabilities of an organization using "management capability" and "organization capability."

5. For instance, as in a clinical case study, viz., Emshoff and Freeman's (1981) analysis of the brewing industry around the issue of beverage container legislation or an in-depth historical study as per Miles (1982) of tobacco companies.

6. The point here is that any theory must explicitly define the range of entities over which the propositions in the theory range. Sometimes it is convenient to speak of "stakeholders" as referring to categories, or sets, of specific groups. But, I insist that, strictly speaking, it is specific groups and individuals which are real, and hence, which can be strictly said to "hold stakes." For a philosophical treatment of the rather nominalistic position taken here see Nelson Goodman (1955).

7. The literature on interorganizational relations is quite enormous and is rich in insights for strategic management. Evan (1976), Negandhi (1975), Nystrom and Starbuck (1981) are excellent collections of articles, each of which contains review articles which summarize the state of the art.

8. See Miles (1982) analysis of the tobacco industry, and Wilson (1981) for analyses of coalitions among interest groups.

9. For a discussion of this grid in the context of corporate governance see Freeman and Reed (1983).

10. The approach to "power" outlined here is quite simplistic, and should be viewed as illustrative rather than definitive. Pfeffer (1981) is suggestive of a more comprehensive analysis of the concept which could be applied to the "power and stakes" grid.

11. For an interesting distinction between economic and political explanations see the work of Hirschman (1970; 1981).

12. For a more complete discussion of portfolio theory see Abell (1980), Rothschild (1976), Lorange (1980), and the literature referenced in these works.

13. The critique of portfolio theory surfaced here is quite general in that it applies equally well to "misuses" of other processes. The point is that the processes must be capable of "fitting" with the other levels of analysis. They must describe the world as it is, and must prescribe transactions that are consistent with such a description.

14. See Schendel and Hofer (1979) for several review articles on the state of the art in environmental scanning.

15. Lorange (1980) explores the communications aspects of strategic management, and recommends a 3 × 3 matrix to diagram such processes.

16. See Freeman (1983), and chapter Four below for an analysis of "what do we stand for" and the relationship of enterprise level strategy to the stakeholder concept and managerial values.

17. Emery and Trist (1965), Pfeffer and Salancik (1978) and many others have looked at the transactional level of organizations. Van de Ven, Emmett and Koenig (1975) describe several different models of transactions.

18. Interview with Professor Currin Shields, University of Arizona, and past President of the Conference of Consumer Organizations, a national consortium of local consumer advocate organizations.

19. The structure of the payoffs of the game outlined here presupposes that the issue is vague enough for there not to be a "clearly optimal" solution, but that a solution which is mutually acceptable is possible, and further that this mutually acceptable solution is preferable by both parties to a solution which is imposed by external parties, such as government.

20. There is a vast literature on the Prisoners' Dilemma, however, a clear discussion of the game can be found in Luce and Raiffa (1957). The game described here is similar to the plight of wheat farmers that is taught in every introductory economics class and chronicled by Garrett Hardin in the "Tragedy of the Commons."

21. I am not claiming that every game that a corporation plays with stakeholders is a Prisoners' Dilemma game, but only that some interactions are Prisoners' Dilemmas. The use of game theory in strategic management, as an explanatory tool, is a long-neglected research issue. McDonald (1977) is one source. Recent work in applying game theory at the conceptual level can be found in Brams (1981) and Muzzio (1982). Both of these works by political scientists yield interesting insights into the workings of individuals in organizations.

Part II

STRATEGIC MANAGEMENT PROCESSES

———————————————————

The purpose of Part II is to explain how the stakeholder concept can be built into the strategic management process that exists in most organizations. In addition, it explores several new processes for explicitly addressing stakeholder concerns. We shall build on Part I — a stakeholder approach to strategic management is both viable and necessary if U.S. business is to be responsive to its environment, and address the "bottom line" issue of how to be more effective.

Chapter Four, "Setting Strategic Direction," addresses two major issues in strategic management. The first is the role of the corporation in its larger context, or the formulation of "Enterprise Strategy." Given the current external environment we must answer the question, "what do we stand for?" One process for answering this question, and thereby formulating Enterprise Strategy, is explained and illustrated. The second issue is the development of a process to explicitly address stakeholder concerns in the more traditional formulation of corporate level strategy, or answering "what business(es) are we in?" The Stakeholder Audit is developed as a means to help managers define their business in a way that is directly responsive to stakeholders.

Chapter Five, "Formulating Strategies for Stakeholders," addresses the problem of how managers can take stakeholder concerns into account when formulating programs to achieve strategic direction. Specific strategies are developed which can be used with a variety of stakeholder groups. In particular we can generalize the generic strategies developed by Porter (1980), to apply to multiple stakeholder groups. Techniques for analyzing stakeholder behavior and possible coalitions are also explained.

Chapter Six, "Implementing and Monitoring Stakeholder Strategies," focuses on the need, recognized by all who have tried to use strategic management models, to pay a great deal of attention to implementation and control. How can we undertake transactions which will lead to the achievement of programs and ultimately corporate mission with respect to stakeholders? And, how can we monitor the implementation activities to be sure that programs are on track, or to make readjustments where necessary? A case study from recent experience is used to illustrate the complicated issues involved in implementing a stakeholder approach to strategy.

Four

SETTING STRATEGIC DIRECTION

INTRODUCTION

We begin with the analysis of how the stakeholder concept can be used to make strategic management decisions. Strategic management is a continuous process, and even though discrete points in time must be chosen for the purpose of making a decision, it must be done year-round, not just during the yearly "planning meetings." I will examine the issue of how direction can be set using the stakeholder concept, and in particular make clear that the concept is useful in looking at the role of an organization in society. The concept of "enterprise strategy" will be used to examine this societal issue. The concept of "stakeholder audit" will build on the enterprise strategy of a firm to enrich the understanding of corporate and business level strategy.

SETTING DIRECTION IN ORGANIZATIONS

One of the major contributions of the implementation of strategic management has been that executives can examine where the firm is headed, what the nature of its businesses will be and how changes in direction can be made.[1] In the early days of strategic management this examination of direction was made via long and involved processes which contained lots of steps and made nice flow charts resulting in binders of data which were for the most part never used.[2] Setting direction was seen as the "front end" of the yearly planning process which ultimately ended in the development of operational goals via "Management By Objectives" for the coming year. With the decentralization of planning and the further decentralization of organizations into strategic business units (Vancil, 1979), direction setting has begun to be seen as one of several strategic tasks that managers must perform in addition to controlling, evaluating, scanning and organizing.

Direction-setting decisions are not one-time decisions to enter a market. They affect every level of the corporation—by shifts in policy, reallocation of resources and changing the nature of the corporation's stakeholder map. New entrepreneurs decide on direction with the decision to enter a particular business, and ongoing businesses can change current direction or explicitly set a direction by examining the businesses they are in and want to be in.[3] Such decisions may represent shifts in the underlying values of the corporation and its managers.[4] New businesses sometimes require new ways of thinking about how to compete in the business, as well as whether the new business fits with the values and beliefs of employees. Decisions to divest or deemphasize a particular business which has long historical roots in the company can also signal that a shift in values has occurred. Perhaps the current direction of the business has proven to be unprofitable, or even illegal.

It is critical for us to carefully examine where the corporation is headed. Decisions to enter new areas of business, or to revise corporate goals, or to emphasize a particular function or strategic issue form the context out of which other strategic tasks can be undertaken and accomplished. Formulating new organizational structures and systems, or trying to get a handle on how well the corporation is performing make little sense without an understanding of the direction of the firm.

Strategic decisions are intentional actions which are designed to exert some measure of control over the future (and the present) state of the corporation. Too often we take too narrow a view of strategy. For instance, viewing the direction-setting task as merely(!) plotting the businesses of a firm on a product/market grid and ignoring the corporate culture and values has led many a firm down the primrose path of portfolio madness, with many unrelated and unmanageable businesses. Conversely, by paying attention only to culture and values and ignoring the "bottom line" implications of the culture, many firms have paved the way to their own obsolescence.[5]

AT&T's recent agreement with the Department of Justice, modifying the 1957 Consent Decree preventing AT&T from entering data processing businesses, is an example of the largest corporation in the world setting a new direction. By agreeing to divest the Bell Operating Companies, AT&T got out of the local telephone exchange business to concentrate on the long distance, terminal equipment and data network businesses. Long standing corporate policies have been called into question with this decision, in particular the way that AT&T accounts for its costs and the way that the Bell Operating Companies charge customers for basic telephone service. Resources will be allocated differently based on the nature of the new businesses. New relationships with key stakeholder groups – including the FCC, state public service commissions, customer segments, competitors and others – will have to be charted. The underlying values of AT&T employees as providers of a public service will need to change, as the business enters new competitive markets. The changes in these values and relationships with stakeholders will form a new context, or culture, for the AT&T of the future. AT&T's dramatic settlement with the Department of Justice on January 8, 1982 leaves no doubt as to whether the action was intentional. However, the consequences of the act will be felt for years to come, and will be watched as a dramatic example of a direction setting decision.[6]

IBM's decision to enter the personal computer business is another example of a large corporation undertaking a shift in its strategy and reversing the course of earlier policies. IBM's decision may have far reaching effects on others in the market, as well as on its own mix of products and services. The related decision to make IBM Personal Computers compatible with other industry products reverses a long standing tradition of setting industry standards at IBM. IBM gains a new set of stakeholders by entering this market, i.e., the morass of software, hardware and other microcomputer vendors, manufacturers, users and home computer "freaks" who previously had little to do with the acknowledged "computer industry leader."[7]

Companies in the U.S. automobile industry have recently gone through changes in direction, induced primarily by competition from Japan and Europe. Chrysler has begun to execute a turnaround from the brink of bankruptcy, and in so doing has changed direction by reallocating resources to the U.S. from its worldwide subsidiaries, and by focusing on the auto business and getting out of the defense and credit businesses. GM and Ford have set new directions by focusing on the development of the so-called "world car," and by paying attention, at least in Ford's case, to the need to change management philosophy and values regarding how to enable workers to be more productive.[8]

Traditionally, direction setting has consisted of defining the business or businesses of the corporation. From the dramatic pronouncements of management consultants ("you're in the packaging business, not the can business") to the more recent scholarly analysis of business definition by Abell (1980), setting direction has included answering the questions in Exhibit 4.1. The complicated nature of the modern corporation entails that we address these questions at several levels. It makes sense to set direction for

Exhibit 4.1   *Traditional Direction Setting Questions*

Corporate Level Questions

- What is our Business?
- What Businesses are we in?
- What Businesses do we want to be in?
- What Businesses should we be in?

Division Level Questions

- What are the synergies among the division's businesses?
- What is our division's Portfolio?
- How do we succeed in this "family of businesses"?

Business Level Questions

- How do we succeed in this business (or with these products)?
- Where are we going with this business?
- Should we be a "low cost producer," or should we "find a niche"?

the corporation as a whole, just as it makes sense to set direction for a division and for a particular organizational subset of a division.

Management theorists have usually divided questions of strategic management into three levels: corporate, division and business unit (or functional). As Exhibit 4.1 shows there are direction-setting questions at each level. The answers to direction-setting questions at the corporate level will form the context for answers at the division level. The answers to division-level questions will serve as context, or possibly constraints, on how to compete in a particular business. What then serves as context for the answer to the corporate-level questions, and how can corporate mission statements be formulated to have real meaning?

At least two separate sets of questions need to be addressed in formulating a statement of mission for the corporation. The first concerns a broad set of issues around values, social issues and stakeholder expectations of the firm. I shall call this level of analysis, "Enterprise Strategy," and discuss how these broad questions can be answered in practical terms. The second set of issues, is that given a broad statement of what the corporation, and we as its managers stand for, we can begin to articulate the range of business opportunities that are available to us. This level of analysis is usually called "Corporate Strategy." We shall see that it rests on an understanding of how the stakeholders of the corporation can affect each business area. I shall discuss a process called "Stakeholder Audit" to help us formulate concrete corporate-level strategy.

ENTERPRISE STRATEGY: WHAT DO WE STAND FOR?

It's late on a winter night, with snowdrifts and ice accumulating on roads keeping all but the most urgent of travellers off the highways. Yet some of those travellers have the blue and gold insignia of the telephone company repair trucks. Almost legendary in its attention to service, Bell Telephone has given its employees a keen sense of the need to keep service levels high, and to keep "the best telephone system in the world working smoothly." In fact Bell has not stopped at "service," but has taken it to its extreme with the concept of "universal service" to insure that virtually anyone can afford to be connected to "the best telephone system in the world." As Bell moves towards the break-up required by the recent settlement with the Department of Justice, and towards being more responsive to changes in the marketplace and new technologies, one of the critical questions for its management is what happens to the traditional values such as "service" and "universal service," the very foundations on which the company was engineered. What does Bell now stand for, and what are or should be the dominant business values of its managers and employees?

The commitment to service at Bell is not an isolated incidence only affordable by a gigantic monopoly business. Peters and Waterman (1982) tell of the myths and stories that have arisen in the Frito-Lay company around the ability of the route salesmen to visit 95% of their customers daily, from large supermarkets in urban areas with high volumes to general stores in Montana. They recount tale after tale of the managers in 3M, Johnson and Johnson, IBM, Citibank and other "excellent companies" who go to heroic limits to serve customers or to act on a particular organizational value. Ouchi (1981) writes of Theory Z and organizational communities built on trust. Pascale and Athos (1981) as well as Peters and Waterman (1982) relate the "Seven S" framework which relies on "shared values" to hold the organization together. Deal and Kennedy (1982) discuss the effect of "corporate culture," and Kidder (1981) tells of the warlike intensity of a group of engineers at Data General committed to building a new mini-computer. A host of social scientists and humanists have begun to worry about "organizational values," "business ethics," "the corporate society" and various other concepts around issues of personal values and ethics.

Most of these studies are couched in an idiom that is explicitly critical of the overreliance on the analytical techniques of strategic management. However, what the authors really point out is that strategic management must be interpreted more broadly to encompass the diverse realm of values. Every manager knows that value judgements are a primary ingredient of a successful strategy. Not only must values be taken into consideration when formulating strategy, but if the strategy is to be implemented the values of those affected by it must also be factored into the equation. When values are shared throughout an organization, implementation or strategy execution is relatively simple. None of these ideas is new. Military and religious organizations have practiced and virtually perfected the principle of depending on the shared values of their constituents. However, the idea is quite novel when we apply it to the conscious formulation of corporate strategy, since by its very nature the corporation is "impersonal" and "logical and rational" rather than "value-laden." Also, the prevailing idiom of strategic management has focused on the "hard facts" available from such disciplines as finance and accounting, economics and marketing.

In the strategy literature, Schendel and Hofer (1979) and Hofer et al. (1980) have identified a level of strategy called "enterprise strategy" which identifies the relationship of the firm with society.[9] Stemming from the research on the social responsibility of business, enterprise strategy, as formulated by these researchers answers the question, "What *should* we do?" In part enterprise strategy, on this interpretation, represents the moral or ethical component to strategic management which was identified by the early researchers in the field (Andrews, 1965; Ansoff, 1965; Chandler, 1962) but which has been largely ignored, except as an addition to the "business" concerns of the firm.

I suggested in chapters One and Two that the distinction between "social responsibility" and "business issues" was not useful in a world where there are multiple demands and stakeholder groups. We need to begin to think about integrating both of these concerns into a notion of "effective management," and in chapter Three we saw how the stakeholder concept can give us a start on this task.

Given the importance of values and management style, as well as the shifts in the business environment, we can redefine the notion of enterprise level strategy to more closely align "social and ethical concerns" with traditional "business concerns." Part of the difficulty in setting direction for a company is understanding the impact of changes in business strategy on the underlying values of the firm, and to understand the new stakeholder relationships which will be charted as a result. Major changes in direction cannot be accomplished without an understanding of the impact on stakeholders, especially those groups which are very "close" to the managers such as employees, unions, customers, etc. Direction setting is inherently tied to understanding what the managers and employees of a corporation stand for.

I propose to define enterprise level strategy as an answer to the question "WHAT DO WE STAND FOR?" At the enterprise level, the task of setting direction involves understanding the role of a particular firm as a whole, and its relationships to other social institutions. Appropriate questions are "what is the role of our organization in society," "what role do we want to play in society," "how is our organization qua organization perceived by our stakeholders," "what principles or values does our organization represent," "what obligations do we have to society at large," and "what are the implications for our current mix of businesses and allocation of resources."[10]

Enterprise level strategy does not necessitate a particular set of values, nor does it require that a corporation be "socially responsive" in a certain way. It does examine the need, however, for an explicit and intentional attempt to answer the question "what do we stand for."[11] The need for thinking about strategy at the enterprise level is reinforced by the analysis of the changing nature of the stakeholder map of many large organizations, and the complexity of organizational life. If this analysis has any merit at all, then the attempt to understand the context of the firm and how this context relates to more traditional direction setting questions must be made. By explicitly examining the "enterprise strategy" of a firm, I believe that intentional actions to change can be made which will yield a "fit" with the other levels of analysis.

Questions of enterprise level strategy have a long history, at least as far back as Berle and Means (1932), and perhaps to Adam Smith (1759).[12] However, there is little research which proposes both how to address the question of enterprise strategy and what kinds of strategies are available, in a systematic fashion.[13] There is a great deal of research on individual questions which need to be answered if enterprise strategy is to be formulated, but no systematic account of both strategic process and content.[14]

Exhibit 4.2 depicts a proposed process for formulating enterprise strategy. (1) Stakeholder Analysis, (2) Values Analysis, and (3) Societal Issues Analysis, must form the foundation for the articulation of enterprise level strategy. Let us look at each briefly, and then describe a range of several alternative enterprise strategies.[15]

Stakeholder Analysis

I suggested in chapters One to Three that managers must seek to gain a more accurate and detailed account of the external environment of which their organizations are a part. In particular, I have argued that the stakeholder concept can be used to better understand, at the rational level, exactly who are the groups and individuals that can affect or are affected by the achievement of an organization's purpose. Exhibits 3.1, 3.2, and 3.3 are examples of how this concept can be applied to construct a preliminary roadmap of

EXHIBIT 4.2   *Enterprise Level Strategy Process*

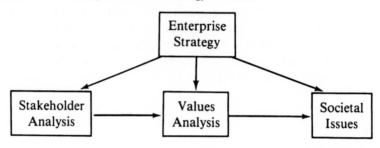

• Who are our stake-holders?	• What are the domi-nant organizational values?	• What are the major issues facing our society over the next 10 years? (economic, political, social, technological, etc.)
• What effects do we have on each in political, economic and social terms?	• What are the values of the key executives and board members?	
• How do these stake-holders perceive these effects?	• What are the values of the key stake-holders?	• How do these issues affect our organiza-tion and our stake-holders?

the firm. In using this analysis to better understand the enterprise strategy of the firm, it is sometimes necessary to take the analysis of "stakes" one step further, and to give it several dimensions.

A particular stakeholder may have "economic" effects on the firm, i.e., its action may affect the profitability, the cash flow or the stock price of the firm. Conversely, actions of the firm may affect the economic well-being of a particular stakeholder, as for instance, when that stakeholder has an economic stake or marketplace power. However, a firm may have economic effects on other stakeholder groups, such as government or activists groups, in terms of their budgets, their ability to raise funds, etc.

Customers and suppliers have economic effects on a business. If raw materials are not of a sufficient quality or price, a manufacturing firm will not be able to attain its normal quality standards. If customers become dissatisfied with a firm's product they can go elsewhere, or find a substitute. More subtly, regulatory agencies can have economic effects on a business by passing rules which involve spending resources to comply, or by preventing competition and allowing a small group of firms to effectively control the price in an industry.

A particular stakeholder group may have "technological" effects on the firm, by enabling or preventing the firm from using core technologies, developing new technologies, bringing existing technologies to market or by constraining what technologies can be "produced" by the firm. The converse is also true, especially if we define "technology" in rather broad terms to include some of the group's "software." The microcomputer industry is fraught with new technologies. The introduction of one technology by an IBM can make another technology obsolete almost overnight. Software firms dependent on the old technology can be made to go bankrupt quite rapidly.

A particular stakeholder may have "social" effects on the firm, by altering the position of the firm in society, changing the opinion of the public about the firm, or allowing or constraining what the firm is able to do with "society's permission." The firm may have social effects on a particular stakeholder as well by helping or constraining the stakeholder to engage in certain activities, or by giving the stakeholder a "cause" around which to rally. Assessments of the impact of products such as automobiles and telephones reveal that they have had a remarkable impact on the way that we communicate with each other, and the way that we think about our lives and careers.

These social effects often translate into "political" effects on the firm. Stakeholder actions often involve the political process in order to achieve some social purpose. Conversely, the firm may have political effects on a stakeholder group by helping or hurting its chances of success in the political realm.[16] Business groups have lobbied in recent years against the formation of a national consumer advocate agency in the government, an agenda item that many consumer leaders feel is necessary to the achievement of their long range goals of making business more responsive to consumer needs.

Finally, a stakeholder may have "managerial" effects on the firm by forcing it to change its management systems and processes, and even its managerial style and values. Managerial effects may well be the most important in terms of a firm's ability to understand its relationships with certain groups and to take these groups into account on a routine basis. The converse is equally true here. Consumer advisory panels have "forced" several utilities to alter their methods of filing rate cases, by having the firm make presentations and enter into negotiations with the consumers before filing the case with the state regulatory commissions. As a result, we would expect the companies to gradually change their beliefs about the consumer groups over a long period of time, from one of "irrational, pain in the . . ." to one of "those folks can help us avoid stumbling blocks with the state commissions and our customers."

By further analyzing the stakes of groups into "economic,"

EXHIBIT 4.3   *"Stakes" of Important Stakeholders: Consumer Advocate (Example from Exhibit 3.3)*

Effects of Corporate Action on Stakeholder		Effects of Stakeholder Action on Corporation
1. Economic Effects		1. Economic Effects
# of members in group		Potential gain (loss) of sales
Ability to raise money		
Ability to get volunteers		Cost of regulation, courts, etc.
		Cost of mgmt. time
2. Technological Effects		2. Technological Effects
none		New product ideas
		Prevent new technologies
3. Political Effects	"Stakes"	3. Political Effects
Relative power of consumer advocate	⟷	Regulation potential
Ability of group to command attention		Spillover to other issues
4. Social Effects		4. Social Effects
Products perceived to affect group adversely		Preconceptions of firm
"Voice of effects"		
5. Managerial Effects		5. Managerial Effects
Ability to deal directly with XYZ		Ability to make decisions
Credibility of group's leaders in dealing with XYZ		Ability to deal directly with consumer groups

"technological," "political," "social" and "managerial" we can understand in more detail the cause and effect relationship between an organization and its stakeholder. Exhibit 4.3 is an example from the "stakes" chart of chapter Three of how this analysis might look, in the case of one stakeholder, "consumer advocate."[17]

The most difficult problem with the analysis portrayed in Exhibit 4.3 is that it represents the perceptions of the analysts or the senior executives doing the analysis. How can managers be certain that their readings of stakeholders' perceptions are correct? I have already shown that to assume that a consumer advocate perceives only an economic stake in the firm may well be mistaken. It is necessary to undertake a validation process using interviews, surveys, the public record, interviews with internal boundary spanners who are stakeholder experts, etc. In cases where we are formulating enterprise strategy for the first time, or where the external environment has changed sufficiently, we may need to undertake an explicit process of verification of the inputs into enterprise strategy. At the very minimum managers must use stakeholder analysis to lay bare their own beliefs about the stakes of each important stakeholder group.

In formulating enterprise strategy, stakeholder analysis is used to help executives think through the effects that their actions have on external groups at a macro level. Without such an analysis, answering "what do we stand for" will be done in a vacuum, and the result may well not be acceptable to those groups whom it will affect.

Values Analysis

One of the most difficult tasks that any of us face is the analysis of our own values. As managers in an organization it is especially hard because of the conflict that is the result of the various roles that we have, as manager, parent, citizen, "expert" or whatever. Each role gives rise to different sets of behavior in terms of those groups or individuals with whom we interact. A cursory examination of our behavior with others reveals the difficulty of finding consistency. Our behavior towards one group is often inconsistent with our behavior towards another group. Yet, if consistency is possible it is because there is something that underlies each of the social roles which we play. If Freud taught us anything it is that what is on the surface is not always what is real. Yet this attempt to "get behind the curtain" and carefully examine our values is fraught with difficulty. Revealing our hopes and dreams and desires involves a great deal of personal risk and relies on our ability to trust those companions who undergo this process with us. The "quickie" values analysis of sensitivity training, est and other methods show how easy and costly mistakes are.

More recently, the analysis of ethical values has become a "hot" topic in business. In the wake of alleged "corporate scandals" in Watergate, the Ford Pinto case and other newsworthy items, several corporations have begun to develop codes of ethics. Business schools have instituted courses in business ethics, and other courses have been questioned on their ethical component. Yet all questions of values are not questions of moral values. While a concern for ethics is a necessary ingredient to the analysis of "what do we stand for," it is not in itself sufficient.

How, then, are we to understand the dominant values that are present in organizations? First, we need to be more precise about the nature of values. Second, we need to understand how personal values and organizational values fit together. Finally we need to know how organizational values fit among several different organizations. By trying to answer questions at each of these levels of analysis we can begin the process of values-clarification.

Values come in many flavors, sizes and shapes.[18] There are aesthetic values about what things are beautiful or what is good art. There are social values about what kinds of institutions are good and just. There are religious values about the worthiness of beliefs in god. There are moral values about the goodness or rightness of certain kinds of actions which affect our fellow persons. There are values about all kinds of things such as what makes an apple a good apple, or what makes a strategic plan a good strategic plan, or what makes a managerial decision a good one, etc. It may help us to sort through this jungle if we distinguish two kinds of values, those which are intrinsic and those which are instrumental.

Intrinsic values are basic. Things which are intrinsically valuable are good in and of themselves. Intrinsic values are to be pursued of their own account and worth. Unless two intrinsic values conflict, we do not usually compromise on them. For many people, belief in a supreme being is an intrinsic value. For some people, freedom to act however they see fit is an intrinsic value. For some, Picassos have intrinsic value. For some, being able to maximize their own or their family's happiness is an intrinsic value. Yet another way of putting it, is that intrinsic values represent the "bottom line" of life and its pursuits.

Instrumental values are means to intrinsic values. We place instrumental value on those things which lead us toward the attainment of things, actions or states of mind which are intrinsically valuable. Religious rituals or services which lead us toward our belief in a supreme being may be of instrumental value. Constitutions which guarantee freedom of action have instrumental value to those who see freedom of action as intrinsically valuable. For some, the creative or artistic process has instrumental value in so far as it leads to the creation of works of art. For some, work itself has instrumental value in so far as it leads to the ability to maximize happiness, or to self-fulfillment, etc.

Therefore, activities which help to bring about intrinsic values also have value which I have called "instrumental value." However, these activities do not have value in and of themselves, but *they have value only so far as they contribute to the achievement of intrinsic values.* It is easy to see how activities which originally have instrumental value gain intrinsic value. As we get more caught up in the process of work, we give it intrinsic value regardless of the outcome. Workaholics abound in organizations. It is easy to replace intrinsic values with instrumental values, over a long period of time. Once values are intrinsic they are difficult to change, for we see those activities as good in themselves, and it does not matter if they lead to the original outcome. Instrumental values are relatively easier to change, for if a time honored method of activity can be shown not to lead to the desired result which is intrinsically valuable, then a new method must be tried.

Many of the activities in which an organization engages daily are instrumentally valuable, because they lead to the attainment of the instrinsic values of the organization and its members.[19]

Yet another useful distinction to make, if we are to understand the tangle of values in which we live, is that between the values of an individual and those of the organization. Organizations exist through time and span generations of members.[20] Culture, tradition, purpose and personality of leaders all help to shape the values of an organization. However, it is not necessary for the values of an organization to be identical with the values of any member of the organization. Even the ultimate "organization man" may not completely and totally identify with his organization. Organizational values will reflect history, will be slow to change over time and may be the amalgamation of the values of many individuals. Thus, organizational values may "fit" more or less well with the values of the individuals who are members of the organization. Executives in an organization should, however, be able to articulate the most important values of the organization, and there should be a high degree of congruence between their personal values and the values of the organization.

This analysis of organizational values is not specific to the business organization and can be applied to virtually any organization. However, it is easy to see why there are so many disagreements among an organization and its stakeholders. If there is dissonance between the values of an organization and its members, and dissonance between the values of a "stakeholder organization" and its members, then it is a small wonder that successful transactions ever occur.

Several managers in XYZ company began to discuss organizational values in a management development seminar. One group of managers insisted that the dominant value must be "survival of the firm," while another group insisted with equal vehemence that the dominant value must be "customer service." A third group believed that "profitability" was the key business value, while a fourth focused on "employee satisfaction." These managers spent a good deal of time trying to clarify the meaning of these values and how their beliefs in them affected their firm. Needless to say, XYZ was undergoing a protracted period of organizational realignment where it was not clear that the old values were still appropriate for organizational survival. As it goes through the slow process of determining its organizational values, much of which cannot be done explicitly, XYZ runs the risk of alienating a large number of its stakeholders.

The first task in the process of "values analysis," as depicted in Exhibit 4.4, is to explicate the intrinsic values of the executives in the organization, and to separate those values from the instrumental values, or activities which achieve intrinsic values. The second task is to explicate the intrinsic values of the organization itself, and to separate those values from the methods that have evolved to achieve those values. The third task is to analyze the differences between the personal values and organization values. The fourth task is to be explicit about where there are conflicts and inconsistencies, recognizing that changes may be hard to undertake. The fifth task is to

EXHIBIT 4.4   *Values Analysis Process*

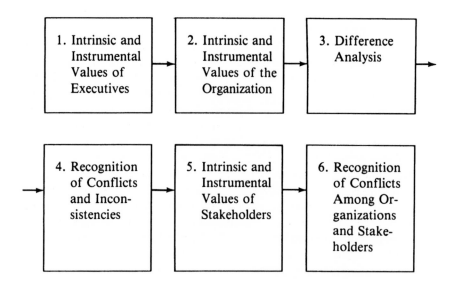

analyze the intrinsic values of important stakeholder groups and to separate these values from the methods those groups use to attain them. The final task is to explicitly recognize the conflicts and inconsistencies among organizational values and values of stakeholders.

Social Issues Analysis

Given that managers understand the stakeholders in their organization, and understand their own and their stakeholders' values, it is necessary to understand the social context of the organization. That is, what are the major issues facing society today? What are the major issues facing our society in the next 5 to 10 years? What are the central differences between these two sets of issues?[21]

Again it might be useful to apply the schema developed earlier and divide these issues into economic, technological, political, social and managerial. The process of thinking through these two lists of issues helps to understand the place of the firm in society as it currently stands and helps to understand where it might lead, or at least what the assumptions are that managers make about where it might lead. Naturally the analysis will contain errors, and 10 years from now it might look silly. However, to formulate strategy at the enterprise level it is just as necessary to look at the future, as it is in forecasting the length of the product life-cycle at the product strategy level. Exhibit 4.5 represents a hypothetical example of social issues analysis.

The analysis of social issues can be combined with stakeholder analysis to look at the impact of current and future social issues on the stakeholders of the firm. Continued acceleration of the micro-chip technology, together with the increased need for business-government cooperation may well give rise to a concern with privacy. The road to "telescreens" and "two-minute-hates" is not so distant as when Orwell wrote of them. The technology, together with the political climate, may well yield a scenario where individual freedom is threatened. If projections of the current state of the art in computer technology are remotely plausible, then it will be possible (at reasonable costs) for every home to be wired together in a nationwide computer network. A computer system is like a bank vault in some sense. If something can be put into it, it can be taken out of it, and not always by the persons authorized to do so. It is not hard to imagine the emergence of stakeholder groups concerned with the safeguarding of citizens' privacy, given the current technology. Any computer company worth its salt must be worried about privacy, now, before there is a crisis.

Several decisions could be taken to be prepared for the issue and

EXHIBIT 4.5   *Societal Issues Analysis (Example)*

Major Social Issues Today	Reasons for Change	Major Social Issues In 5–10 Years
1. Economic 　　Role of govt. in redistribution 　　Ability to sustain growth 　　Role of US economy in world		1. Economic 　　Role of private sector in redistribution 　　World economy management
2. Technological 　　Uses of integrated circuits 　　Robotics 　　Biotechnology 　　Basic R&D		2. Technological 　　Computer Age "Artificial" intelligence 　　Space exploration
3. Political 　　Right vs. left 　　Military role and threat of war	Reasons for Change 1. Acceleration of application of new technologies 2. Growth of large organizations 3. Business/Govt. cooperation 4. etc.	3. Political 　　Business-government organization 　　Freedom parties 　　Military role and threat of war
4. Social 　　Urban vs. rural 　　Developed vs. undeveloped nations 　　Aging of US population		4. Social 　　Privacy 　　Power of business
5. Managerial 　　Ability to manage in turbulence 　　Ability to manage in global economic system		5. Managerial 　　Power of business 　　Manager as public official

stakeholders that will emerge. The first is for executives in major computer companies such as Digital Equipment, IBM, Control Data, etc. to individually decide how the privacy issue affects their firm, now and into the future. The second would be to sponsor joint research on the concept of privacy, to find out how current stakeholders feel. Finally, we could initiate programs of development and education to find solutions to commonly voiced concerns. These decisions are necessary now, before some Luddite backlash emerges, and regulations are passed which limit the beneficial uses of computer technology; however, they should only be made within the context of a careful understanding of what an individual business stands for in terms of its values on issues such as privacy.

The purpose of these pieces of analysis is to lay the groundwork for the formulation of enterprise level strategy, or a statement of "what do we stand for." By combining an understanding of the stakeholders in an organization, the values of the organization and an account of the social issues which affect the firm now and in the future, we can articulate a statement of either where the organization currently is, with respect to its enterprise strategy, or we can formulate a new direction for the enterprise.

A Typology of Enterprise Strategy

There are many ways to put these pieces of analysis together into a statement of enterprise level strategy. Stakeholders, values and social issues are all important ingredients and can be mixed together in a variety of proportions. However they are put together the outcome should be some sort of "fit" with the society in which managers find themselves.[22] Organizations which do not have an appropriate enterprise strategy over time are not socially viable, and experience a great deal of both internal and external turbulence. What the organization stands for is not consistent with the values of its members causing internal stress, and is not consistent with the needs of its stakeholders or the social issues of the time causing external stress.[23]

There are at least five generic enterprise level strategies which can be seen as achieving "fit" among stakeholders, values and social issues. Each of these strategies represents a whole set of particular responses and actions to the circumstances facing an individual firm. Hence, these generic strategies are broad descriptions of answers to "what do we stand for," and involve tradeoffs about the relative importance of stakeholder concerns, values and social issues. I shall briefly discuss each of the following: (1) specific stakeholder strategy; (2) stockholder strategy; (3) utilitarian strategy; (4) Rawlsian strategy; and, (5) social harmony strategy. Exhibit 4.6 illustrates the key differences among the strategies. Other enterprise level strategies are

EXHIBIT 4.6 *A Typology of Enterprise Strategy*

Specific Stakeholder Strategy

• Maximize benefits to one or a small set of stakeholders

Stockholder Strategy

• Maximize benefits to stockholders
• Maximize benefits to "financial stakeholders"

Utilitarian Strategy

• Maximize benefits to all stakeholders (greatest good for greatest number)
• Maximize average welfare level of all stakeholders
• Maximize benefits to society

Rawlsian Strategy

• Act to raise the level of the worst-off stakeholder

Social Harmony Strategy

• Act to maintain or create social harmony
• Act to gain consensus from society

possible in addition to those mentioned here, which I have singled out to be of particular interest.

Specific Stakeholder Strategy

One response to "what do we stand for" is to concentrate the efforts of the firm towards satisfying the needs of a small number of specific stakeholder groups, or the needs of one or two generic stakeholder groups. For example, if "Customer Service" and "Employee Welfare" are the basic values for a particular organization, and if everything the firm does is aimed at achieving these intrinsic values, then in some realistic sense that firm stands for improving the welfare of customers and employees. Since these are but two of many stakeholders, I have dubbed this kind of enterprise strategy, "specific stakeholder strategy." To adopt such a strategy is to try and maximize the benefits of the firm to a relatively narrow group of stakeholders.

The concept of "specific stakeholder strategy" leads to the following hypothesis:

If the actions of the firm have a relatively narrow range of effects on a relatively small number of stakeholders, and if the values of the managers of the firm are closely aligned with the values of these stakeholders, and if there is little relevant social change, then the firm is likely to adopt a specific stakeholder strategy of maximizing the returns to a small set of stakeholders.

An example of firms adopting specific stakeholder strategies would appear to be several firms in the computer business who align themselves almost totally with the customer. Hewlett-Packard, IBM and Digital Equipment are almost legendary for their customer relationships. From published accounts it is difficult to tell if this customer alignment is an end in itself or a means to an end, but there is some evidence that it is an end in itself (Peters and Waterman, 1982). The history of the industry involved creating a demand for its products. The resulting attention to customer needs and customer service has become the criterion for success and leadership in the industry. We could hypothesize that as managers come up through the ranks in a company oriented towards customers they identify with the customer and its needs so much that it would be impossible to change the orientation of the company. Social issues have had little effect on these companies as they have developed. Perhaps with the advent of the personal computer and large computer networks available to the public for little cost, the impact of social issues such as privacy and "1984" will increase, thereby necessitating a reexamination of the enterprise level strategies of these firms.

Stockholder Strategy

The second type of enterprise strategy is really a special case of the specific stakeholder strategy. However, it so pervades our way of thinking that we can list it separately. It is the concentration of effort by managers towards satisfying the needs of the stockholders of the firm.[24] The stockholder strategy is perceived to be so pervasive as to warrant extra attention, even though its logic is identical with that of the narrow stakeholder strategy where "stockholder" is substituted for "narrow range of stakeholders."

The essence of the stockholder strategy is "to maximize returns to stockholders," or if interpreted more broadly, "to maximize the market value of the firm." Executives in firms who adopt the stockholder strategy usually believe that they have a fiduciary obligation to stockholders, that is, they must always seek to act in the interests of the stockholders. However, it must be noted that the legal concept of management as bearing a fiduciary obligation to stockholders is undergoing some change. Taken to its logical extreme, such an enterprise strategy could involve actions which are immoral or unethical, as well as illegal. When questioned about payments to the Committee to Reelect the President in 1972, one Chief Executive responded that he was doing what was necessary to protect the interests of the company and its stockholders.[25] (Some of these issues are addressed in chapter Seven on board behavior and stakeholder analysis.)

A closely related variant of the stockholder strategy might be called "the financial stakeholder strategy." This version relies on satisfying the interests of the set of stakeholders who have financial stakes in the firm, or who can heavily influence those stakeholders who have financial stakes. Thus, management actions are aimed towards stockholders, banks (both commercial and investment), other holders of debt, investment analysts, etc. The values of management in this case must dictate that "financial stake" counts for more than other kinds of interests. Management recognizes that "ownership" needs to be broadened to include any group who is risking its capital in the firm.

One hypothesis suggested by the above analysis is:

If the actions of a firm have effects which are perceived by its managers to be primarily economic, and if the values of management are oriented towards satisfying a fiduciary obligation to the owners of the firm, and if the relevant social issues are perceived by managers to be economic growth and prosperity, then the firm will adopt a stockholder strategy, to maximize the returns to stockholders (or to financial stakeholders) or to maximize the market value of the firm.

Examples of the stockholder strategy are abundant. Firms who pride themselves on the increase in the quarterly dividend above all else, who pay constant attention to short term measures of performance and who run their businesses as if the corporation were an investment company with its businesses as its portfolio of stocks are all candidates for the stockholder strategy.

Utilitarian Strategy

A third enterprise level strategy is one that tries to improve the general quality of life in society. Actions are undertaken which raise the general welfare of society. Such firms answer "what do we stand for" with "improving society," or "doing something that is socially useful."[26] Managers in these firms usually believe that the firm does (or can) have a wide range of effects on stakeholder groups. They believe that the purpose of the corporation is to produce the greatest good for the greatest number of people in society, that business is fundamentally a social institution and thereby incurs obligations which must be discharged by seeking to produce social good.

Such firms will be responsive to social issues and will seek to contribute to the development of these issues. Thus, my hypothesis is:

If the actions of a firm are perceived by its managers to have a wide range of effects on stakeholders, and if the managers have utilitarian values, i.e., that they should maximize the social welfare as far as is possible and if there are a wide range of social issues that affect the firm, then the firm will adopt a utilitarian strategy to maximize the welfare of as many stakeholders as possible.

One example of this strategy might be AT&T's development and implementation of "universal service" as a guiding principle for managing the telephone business. "Universal service" means that telephone service is made available to as many people as possible because the telephone is socially desirable (it is economically desirable as well). Policies, including pricing, are adopted to make telephone service available to everyone regardless of income level or location. Accounting practices, service organizations, internal measurements are all oriented towards maximizing the availability of the telephone and thereby raising the general quality of life in society (Kleinfield, 1981). It can be argued that AT&T adopted such a strategy in its early days to appease the government officials worried about anti-trust, etc. But, this does not invalidate the strategy, if AT&T is genuinely concerned with "universal service" as a method for improving social welfare and if such a concern has become the guiding intrinsic value for its managers (Freeman, 1983a).

Rawlsian Strategy

A fourth generic strategy at the enterprise level is for the managers of a firm to see themselves as agents of social change. In particular in the U.S. they might see themselves as seeking to bring about true equality of opportunity or seeking to maximize the amount of freedom that individuals have to live their own lives. Rawls (1971) has argued that social institutions (including, I shall assume, the corporation) are just only in so far as they insure individual liberties that are compatible with "a like liberty for all," and that the offices and privileges are open to anyone regardless of race, sex, etc.[27] Rawls argues further that inequalities in the distribution of goods and services in a society are justified only if the inequalities raise the level of the least well-off social groups. A crude application of Rawls's theory to the issue at hand, the development of enterprise level strategy, would possibly dictate that a firm seek to raise the level of its least well-off stakeholder and to insure that its employment and promotion practices encourage equal opportunity to all social groups.

In order for a Rawlsian strategy to be appropriate managers must share the values which underly the theory; namely, they must believe that the just society does not discriminate among social classes in its allocation of basic goods and services. Furthermore, managers must believe that the corporation can have some effect in correcting current inequalities if any exist, and that these basic values of equality of opportunity and freedom underlie a host of current and future social issues. Thus, my hypothesis is:

If the actions of a firm are perceived to have a wide range of effects on stakeholders of differing social positions, and if the values of the managers are oriented towards freedom and equality of opportunity for all members in society and if social issues which affect the firm are concerned with freedom and equality of opportunity, then the firm will adopt a Rawlsian strategy, i.e., it will seek to raise the welfare of the least well-off stakeholder groups and to insure that the positions in the firm are open to all members of society.

One example of a Rawlsian strategy might well be Control Data's undertaking to improve the lot of inner cities through their City Venture subsidiary. Projects are undertaken which help to renovate portions of the inner core of decaying cities, usually as a subcontractor to, or in conjunction with, government. Additionally, Control Data has undertaken to train and employ the "hardcore" unemployed in several cities. In short they have looked for business opportunities which are not only profitable but which raise the level of the least advantaged groups in society.

Harmony Strategy

A fifth generic strategy comes from a cursory analysis of some other societies and the methods businesses have in aligning themselves very closely with the local communities. It is possible to adopt an enterprise strategy based on the principle of social harmony, that is, to insure that whatever action is taken, it is agreeable to and supported by a large, near unanimous group of stakeholders. The emphasis on social harmony comes from the basic values of communitarianism, where we value being a respected member of the community over all else. Under such a strategy, the company gets its essential identity from the community, and is unwilling to go along a divergent path. When conflict arises with stakeholders, major efforts are undertaken to resolve the conflict to the "mutual understanding" of all parties.

During an executive development program with several Japanese managers I posed the question of what they would do when a conflict arose between their company and the local community. One manager replied, "we would talk with them until we reached a mutual understanding." I pressed on and asked what would happen if no such understanding were achieved. He replied, "we would talk some more until we reached a mutual understanding." I then asked him what would be done if the company's interest was diametrically opposed to the community's interest. And, he replied once again, "we would talk until we reached a mutual understanding of our interests." Such an approach depends on values very much like those described in a harmony strategy.

My hypothesis is:

If the actions of a firm are perceived to have wide ranging effects on society, and if the values of the managers are oriented towards communitarianism, i.e. an identification with the local community, and if social issues concern the promotion of community interest, then the firm will adopt a harmony strategy. It will seek to minimize the amount of friction between the firm and the local community, and to identify the interests of the firm with the community.

The Necessity of Enterprise Strategy

It is very easy to misinterpret the foregoing analysis as yet another call for corporate social responsibility or business ethics. While these issues are important in their own right, enterprise level strategy is a different concept. We need to worry about enterprise level strategy for the simple fact that corporate survival depends in part on there being some "fit" between the values of the corporation and its managers, the expectations of stakeholders in the firm and the societal issues which will determine the ability of the firm to sell its products. For instance, if we are to be able to innovate with new technology and bring new products to market, we must understand how such changes affect the people in our business, as well as whether it helps us to meet continuing expectations of stakeholders. To return to our earlier example, if Bell wishes to survive, its managers must understand the changes in their values that are necessary to compete in the new telecommunications environment. Whether such changes are socially responsible or morally praiseworthy is an important question, but it is yet a further question which an analysis of enterprise strategy does not address.

Enterprise strategy is concerned with the question of "consistency" among the key elements of a firm's relationship with its environment. The formulation of enterprise strategy helps us to begin to clearly articulate corporate values, and to insure that they are in touch with the expectations of those groups who have a stake in the firm. Corporate strategists have ignored this level of strategic thinking for too long. It can be the difference between success and failure in today's business environment. By addressing the issues in an "upfront and tough-minded" manner, we can avoid the worst case that is prevalent in many firms: self-deception. Self-deception occurs when we do not honestly ask the tough questions, and do not accurately assess our own values and the stakeholder picture that we face. It involves saying one thing and acting on another. Self-deception is the difference between those values that we espouse and those that are really in force, and is one of the main reasons for a credibility gap between management and its stakeholders. Here are a few examples:

1. XYZ Company espoused quality of work life in its brochures and other communications to its employees. The president of XYZ made a speech in which he articulated "the moral responsibility" of XYZ to its employees, and commended the employee body of XYZ for serving the company well during its history. However, soon afterwards the company began to offer early retirement in an effort to reduce the number of employees, and later began to lay off employees. The actions of the company did not match its words.

2. ABC Company espoused the need to work closely with a particular government agency to find ways of regulation that benefitted ABC, the agency and the local community. Yet resources were not allocated and time was not spent to deal with the agency. "Good intentions" led nowhere, and the company was slow to deal with a nonproductive adversarial relationship with the government.

3. JKL Company espoused the value of doing what was in the shareholder's best interest. The management of JKL made many public statements, and quite probably private ones to each other, about the need to work for the shareholder. Yet when a merger proposal was put on the table by another company which would give JKL shareholders roughly a 300% premium over the current value of the stock, it was turned down by management as "not in the shareholder's interest." Self-deception, on a large scale, had occurred.

Each of the enterprise strategies outlined above holds possibilities for self-deception. With the separation of ownership and control (Berle and Means, 1932), it is easy for the intrinsic value involved in carrying out this fiduciary obligation to take on less and less importance over time. One "bad faith" variation of the stockholder strategy is described by Burnham (1941) whereby managers maximize the control that they can exert over the affairs of the firm, regardless of the effect on the interests of the stockholders. Williamson (1964) has investigated the conditions under which such managerial discretion arises and becomes pervasive. "Acting in the interests of the stockholders" becomes the rationalization (as opposed to the justification) for exerting control over the affairs of the corporation. Tender offers which appear to increase the stockholders' returns will be rejected. Joint ventures which have potentially high payoffs will be spurned when they require a sharing of control. Management will act defensively to regulatory attempts to change the practices of the firm, and it will ignore social issues and critics as inappropriate and as not in the interests of the stockholders.

Bad faith versions of utilitarian strategies are possible as well. Here, we could claim that whatever is done in the interests of the stockholders is automatically in the interests of society. Therefore, since our basic values are utilitarian, every action must be evaluated in terms of being in the interests of the stockholders. An even more deceiving situation can occur if our basic values are really oriented towards control of the affairs of the corporation. A double bind resulting from the deceptive version of the stockholder strategy occurs whereby almost any action can be justified in either the interests of the stockholders or the interests of society, or in short, in the interests of any group other than management, which is of course the real group in whose interests the action is undertaken.

There is, of course, a similar version of the Rawlsian strategy, for it is possible to exploit the least well off groups in society under the guise of making them better off. We might believe that sweat shops, below subsistence wages, selling inferior quality products in ghettos, making nonnutritional food available in poor areas, etc. are examples of business practices which are possible to rationalize through an application of Rawlsian principles. It is also possible to argue, albeit not logically, that raising the level of the least well off groups occurs when there is more for everyone, i.e., when we try to maximize the greatest good for the greatest number of stakeholders, and that more for everyone is accomplished only when actions are taken which maximize the interests of the owners of the firm. Here we are right back to the original pathology in the stockholder strategy, but with a level of rationalization and rhetoric possible to confuse even the most enlightened stockholder.

The harmony strategy presents equally thorny problems, for we can use the unwillingness of the community to change as an excuse for not finding alternative methods of accomplishing our goals. The harmony strategy can act as a rationalization for the status quo, when in reality we need to work very hard at "reaching a mutual understanding."

Socrates said that the unexamined life is not worth living and that the secrets of life are knowable only if "know thyself" is followed. I believe that Socrates' advice is applicable to us as managers. Only by understanding "what we stand for" can we clearly articulate business issues which are important and address those issues in a manner which is rational. It is easy for us to deceive ourselves, whether we are making decisions about beginning a personal exercise program or launching a new subsidiary.

The purpose of analyzing enterprise level strategy and claiming that there are at least five generic strategies which can be consistently or inconsistently applied from the analysis of stakeholders, values and social issues, has not been to argue for one or another of the five strategies. Rather, I believe that it is important for us to understand honestly whatever our enterprise strategy happens to be. So little is known about the values as they exist in organizational life that I believe it is premature to argue for the preference of one strategy over another.

By attempting to articulate enterprise level strategies, executives set the context for the next round of development of corporate level strategies, and the organization moves slowly towards a unified purpose that both produces bottom line results and serves the purposes and values of executives and other organizational members and stakeholders. Enterprise level strategy is no panacea. But, it is necessary if we are to survive in the world as it exists today.

SETTING DIRECTION AT THE CORPORATE LEVEL: THE STAKEHOLDER AUDIT

A more traditional approach to setting direction for the corporation involves answering the corporate level questions from Exhibit 4.1. At least two methods have evolved in the literature and in practice for analyzing the business, or set of businesses, in which a firm competes. Each of these methods seeks to determine the "proper" set of businesses for the firm, and each has been used in most major U.S. corporations.

Following Andrews (1965) and Christenson, Andrews and Bower (1980) situational analysis identifies "the pattern of purposes and policies defining the company and its businesses." Strengths, weaknesses, opportunities and threats are determined, corporate resources are analyzed, and a rigorous set of questions is answered, including, "where are we now," "what can we do," "what do we want to do," and "what should we do."[28] The bottom line to situational analysis is that many different factors are important in determining the strategic position of a firm, and the set of relevant factors may depend on the industries in which the firm has historically competed, the individual strengths of the managers and other contingencies.

An alternative approach to setting direction at the corporate level is the use of a "portfolio approach," whereby the individual business elements of a multi-business firm are plotted on a grid which measures relative market share versus industry growth. The idea behind portfolio theory is that at the corporate level the strategic task is to achieve a balanced portfolio, where "balanced" is to be understood as "smooth overall cash flow" or "the achievement of a maximum overall return for a given level of risk" or "an acceptable level of overall growth." Resources are allocated among the corporation's set of businesses according to how each "fits" with the overall portfolio.

We noted in chapter Three that neither of these approaches is sufficient, in and of itself, to take account of the business environment that most executives face today. They do not automatically account for, nor measure, the influence of multiple stakeholder effects on the firm. It is easy to overlook the stakeholders in the firm using only situation analysis; however, we might explicitly add more questions to make the analysis even more complex and to collect and analyze a host of data on stakeholder influences. The major concern with situational analysis is then compounded. It offers no systematic way to put the pieces of the analysis together. On the other hand, portfolio theory simply ignores, or at least discounts, the ability of non-marketplace stakeholders to affect the businesses of the firm. Hence, if rigidly followed, portfolio theory leads to decisions to invest in businesses which give little incentive to a firm's stakeholders to offer their support for the firm.

Both of these methods of setting corporate direction can be enriched to yield a better understanding of the firm's stakeholders. One such process that has been developed is the "stakeholder audit."[29] Just as the financial audit creates and certifies a financial roadmap for the firm, so does a stakeholder audit create and certify a roadmap of the external environment of the firm. The stakeholder audit process builds on the analytical techniques developed in chapter Three of identifying the stakeholders and their stakes in the firm, as well as the analysis conducted in setting direction at the enterprise level. However, the stakeholder audit process does not assume that a firm has a carefully articulated enterprise strategy, nor does it assume that a firm has a good idea of who its stakeholders actually are. Rather, in keeping with the framework developed in chapter One, this type of audit assumes that there are stakeholders in the external environment of the firm whether its managers are aware of them or not. This is similar to the fact that a financial audit can be done, albeit with difficulty, whether a business follows generally accepted accounting principles or not.

Exhibit 4.7 depicts one such "stakeholder audit" process consisting of four main strategic tasks: (1) stating the corporate mission; (2) identifying stakeholder issues and concerns; (3) assessing corporate strategies for stakeholders; and (4) adjusting stakeholder priorities. In addition, as Exhibit 4.7 shows, there are several feedback loops in the process. This process can be tailor-made depending on the particular situation of a firm, and thus

EXHIBIT 4.7   *Stakeholder Audit Process*

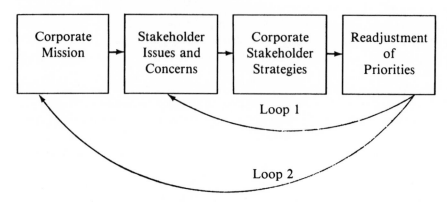

it should not be viewed as a rigid set of steps to be followed at all costs. Rather, Exhibit 4.7 is meant to serve as a conceptual guideline for managers who want to understand their environments in stakeholder terms. A brief discussion of each of these tasks and feedback loops and some examples of how this process can be used follows.

Task 1: Stating the Corporate Mission. Many hours of executive time have been spent trying to formulate a statement of corporate purpose which is both meaningful and acceptable to a majority of the top executives in the firm. Oftentimes it is simply impossible for them to agree on the definition of the firm's business. Such conflict is good for the organization as long as it is productive and dealt with openly. The stakeholder audit process begins with a provisional statement of the mission as it appears in the annual report, has been articulated in the business press or has been explained in the corporate planning process or to financial analysts. From this provisional statement of mission the businesses of the corporation are identified, again, as they have been traditionally arranged. Thus, a company whose mission is to achieve a dominant position in the micro-computer business, may have several distinct business areas such as "business software," "games," "computers" (which may be segmented several ways) and "peripherals." These businesses may or may not be segmented by strategic business units, again depending on the degree of sophistication of the company's planning system.

Once mission and businesses have been identified a generic stakeholder map can be drawn similar to those in chapters One and Three. From the analysis of mission, business and generic stakeholders a matrix similar to Exhibit 4.8 can be constructed which shows in grid form the importance of each class of stakeholder to achieving success in each business. This generic

EXHIBIT 4.8   *Stakeholder/Business Success Matrix (Hypothetical Example)*

Business Stakeholder	Business A	Business B	Business C		Business N
Employees	5	2	1		3
Unions	5	2	1		4
Stockholders	2	1	5		2
Government	1	5	5		1
Suppliers	3	5	1		3
Customers	1	1	5		1
Banks	NA	11	3		2
Activist Groups	NA	4	4		3

1 = Critically important to achieve business success
3 = Somewhat important to achieve business success
5 = Not very important to achieve business success
NA = Not a stakeholder issue in this business

stakeholder/business success matrix is useful, not only in initially thinking through the relative importance of each stakeholder category, but it organizes the information in a way that allows executives to readily determine which stakeholders will have an impact on the implementation of specific business goals and objectives.

Task 2: Identifying Stakeholder Issues and Concerns. Once the generic stakeholder analysis has been completed, specific stakeholder groups for each business need to be identified. Here a stakeholder map for each business can be drawn, and a table similar to Exhibit 3.2 can be constructed. Again, a ranking procedure may be used to deduce importance of particular stakeholder groups for success in a business. From the analysis of specific stakeholders, several versions of the stakes of each group can be deduced, again similar to Exhibits 3.3 and 3.4. The degree of detail should vary by the depth of understanding that managers have vis-à-vis stakeholders. The degree of detail need not be uniform for all stakeholders, with more effort spent on those groups which managers feel they understand relatively less well.

Once this initial analysis is completed a list of key concerns or issues must be developed for each stakeholder group. In many cases the informa-

tion required to complete this step will be readily available from historical records and the experiences of individual managers. In some cases,
however, the information must be systematically gathered by interviewing individual stakeholders, briefing sessions with managers who are
"stakeholder experts" or "boundary spanners" responsible for a particular
stakeholder relationship and by an analysis of the public record to determine positions of stakeholders on key issues. Again, this information can be
aggregated at the corporate level and displayed in a matrix of stakeholders
vs. issues and concerns. Exhibit 4.9 is one example of how that matrix might
look. Completion of a stakeholders/issues matrix enables the managers involved in the audit process to orient themselves externally towards the issues
and concerns of key external groups. The managers can identify the sensitivity points in their external environment and pinpoint the issues or concerns which must be resolved if success in particular businesses can be
achieved. The matrix also allows an aggregate look across businesses at the
concerns of employees, consumer advocates or local communities, enabling
managers to think about the strategies which the firm as a whole may have
with these stakeholder groups.

Task 3: Assessing Corporate Strategies for Stakeholders. Tasks 1 and 2

EXHIBIT 4.9   *Stakeholders/Issues Matrix (Hypothetical Example)*

Issues \ Stakeholders	Employees	Unions	Stockholders	Government	Suppliers	Customers	Consumer Groups	
Truth in Advertising	3	3	NA	1	NA	3	1	
Product Safety	1	1	NA	1	1	1	1	
Pricing Policies	3	3	NA	1	1	1	1	
Product Service	3	3	NA	4	NA	1	1	
Financial Returns	1	1	1	4	1	NA	NA	

1 = Critically important to stakeholder
3 = Somewhat important to stakeholder
5 = Not very important to stakeholder
NA = Stakeholder not concerned with this issue

create an external view of the firm by analyzing stakeholders and the key concerns of each. The purpose of Task 3 is to identify how the firm is currently meeting the needs of its stakeholders, i.e., what is the current strategy of the firm with regard to each stakeholder or group of stakeholders. This strategy statement must not only include what the firm is currently doing with respect to a stakeholder but how the firm is accomplishing the strategy or the process of achievement, and what organizational unit within the firm has responsibility.

Identifying existing stakeholder strategies can normally be accomplished by a review process with the SBU, division or functional managers responsible. However, in large and complex organizations it may be the case that no one is responsible for a particular stakeholder group at the corporate level, with responsibility residing at the "strategy center" level. Corporate staff in public relations or public affairs may have functional responsibility for non-traditional stakeholder groups such as consumer advocates, the media and government, and may be formulating programs in virtual isolation from the strategy center managers. It will be difficult, in such cases, to articulate a strategy for the corporation as a whole towards a particular stakeholder or set of stakeholders. Also, the corporate strategy may well be inconsistent with the programs undertaken at the lower levels in the firm.

Once a statement of purpose and an action plan for each stakeholder has been identified at the business and corporate level, the response of stakeholder groups can be determined. Again, interviews with stakeholders or internal experts, as well as searching the public record needs to be undertaken. The effectiveness of each strategy can then be rated on a simple scale of effective, somewhat effective, somewhat ineffective, ineffective and undetermined. Exhibit 4.10 illustrates a stakeholder strategy matrix to display this information for the firm as a whole. Depending on the circumstances of a particular firm, many of the cells of Exhibit 4.10 may well be blank, or contain words such as "currently ignoring this stakeholder."

Task 4: Adjusting Corporate Priorities. Obviously, the desired result in the stakeholder audit process is to readjust the corporate priorities to more closely align the firm with satisfying stakeholder needs, or towards changing the mission of the firm. Given the assessment of firm's environment and the effectiveness of current strategies in dealing with stakeholders in Tasks 1–3, the senior managers conducting the audit must decide where to put the firm's priorities. Ideally, the enterprise level strategy will set the context for this analysis, but realistically, many firms have not articulated their strategy at such an abstract level. Thus, particular corporate level strategies may need revision giving rise to Loop 1 in Exhibit 4.6 and the need to reassess the position of a particular business and the programs it is using to achieve success with its stakeholders. Or, if there are enough ineffective or ques-

EXHIBIT 4.10   *Stakeholder Strategy Matrix (Hypothetical Example)*

Business/ Corp. Stakeholder	Strategy of Business 1 w.r.t.:	Strategy of Business N w.r.t.:	Corporate Strategy w.r.t.:	Effectiveness 1–5
Customer	Increase sales by 15%	Maintain current market share	Be market leaders (#1 or 2) in all businesses	3
Employer	Get employee commitment to improve productivity Start quality circles	Reduce headcount by 15%	No overall corporate strategy with this group	3
Government	Minimize government interference	Currently ignoring stakeholder	Accept no government interference in marketplace	5
. . .	.	.	.	.

tionable strategies, then the executives need to travel down Loop 2 and to reexamine the mission of the firm.

By undertaking a stakeholder audit on a regular basis managers can gain a good understanding of how effectively the firm is meeting the requirements of its environment and meeting the stated mission of the firm.

The length of time to complete an audit varies by size and degree of complexity of the firm. However, it should be relatively easy to integrate the process into the front end of the planning cycle. Alternatively, the audit can be performed as a one-time snapshot of how well the organization is meeting stakeholder concerns. The latter process is more in the mode of validation, and should be undertaken only if the firm has some idea of its entire array of stakeholders.

TAILOR-MAKING THE STAKEHOLDER AUDIT: SOME EXAMPLES

CD Insurance Co.

CD Insurance Co. is a relatively small insurance company whose primary business is health insurance. CD writes both group and individual policies, and is in a few other peripheral businesses which are a small part of its total sales. A limited number of large customers account for a high proportion of CD's business. CD operates in a limited geographical area and for the most part has a very good reputation in this area as a good corporate citizen. In fact, the enterprise level strategy can probably be classified as utilitarian, as CD managers were quite conscious of promoting the welfare of the community, as well as the health of its policyholders. A new CEO at CD became worried about the changes that the insurance industry in general, and the health care industry in particular, were undergoing. The new CEO also began to change the enterprise level strategy towards spreading what he perceived the financial risks to be, and hence more towards a stockholder strategy.

High inflation and the availability of other financial instruments made the workhorse of the industry, the individual life policy, virtually obsolete. At the same time corporate customers began to see the need for broader services involving employee benefits, health coverage, group life and even corporate financial services which large data processing oriented companies could provide. Large insurance companies were beginning to offer a full product line which would compete with CD's market niche, in terms of both products and geographies. Some large firms were beginning to move into data processing, communications and business services, threatening to make CD's group insurance business obsolete.

Aetna and IBM had formed a partnership to operate Satellite Business Systems. American Express and its Fireman's Fund subsidiary were clearly in the same "complete business services" market. Other large firms such as Prudential, Connecticut General, etc. were experimenting with innovations such as group legal, dental and even group auto insurance in efforts to woo large corporate clients. Within the context of the health care industry the recent regulatory pressure began to drastically affect the cost of health care. Medicare and Medicaid programs were increasingly going to the "low cost producer," and the ability to win those contracts was based on the efficiency of a company's data-processing operations. New technological advances in data-processing were beginning to outstrip the availability of systems, therefore firms who could afford substantial capital investment had an advantage. Thus, the competitive structure of the industry began to change. New stakeholders emerged, as well as new issues, and the picture of the external environment of traditionally staid and conservative insurance companies began to radically shift. As a relatively small player, CD needed to take stock of this environment and attempt to position itself favorably for the future.

Executives at CD saw its mission as maintaining its current position in the market, while seeking to find a niche in some other industry for the future. A stakeholder analysis of CD showed five major generic groups of stakeholders, or five separate environments, in which CD could possibly operate. These five areas were (in the order of importance): (1) Health Insurance; (2) Other Insurance; (3) Local Community; (4) Financial Services; and (5) Data Processing. Exhibit 4.11 is a picture of some of the key stakeholders in each area. East set of stakeholders yielded several major issues and a set of questions for CD managers to answer in terms of the strengths and weaknesses of the company in dealing with the issues and stakeholders in a particular area such as data processing, as well as the opportunities and threats which that area held for the company.

The net result of this stakeholder audit process, tailor-made to examine the future stakeholder environment of CD, was the formulation of several alternative corporate missions. The alternatives considered included: (1) becoming a data processing consulting firm in the local community; (2) developing a more complete line of insurance products; (3) opening an HMO, and going into the "wellness" business; (4) expanding the health insurance business into other markets; and (5) looking for a merger partner. The generation of these options caused a great deal of conflict at CD. The CEO and his top management team had to choose a path to follow. They picked the relatively safe alternatives of opening an HMO and expanding into some new markets, while keeping an eye open for a merger partner. Such alternatives were not acceptable to all managers, and some did leave the company. While the managers at CD are still in the process of shifting the priorities in the company to achieve a shift in corporate direction, their stakeholder audit helped them to better understand how the external environment was changing, and the strategic options that were available to them.

EXHIBIT 4.11   *Stakeholder Audit Map for CD Insurance*

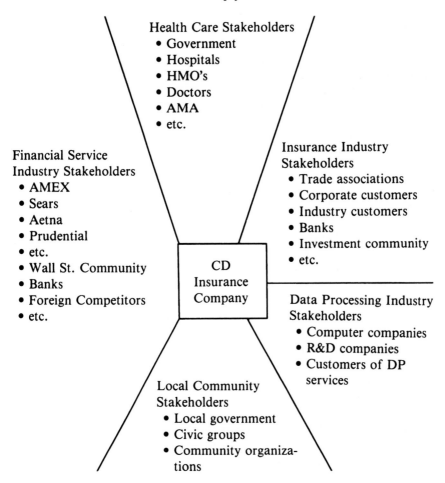

Health Care Stakeholders
- Government
- Hospitals
- HMO's
- Doctors
- AMA
- etc.

Financial Service
Industry Stakeholders
- AMEX
- Sears
- Aetna
- Prudential
- etc.
- Wall St. Community
- Banks
- Foreign Competitors
- etc.

Insurance Industry
Stakeholders
- Trade associations
- Corporate customers
- Industry customers
- Banks
- Investment community
- etc.

CD
Insurance
Company

Data Processing Industry
Stakeholders
- Computer companies
- R&D companies
- Customers of DP services

Local Community
Stakeholders
- Local government
- Civic groups
- Community organizations

Major Oil Inc.

Major Oil Inc. is a large international petroleum products company with operations worldwide.[30] To help its managers understand how the external environment had changed during the past decades, and thus understand the necessity for acquiring new management skills, some executives at Major undertook a project to construct a thirty year history of the company from 1950 to 1980. The purpose of the history was to understand the direction of the company in the past and how shifts in direction had occurred. The stakeholder audit process was tailor-made to look backwards in time, and to construct stakeholder maps and sets of strategic issues from the past.

Exhibit 4.12 is a stakeholder map of Major Oil Inc. in the late 1950s. The focus of the company was primarily as a production company, to explore new sources of crude oil and to get it out of the ground and to market as quickly as possible. The market for Major's products was growing rapidly, and Major was expanding its distribution network to include almost 40,000 outlets by the mid-1950s. By the late 1950s Major had begun to diversify "downstream" into petrochemicals and other uses for the basic product, crude oil. Some regulatory pressures occurred during this point in time as a 1954 Supreme Court decision established the Federal Power Commission's regulatory control over the wellhead price of natural gas. Additionally foreign policy continued to play a major role in the industry, as Major and other companies searched for oil in less developed countries including the Arab world. The Iranian crisis of 1951–54 prompted State Department intervention in the industry, and at the same time the Justice Department began preparing a major anti-trust suit against members of the industry.

In the 1960s and early 1970s growth for Major's products continued, but the overall rate of growth in the industry was below the rate of the increase in supply. Therefore competitive pressures mounted. One response to these pressures was the formation of OPEC by Iran, Venezuela, Iraq, Kuwait and Saudi Arabia in 1960 to advocate the interests of the producing nations, whose revenues were highly dependent upon tax and royalty payments from the large oil companies. Thus, OPEC's primary goal during the first phase of its existence was the support and stabilization of posted prices.

The story of OPEC's development and the subsequent changes in the industry are well-documented and will not be rehashed here. The important issue for Major Oil Inc. in looking forward, was to understand what were the key environmental signals which existed during this period of time, and what were the causes of the changes in the stakeholder map of Major from the relatively stable picture in Exhibit 4.12 to the turbulent one in Exhibit 4.13.

By examining the shifts in stakeholder maps, major issues and strategies which the company used to manage (or ignore) certain stakeholder groups, managers at Major can better equip themselves to understand the criteria for success in the future, and go about the process of setting direction in a more effective fashion. The use of the stakeholder concept as a vehicle for historical analysis, and in particular the stakeholder audit as a vehicle for the construction of corporate case studies, can yield both new insights and an understanding of old methods of operation.

EXHIBIT 4.12 *Stakeholder Map of Major Oil Co. in late 1950s*

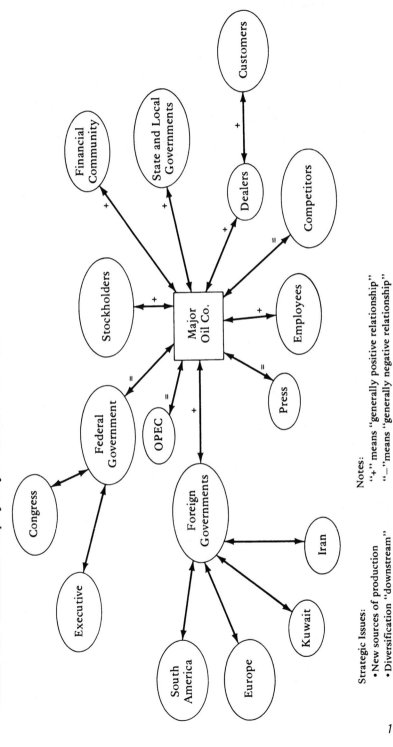

Notes:
"+" means "generally positive relationship"
"—" means "generally negative relationship"
"=" means "generally neutral relationship"

Strategic Issues:
• New sources of production
• Diversification "downstream"
• U. S. Government Policy

EXHIBIT 4.13 *Stakeholder Map of Major Oil Co. in 1980s*

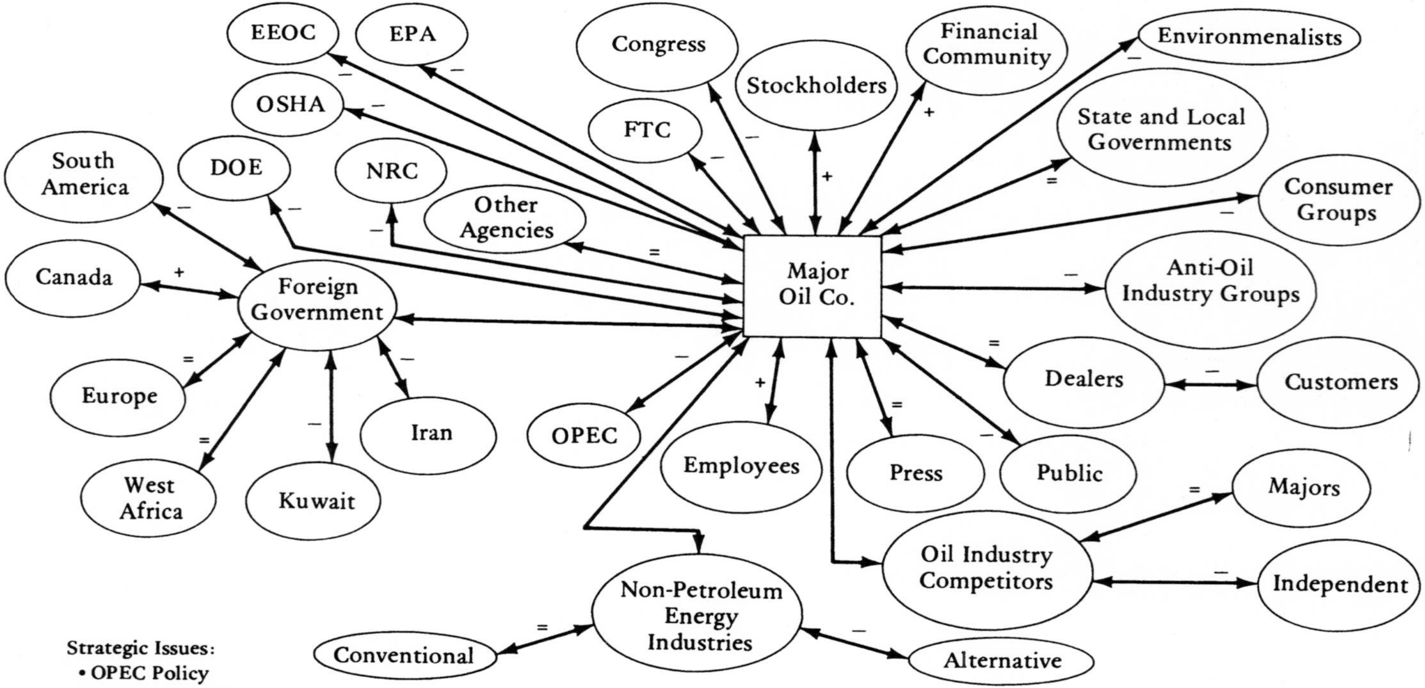

Strategic Issues:
- OPEC Policy
- New sources of supply
- U. S. Govt. policy on energy
- Managing "regulation"
- Public image

Notes:
"+" means "generally positive relationship"
"—" means "generally negative relationship"
"=" means "generally neutral relationship"

SUMMARY

Setting direction in today's business environment is a complicated strategic task. The purpose of this chapter has been to explore how direction can be set at two levels in the firm, and how the stakeholder concept can be used to construct managerial processes which can assist in this task. Setting direction forms the context from which the accomplishment of other strategic tasks are possible. In particular I have shown that an answer to "what do we stand for," or an articulation of enterprise strategy, is necessary if a corporation is to truly understand the environment in which it exists. This relatively new and little understood level of strategic management addresses the question of organizational direction at the highest level of abstraction, by including an analysis of stakeholders, managerial values and social issues. Also, the stakeholder audit can be used to enrich the more traditional direction setting processes such as situational analysis and portfolio analysis. Hence, the stakeholder audit represents one way to conduct a "front end" analysis for a planning process to make it more sensitive to the external environment.

NOTES

1. It is open to question how important strategic decisions are to constructing an explanatory model of organizational behavior. Pfeffer and Salancik (1978) can be read as saying that the intentional acts of managers pale beside the explanatory force available from analyzing the external environment. I do not believe that management need join economics as a dismal science, but if it is not to do so, then theories must prescribe "rational action" or explain "rational action," and not be tempted to conflate "whatever the firm does," or "those firms which survive" with rational choice. It seems that population ecology models do just this by attributing effectiveness to those firms which survive. See Aldrich (1979) for an analysis of this approach, and Van de Ven and Astley (1983) and Van de Ven and Freeman (1983) for a critique and some alternatives.
2. See Ansoff (1979) for a number of more recently complicated planning diagrams.
3. Schendel and Hofer (1979a) distinguish between means and ends as a way of determining the domain of strategy. Their concept of "grand strategy" is closer to the notion of setting direction at the corporate level, which certainly encompasses ends as well as means.
4. However, not all direction-setting decisions represent shifts in values. Some may be "decisions" to carry on as always.
5. The argument is quite complicated here. Perhaps the domain of strategic management is manifestly unclear, for what counts as "the soft stuff" i.e., values and culture, and what counts as the "hard stuff" i.e., no nonsense

business strategies. I shall systematically confuse the issue here, for I believe that it is the wrong issue to address. Surely strategic management, conceived of simply as setting and implementing direction has both of these components. Theories and models must address "hard business" issues and "soft culture and value" issues.

6. AT&T's story is chronicled almost daily in the *Wall Street Journal* for 1981 and 1982. See also Kleinfeld (1981).

7. The story of IBM's development of the personal computer is chronicled in *PC*, Volume 1, an independent trade magazine for the IBM Personal Computer.

8. Jim Sayre and Roberta Wilensky prepared notes on the auto industry, and a draft of a case study on Chrysler from analyzing 30 years worth of newspapers, business press articles and other sources.

9. The development of the concept of "enterprise strategy" is difficult to determine. Ansoff (1979a) uses the concept as a way of broadening the "product-market" focus of strategy research. His concept of "Environment Serving Organizations" is also close to the concept which I have in mind. However, an important difference is that the notion of enterprise strategy discussed here specifically addresses the value-systems of the managers and the stakeholders in rather concrete terms.

10. I owe the use of "what do we stand for" to Professor Andrew Van De Ven.

11. I want to emphasize the need for strategic management processes here. There is a void in the literature in terms of understanding values, and in terms of relating these values to the external environment.

12. Surely Barnard (1938) can be said to be concerned with enterprise level questions when he argues that the obligation of the executive is to instill a service orientation in his subordinates.

13. Post (1978) and Sethi and Post (1982) have formulated processes for understanding social issues.

14. For instance, one attempt to take an issue and account for both process and content is Emshoff and Freeman (1981).

15. This process should be viewed as consisting of several strategic tasks which yield many specific ways of answering the questions posed by the tasks. Organizations can, and should, tailor-make the process to their specific situations.

16. I am grateful to Professor Edwin Epstein for this point.

17. There may well be other relevant categories for particular firms.

18. There is a vast literature on values and ethics. For an introduction see Frankena (1963). Other more recent works which are relevant are Brandt (1979), MacIntyre (1981), Singer (1979) and White (1981). There is a growing literature on "business ethics" which can be helpful as well. See Nash (1981), Goodpaster and Mathews (1982), Beauchamp and Bowie (1979), Bowie (1981), Goldman (1980), Donaldson (1982), Goodpaster and Sayre (1979), De George and Pichler (1978), as well as two recent journals that have been started, *The Journal of Business Ethics,* and *Business and Professional Ethics.*

19. Of course it is possible for a value to be both intrinsic and instrumental. Two intrinsic values could conflict and one could lead to the attainment of the other. I

am indebted to Edwin Hartman for saving me from some of the more stupid ideas which appeared in an early draft of this chapter.

20. Whether organizational values can be said to differ meaningfully from the values of the members of the organization is a difficult question. French (1979, 1982) has addressed this question and argued that collectives like corporations can, and should, be held morally accountable, and hence could be said to have values. His argument is quite controversial.

21. Sethi (1982) has proposed a model of issues and their life-cycles. See Horwitch (1982) for an account of the unfolding of a social issue over time, the SST.

22. The approach developed here seems to be consistent with a "contingency theory" of enterprise strategy.

23. Another way of reading chapter One is to claim that the enterprise level strategies of most U.S. firms are both inappropriate and ineffective.

24. Friedman (1962) has propounded a sophisticated version of this view whereby it is the moral obligation of the manager to maximize the market value of the firm. To do otherwise is to run the risk of concentrating too much political power in the hands of the private sector.

25. See "The Corporation" a film produced by CBS News on the Phillips Petroleum Co.

26. For a critique of utilitarianism see two recent collections of essays, Sen and Williams (1982) and Miller and Williams (1982). For an interesting attempt to apply utilitarian reasoning to problems in business see Sturdivant (1979).

27. The literature on Rawls is enormous. See Daniels (1975) for a sample. My attempt to work out a Rawlsian approach to enterprise strategy is quite crude given the amount of work that needs to be done.

28. There are many ways of asking these questions. Andrews (1980) contains several useful sets of questions.

29. Lawrence Richards has applied this concept in several organizations and I am grateful for his ideas on this chapter.

30. A draft of the Major Oil Co. case was prepared from published materials by Emily Susskind, Mark Kramer and Marci Plaskow. Subsequent interviews with executives at Major Oil were most helpful in finding our way through a maze of literature. Rather than recite the long bibliography here, I shall only mention that Sampson (1975) is a readable introduction, and according to some people in the industry which I interviewed, a reasonably accurate account, "even if prejudiced against us."

Five

FORMULATING STRATEGIES
FOR STAKEHOLDERS

INTRODUCTION

This chapter shows how the stakeholder concept can be used to formulate specific programs for dealing with a broad range of stakeholder groups. In order for the implementation of "stakeholder thinking" to become a reality, the broad prescriptions and philosophical meanderings of the previous four chapters must be narrowed. Specifically, I shall explain how the stakeholder concept can be used at the process level to begin the task of implementing concrete action programs. This chapter explicitly addresses the program formulation task, while chapter Six addresses more directly, the question of implementation.[1]

In the previous pages I have shown that managers need to see the big picture in terms of those groups and individuals who can affect, and are affected by, their actions. I have shown how the stakeholder concept can be used to construct an enterprise strategy for the firm, and how the more traditional direction-setting processes can be enriched.

While this "larger systems" view of the corporation is a necessary condition for managerial success in the current environment, I do not believe that it is sufficient. If managers merely(!) understand the role that their organizations play in society at large, and merely(!) understand their own values, we are not guaranteed that responsive action will occur. If the argument in chapter Three has any merit, then we must seek to understand how lower level organizational processes can also be enriched, and ultimately we must undertake an analysis of the actual transactions which an organization has with its stakeholders.

Setting direction is not the only strategic task, though it has garnered a high market share of the strategic planning literature. Given an overall understanding of "what we stand for" or even an understanding of "where we are going" in terms of our stakeholders, "how do we get to where we want to go" is a most relevant question. Lorange (1980) puts the necessity for looking beyond strategic direction quite simply as, "we have decided during the previous objectives-setting step where we intended to go; now the issue is how to get there." Lorange calls this intermediate step between direction setting and budgeting or resource allocation, "strategic programming." Exhibit 5.1 highlights the questions from the strategic management schemata developed in chapter Three, in terms of strategic programming as well as the subsequent questions on resource allocation.[2]

EXHIBIT 5.1   *Strategic Management Schema*

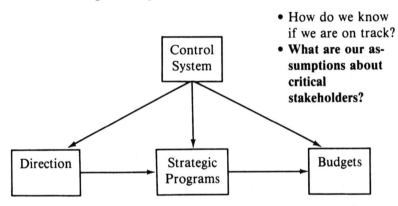

- How do we know if we are on track?
- **What are our assumptions about critical stakeholders?**

- Where are we going?
- What businesses are we in?
- What businesses should we be in?
- **Who are our stakeholders?**

- How do we get to where we want to go?
- What are the cross-functional programs needed?
- **How do stakeholders affect each division, business and function, and its plans?**

- What is our blueprint for action?
- How do we allocate resources for this year?
- What is our operating budget? Strategic budget?
- **Have we allocated resources to deal with our stakeholders?**

When inadequate attention is paid to the strategic progamming phase, or when little regard is given to the linkage between strategic programming and direction setting on the one hand and resource allocation on the other, the strategic management system becomes disconnected from the operational structure of the business. Planning will become an exercise, and stakeholder analysis will be only a part of the yearly ritual undertaken to satisfy the corporate planners. Thus, the logic of strategic management requires that if the stakeholder concept is to have meaning for the "front end" of planning processes, it must also have meaning for the "back end" of the processes. This chapter develops the concept and related processes for formulating strategic programs for stakeholders, and explores the linkage of these programs with direction-setting decisions of the firm as well as the budgeting process.

A PROCESS FOR FORMULATING STRATEGIC PROGRAMS FOR STAKEHOLDERS

Lorange (1980) has argued that there are four basic kinds of strategic programs which can be used to achieve direction: (1) existing revenue programs; (2) new revenue programs; (3) efficiency improvement programs; and (4) support programs. Of course, in setting objectives or direction for the firm, we need not be wholly concerned with revenue. The extent to which revenue is important will depend on the strategy of the firm at the enterprise level. We might be equally concerned with programs which deploy human resources in an effective manner. Indeed, any set of strategic programs must consider how the resources of the firm can be used to implement the business mission. These resources will include financial, technological, human and others. Therefore, we can generalize Lorange's schema for strategic programs along the following lines:

1. *Existing Programs for Stakeholders.* These programs are the strategies which the firm is currently undertaking to manage its stakeholder relationships. A subset of these existing programs will be "existing revenue programs." Hopefully, these existing programs will be uncovered and cataloged during the Stakeholder Audit.[3] If not, then a preliminary analysis to the process described below must be conducted to be able to articulate the intended relationship between a firm and its current stakeholders. For example, a firm may have as a strategic program a media relations program, whereby members of the media are informed on a regular basis about new and upcoming product announcements, or other events affecting the firm. The justification for such a program is

hopefully found in an analysis of the direction of the firm and its desire to improve its image as portrayed in the media, or else this program is a waste of resources. Programs for customer service, filling out a product line or increasing the dividend over time exist in almost every major corporation and represent existing methods of dealing with key stakeholder groups.

2. *New Programs for Stakeholders.* These programs seek to establish new stakeholder relationships or to change the ways that current stakeholder relationships are handled. Sometimes new products create new stakeholder groups, and the repositioning of old products through new markets or new uses of the product also redefine existing programs. For example, a utility redefined its relationship with consumer advocates by forming a consumer advisory panel, consisting of consumer advocates who usually opposed the company in rate filings. The purpose of the program was to achieve, over time, a more cooperative relationship with consumer groups, and hopefully to mitigate the intervention of these groups in the formal rate proceedings by designing rate structures which take consumer advocates' concerns into account.

3. *Programs To Improve Efficiency of Current Operations.* Strategic programming must be concerned not only with what the firm can do differently, but with how it can be more efficient in its current operations with certain stakeholder groups. Capital investment programs to improve the efficiency of plant and equipment, or studies of improvements in the production process or purchasing process are normal examples of programs to improve the current operational expertise of the company. Some firms seem to see changes in management style as a means of improving efficiency, and have called on their unions to support quality of worklife programs to make the shop floor more productive. However, "productivity" is not identical with "efficiency," and QWL programs which are aimed solely at efficiency considerations are ultimately misdirected. Another example of the need for programs to improve efficiency is in the area of government regulation compliance. The burden of compliance with a host of reports from the Bureau of Labor Statistics, OSHA, EPA, IRS and other agencies at multiple levels of government is enormous. For the most part, we know little about how efficiencies in this area are possible. Some firms have established a senior executive as a "chief compliance officer" as a beginning program aimed towards more efficient management of the government agency relationship.

4. *Support Programs for Other Stakeholder Relationships.* Support programs are formulated to help other managers achieve their goals with their own stakeholders. As Lorange argues, these programs are usually

integrative in nature, and often times revolve around the creation of a more favorable managerial climate. Thus, employee communications programs support the programs of both production and labor relations programs, even though they do not seek the direct management of the employee relationship. Organizational change and development programs can be viewed as support programs. Indeed, undertaking to do stakeholder analysis can be viewed as a second-level support program, which supports the business as it is usually operated. The integrative aspect of support functions is especially important in the stakeholder context. Programs for stakeholder groups cannot be developed in isolation, since there are connections externally among various stakeholder groups. The cross-functional nature of strategic programs allows their development at lower levels of decentralized organizations, and in particular at the division (business family) and the business element (SBU) level. In order to successfully compete in the long distance telephone business, a company must have strategic programs for customers, employees, suppliers, government, etc., and there must be some degree of fit across these programs.

The following analysis will concentrate on new programs and support programs, since I have already covered some aspects of existing programs and how to understand them in looking at the stakeholder audit process. There is, of course, more to be said about both existing programs and efficiency improvement programs. However, I believe that new programs and support programs will give a better flavor of how the stakeholder concept can be applied in this area.

In general there are at least two levels of analysis. The first level of analysis differentiates as much as possible among stakeholders and treats the development of programs for stakeholders in a relatively isolated manner. The second level of analysis tries to integrate the requirements of specific stakeholders into general programs which serve multiple groups. The link between individual and integrative analysis is the development of generic strategies, or strategies which work for multiple situations and multiple stakeholders, regardless of the specific peculiarities of an individual stakeholder.

Exhibit 5.2 depicts a process consisting of six major tasks: (1) Stakeholder Behavior Analysis; (2) Stakeholder Behavior Explanation; (3) Coalition Analysis; (4) Generic Strategy Development; (5) Specific Programs for Stakeholders; and (6) Integrative Strategic Programs. Once again, this process can be tailor-made for the individual needs of a specific organization, and it should not be viewed as a rigid set of steps to be followed at all costs. It is an exercise in strategic thinking. The final output of this process is an action plan for stakeholders. Hopefully this plan will be

EXHIBIT 5.2   *Stakeholder Strategy Formulation Process*

helpful in achieving the direction in which the business is headed. The analysis in the following sections assumes that managers have some idea of where they want to go, though it does not assume in the explanation of the process that the organization has explicitly formulated an enterprise strategy, nor conducted a stakeholder audit.

FORMULATING STRATEGIES FOR SPECIFIC STAKEHOLDERS: ANALYSIS

Stakeholder Behavior Analysis

The first step in the construction of strategic programs for stakeholder groups is the analysis of behavior. Most of us have a tendency to assume far too quickly that a group has a particular attitude or set of values, especially when we have a disagreement with them.[4] The inference from "that activist group is demonstrating against our new nuclear facility" to "that activist group is made of anti-American Communists" is an easy, yet fallacious, trap in which to fall. When there are many conflicting stakeholder groups on a particular issue, it is important to sort the varieties of behavior that are present. There are at least three categories of behavior for any stakeholder group on each issue, or as these behaviors relate to some directional objective or other.[5]

The first, *actual* or *observed behavior,* asks the manager to set forth those behaviors that have actually been observed of a particular stakeholder. The set of actual behavior describes the current state of the relationship between organization and stakeholder on the issue in question. It may even describe responses to existing strategic programs, where there are such programs underway.

The second category of behavior, *cooperative potential,* asks the manager to list concrete behaviors that could be observed in the future that would help the organization achieve its objective on the issue in question. Or, what could a stakeholder group do to assist the organization along its desired direction? Cooperative potential sets forth "the best of all possible worlds" in terms of what a stakeholder could do to help. It is useful to look at cooperative potential as relative to actual behavior. Thus, *cooperative potential represents the changes in actual behavior which would be more helpful to the firm.*

The third and final category of behavior, *competitive threat,* asks the manager to list those behaviors that could be observed in the future, that would prevent or help to prevent the organization's achieving its goal. Competitive threat represents "the worst of all possible worlds," and again it is useful to consider it as relative to actual behavior. By thinking through what a particular group could do to hurt an organization's chances of success, a manager can understand the "downside" risk associated with dealing with stakeholders.

By dividing the analysis of behavior into these three categories, the manager, in essence, thinks through the range of options that a particular stakeholder group has in terms of possible behaviors. Not all of the behaviors under cooperative potential and competitive threat will be actually observed in the future, nor will some of them be very likely. However, if a broad range of options has been considered, the manager will be psychologically prepared for virtually any outcome, and will avoid what Ansoff (1979) terms "strategic surprise." By seeking to avoid strategic surprise, the organization is automatically committing itself to a non-reactive philosophy of dealing with its environment. By adopting the schema of cooperative potential and competitive threat, the organization can undertake strategic programs which seek to maximize cooperative potential or prevent (minimize) competitive threat. Above all, it does not assume that stakeholder behavior is a fixed constraint around which it must work. Rather, active programs to bring about cooperative potential can be formulated. Before such programs can be constructed to change behavior, we must understand the underlying causes of behavior, and what changes might lead to cooperative potential or competitive threat.

Stakeholder Behavior Explanation

The second task in beginning the construction of strategic programs for stakeholders is to build a logical explanation for the stakeholder's behavior. It is quite easy to claim, "that stakeholder group is irrational," especially when there is a high degree of conflict between the firm and the stakeholder. (Critics of business pose an excellent example here.) The phrase "I don't understand that stakeholder's point of view" should be substituted whenever a manager is tempted to say that a group is irrational. It may be that a group's objectives are quite different from those of the firm, but rationality involves efficient means to whatever end a group might have. I believe that it is management's job to understand stakeholder behavior whether or not there is agreement on the appropriateness of that behavior. Managers must construct "theories" about stakeholder behavior which try to explain how a stakeholder could possibly act in the way that has been observed. To attribute "irrationality" to a stakeholder is to take the easy way out.[6]

Stakeholder Behavior Explanation asks the manager to put himself/herself in the stakeholder's place, and to try and empathize with that stakeholder's position, i.e., to try and feel what that stakeholder feels and to see the world from that point of view. It does not ask the manager to sympathize or express a genuine liking for a point of view. In essence the manager must undertake to play the role of a particular group. (Chapter Six explains how one company undertook to instill this empathy-building process in its managers.) By trying to play the role of a particular stakeholder the manager can more fully understand the "why" of a stakeholder's behavior, and thus construct an explanation of that behavior.

First the manager must try to state the objectives of a stakeholder group. It may be useful to look at objectives in terms of: (1) what the stakeholder group is trying to accomplish over the long term; (2) what the stakeholder group is trying to accomplish on the issue under analysis; and (3) what is the linkage between the current issue and the stakeholder's longer-term objective. Now, some stakeholder groups are so amorphous as to not have cohesive "group objectives." For instance, a particular customer segment is usually not a group that has a set of objectives in any normal sense of "objectives"; rather, individual customers have objectives. Each customer is thus treated as a "representative of a customer segment," and we act as if the customer segment had a set of objectives. When we find too much of a difference among representatives of a customer segment, then it is time to resegment the market.

The second step in explaining a stakeholder's behavior is to conduct a stakeholder analysis of that stakeholder. Put the stakeholder group in the middle and draw a chart of its stakeholders. By understanding the external environment of a particular stakeholder group, the manager can see the external forces and pressures that are acting on that stakeholder. This second-order stakeholder analysis also gives insight on the pressure points and vulnerabilities of a particular group. While a particular issue may be the most important thing to a manager, it may have low priority to a stakeholder because of all of the other external demands on the group. If one can gain insight into the behavior of a particular organization by understanding the stakeholders in that organization, then one may as well apply that rule to the stakeholders. That is, we gain insight into the workings of a stakeholder group by seeking to understand that group's external environment.

The third step in explaining stakeholder behavior is to examine that group's beliefs about the firm. Does a group believe that the firm is unresponsive to their point of view? Or, does a group believe that the firm pays too little attention to them? Does the group believe that the firm is incompetent, or irresponsible on the issues?

By completing an analysis of objectives, stakeholders and beliefs about the firm, the manager constructs a "mental model" of a stakeholder group that generalizes that manager's experience with the stakeholder (Emshoff, 1978). It should now be possible to explain the stakeholder's actual behavior, and to more fully understand why or why not cooperative potential and competitive threat are likely. The reasoning should go as follows:

> Stakeholder S has exhibited behavior B because S's objectives are O. S's stakeholders are S' and S believes A about us.

If this explanation is not logical, or if it does not seem to explain the behavior of a group, then more work must be done in the preceding steps. The data for this model of a stakeholder may well be biased. Remember that all of the data comes from the perceptions of the manager, and its validity is dependent on the ability of the manager to truly empathize with that stakeholder group. If there are errors in the manager's attribution of objectives, stakeholders and beliefs to a group, then the model will not explain the group accurately. Hence, these explanatory models must be iterative, constantly being revised when new data is found. Perhaps a newspaper story on a stakeholder group makes the manager realize that the group's objectives are different from those in the original model. Perhaps a conversation with a colleague gives the same result. The point is that managers must constantly think critically about what makes a particular stakeholder group tick.

Explaining stakeholder behavior is not logically independent of the behavior itself. By constructing an explanatory model we may come to see a particular piece of behavior in a different light, and hence, we may need to revise our statement of that behavior.[7] Additionally, by drawing a stakeholder map of a stakeholder we may think of new cooperative potential and competitive threat behaviors. Again, while the process depicted in Exhibit 5.2 must be undertaken in sequential steps, the logic of the process is not sequential; rather, the tasks fit together like pieces of a puzzle.

Coalition Analysis

The final analytical step in constructing strategic programs for stakeholders is to search for possible coalitions among several stakeholders. The preceding steps of the analysis give at least two ways of analyzing coalitions. The first is to look for commonality in behavior, in all three categories. Thus, stakeholder groups who have similar actual, cooperative or competitive behavior may well be candidates for a coalition. In addition, managers should think through existing strategic programs to determine if there are currently coalitions among stakeholders. The second basis for coalitions forming is through a commonality of interests. Certain groups will share objectives, stakeholders or beliefs about the firm. These groups will be more likely to form coalitions.

Coalitions may be explicit, whereby stakeholders get together and plan a joint initiative. Coalitions may also be tacit, whereby there is an implicit understanding among several groups that they will not interfere with the others' goals, or that they will support each other on key issues. By analyzing stakeholder behavior, explaining that behavior and searching for coalitions, managers can better understand what strategic programs will be successful. They will also be better positioned to develop programs which will appeal to stakeholders. Before showing how such programs can be constructed, however, an example may help to illustrate the kinds of analysis which tasks 1–3 require. By taking an historical example that has been analyzed in the literature and that is familiar to a number of managers we can get an appropriate level of detail in the analysis. Horwitch (1982) has completed a comprehensive analysis of the attempt to build a supersonic transport airplane during the 1960s and early 1970s. His analysis is sufficiently rich and detailed to give the flavor of this strategic program formulation process.[8]

STAKEHOLDER ANALYSIS EXAMPLE: THE U.S. SUPERSONIC TRANSPORT

Background

In 1963, after much study, President Kennedy announced that the U.S. would build a supersonic transport airplane (SST) capable of transporting passengers at speeds of up to three times the speed of sound (Mach 3). Similar programs were underway in Europe with a consortium of British and French firms working on the Concorde, and in the Soviet Union working on what became the TU-144. The U.S. project was to be a joint initiative between government and private industry. The project managers from government were in the Federal Aviation Administration (FAA), and the key private actors were Boeing, Lockheed, G.E., Pratt and Whitney, etc. Initial attempts at design of the airplane were flawed and delayed for a variety of reasons. Funding for the program had to be secured through the Congress. The technology for building the SST was untested. Also, the FAA had been primarily an administrative regulatory agency and had little experience in managing contractor relationships. Such partnerships were normally handled in the airline industry with the Department of Defense. In 1964 President Johnson created a Presidential Advisory Committee (PAC) on the project, chaired by Secretary of Defense Robert McNamara. The PAC began to ask many questions about the feasibility of the program, which up until 1964 had been ignored or assumed to be not an issue.

Thus, The Department of Commerce and the Institute for Defense Analysis were called upon to make economic studies. The PAC met often and asked tough questions of the program managers and the contractors who were bidding on the final contracts. Indeed, by 1967 there was no agreed upon design for the plane and every deadline had been missed. In addition, by 1967 the sonic boom that the SST would produce became an issue and the National Academy of Sciences got involved in evaluating the effects of the boom, as did a special Sonic Boom Coordinating Committee of the Office of Science and Technology. Hence, the management of the program began to fragment, as new stakeholders emerged and as design issues were not yet solved.

The late 1960s saw the emergence of the environmental movement. The SST became a symbol of a technology which would do environmental harm and which was not really needed, at least according to the environmental critics, led by Dr. William Shurcliff, a physicist from Harvard. As a result of the internal focus of the project managers towards answering questions posed by PAC, the environmental critics were basically ignored and were ultimately victorious in killing the program in 1971.

Stakeholder Analysis

While the SST is obviously more complicated then the preceding three paragraphs, it is useful to illustrate how the analytical methods described above could have been used to develop strategic programs for key stakeholders. Let us assume that we are senior managers at Boeing, GE or Lockheed, and our objectives include proceeding with the SST. We shall leave aside the question whether this is a "proper" objective. From our general knowledge let us analyze several key stakeholders at several points in time. First, let's take Secretary McNamara in his role as chairman of the PAC, a group which in the 1964–65 time frame was instrumental in delaying the program.

Actual Behavior of McNamara and PAC in 1964–65

- Group met often
- Asked questions about the economic feasibility of the program
- Commissioned economic studies by other actors such as the Department of Commerce
- etc.

Cooperative Potential

- Disband (not likely)
- Give favorable support to the program to LBJ and the Congress, to expedite the program
- Agree on the economic feasibility, and stop commissioning studies
- etc.

Competitive Threat

- Recommend the abandonment of the SST to LBJ and the Congress
- Continue to delay the program
- Change the criteria for acceptance of a particular design
- etc.

Objectives of PAC and McNamara

It is difficult to sort out the objectives of PAC and McNamara. Perhaps they wanted to maximize their clout with respect to this program. It seems equally likely that they merely wanted to serve the President by getting the facts together, and by making a rational decision. Perhaps they wanted to save Johnson potential political embarrassment concerning what was essentially a Kennedy program. While it is impossible to precisely determine the objectives of PAC, we do know that they were driven by a need to get the facts and that McNamara was the paradigm of the "rational manager," being a "Whiz Kid" proponent of systems analysis, etc. We also know that McNamara, by virtue of his being President of the Ford Motor Company, understands the importance of timely action in business.

Stakeholder Analysis of PAC and McNamara

A stakeholder analysis of McNamara and the PAC reveals an impressive list of stakeholders. McNamara, himself, had to be concerned with Defense Department stakeholders, such as contractors, internal groups such as the military services and the civilian workforce, NATO, SEATO, and the related governments such as Vietnam, Cambodia, etc. In addition, LBJ's programs and the associated stakeholder groups were important to other members of the PAC. The stakeholder analysis reveals that the SST was but one relatively small item on the agendas of these quite busy government officials.

Beliefs About Key Stakeholders

It is probably true that the PAC felt that the project managers at the FAA were not capable of seeing the big picture—of which the SST was only a small part. Thus, PAC may have believed that left to their own devices, and encouraged by the industry, the program would have been shoved through devoid of careful analysis and justification. PAC may well have believed that the industry managers such as those at Boeing and GE, were only interested in making sure that the program continued. After all they had a great deal of resources committed to the program.

Coalition Analysis

The possibilities for coalitions were strong, as the PAC contained some of the most powerful people in Washington. Coalitions with the Congress, or at least with key committees in the Congress, LBJ, other departments in the government, etc. were a definite possibility.

Given this stakeholder analysis it is relatively easy to construct a strategic program for dealing with the PAC. Of course, since we are viewing this case with 20-20 hindsight, we know that the PAC played a vital role in the program and that the delays in the initial stages of the program were critical. Nonetheless, given the rather high level and power of the members of the PAC, and their penchant for asking questions, we should realize early on that we need to change the rules of the game as they now stand (in 1964-65). Thus, one strategic program to achieve cooperative potential, and to prevent competitive threat would be to set up a joint panel of experts to try to raise and answer the critical economic and technical questions quickly. Resources would be allocated to these experts, and a number of interested parties would participate in their selection. We would appeal to McNamara's business sense to try and gain agreement to abide by the results of the study, so that the questions could be settled once and for all. The risk of this strategic program is that the questions turn out not to have answers, or that the economic and technical feasibility turns out to be negative. However, it would be better for Boeing and GE, etc. to know that now, as opposed to continuing to expose the firms to future uncertainties.

What actually happened is a long story, and Horwitch (1982) tells all of the complications. Suffice it to say that the managers of the program did not address the concerns of environmentalists before it was too late. I believe that they paid little attention to the pressure groups because they spent too much of their time dealing with the issues of power and politics internally, *as if they were separate issues.* If the managers had developed an integrated set of strategies for all stakeholders, including PAC and McNamara, then they would have been more likely to see the rise of the environmentalists, and to enter into productive negotiations with them. I am not certain that the program could have been (or even should have been) rescued. However, a great deal of time and resources could have been saved if the program had been managed more effectively.

The SST is only illustrative of how stakeholder analysis can be used to formulate strategic programs for stakeholders, and in particular how the analytical concepts can be used. We need to look at the kinds of stakeholder positions which are possible, and the generic strategies which can be used to address these positions.

GENERIC STRATEGIES FOR STAKEHOLDERS

Research in strategic management has recently concentrated on the development of prescriptions for what a firm should do, given certain general situations. Thus, we can develop generic strategies which are valid regardless of industry, and which are keyed to the strategic position of a firm within an industry or industries.[9] Both situationalists and portfolio theorists have developed generic prescriptions for what a firm should do in a particular business. Often these prescriptions are at the level of, "which direction should we take a particular business," and for the most part they ignore the influence of external stakeholders that are not directly a part of the marketplace. Exhibit 5.3 illustrates some of the prescriptions available from situational and portfolio theories.

In a recent book, Michael Porter (1980) claims that industry structure alone determines the appropriate generic strategy. Specifically, he argues that there are five forces that shape competitive strategy. The first force is the internal jockeying for position among the firms competing in a particular business. Relevant variables include the number of competitors, the concentration ratio in the industry, the "competitiveness" of the firms, the segments in the industry, etc. A second force is the relative power of customers, i.e., can the customers exert a great deal of influence over competitors by playing one off against another, by requiring special services or by threatening to integrate backwards and become a competitor. A third force is the relative power of suppliers. Are the suppliers an oligopoly or a cartel? Do they control price? Is there the threat of forward integration and becoming a competitor? A fourth force is the threat of new entrants. In addition to suppliers and buyers, there may be others who can overcome barriers to entry and become competitors. A fifth force is the threat of

EXHIBIT 5.3 *Generic Strategies: Some Examples*

Andrews, et al.	Portfolio Theory
No change	Grow (invest) in high growth high share businesses
Retreat	
Focus on limited special opportunities	Divest low growth/low share businesses
Acquire	Build position in high growth/ low share businesses
Geographical expansion	"Hold" low growth/high share businesses
Diversify	
—	—
—	—
—	—

substitutes, making current products obsolete or making profits more difficult to obtain. According to Porter, a careful analysis of these forces will dictate the proper generic strategy, either "change the rules of the game," "exploit advantage and opportunity," "defend current position by taking competitors head-on," etc. We can make a particular business competitive by being the low cost producer in a market, focusing on a particular market niche or by product differentiation.

Porter hints at, but does not develop, the role of other stakeholder groups in formulating generic strategies.[10] If we add a sixth force to Porter's model, we can generalize it to include a variety of stakeholder groups. While such a careful generalization of Porter's theory is beyond the scope of the present analysis, [see Freeman (1983a) for more] it may be useful to see how generic strategies can be developed for stakeholders. The resulting analysis fits quite well with Porter's theory, even though we have gone beyond industry structure towards "stakeholder structure," and firms in an industry need not necessarily share common stakeholders. Exhibit 5.4 illustrates the "six forces that shape competitive strategy."

By analyzing cooperative potential and competitive threat of each stakeholder we have a surrogate for the potential of a stakeholder to affect any strategic program that is developed. Obviously, we want to treat those stakeholders who have high cooperative potential and low competitive

EXHIBIT 5.4   *Six Forces That Shape Competitive Strategy*

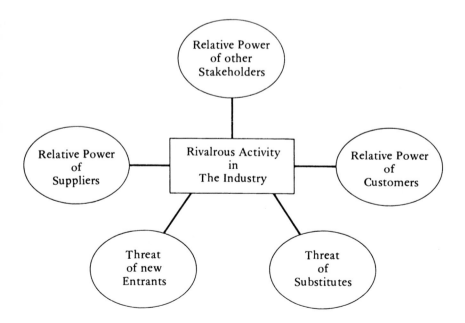

threat differently from those groups who have low cooperative potential and high competitive threat. Thus, we might first want to rank stakeholders in terms of their relative cooperative potential. This is done by asking the question, "which groups could most help us achieve our objective," or simply by classifying the groups by a simple scheme such as "high CP," "somewhat high CP," "somewhat low CP" and "low CP." The same can be done for competitive threat. (It is an enlightening exercise to go through a similar analysis as if we were our competitors. Competitors often have differing sets of stakeholders, and therefore, will adopt different generic strategies.)

There are at least four categories of groups: (1) those groups with relatively high cooperative potential and relatively high competitive threat, let's call them "swing" stakeholders; (2) those groups with relatively low CP and high CT, let's call them "defensive" stakeholders; (3) groups with relatively high CP and relatively low CT, let's call them "offensive" stakeholders; and (4) groups with relatively low CP and CT, let's call "hold" stakeholders. We would next check our classification and discount the CP and CT of groups which are not even remotely possible. That is, if a stakeholder group has high cooperative potential, but we know from past experience that we cannot turn it around within the time frame of the strategic program we are developing, we must discount the CP of that group and perhaps cycle it to a higher level in the corporation. Thus, we get a final matrix such as Exhibit 5.5.

Generalizations of Porter's generic strategies seem to be appropriate. Swing stakeholders have a strong ability to influence the outcome of a particular situation. Hence, strategic programs which seek to change the rules by which the firm interacts with those stakeholders are appropriate. Note that a change-the-rules strategy was suggested for Boeing/GE with respect to the PAC. In general, new strategic programs are called for, and sometimes support programs are necessary to help.

Defensive stakeholders can be of relatively little help, but can take steps (behaviors) to prevent the firm from achieving its objectives. Defensive stakeholders often have current or actual behavior which is quite helpful, thus their possibilities for improvement, and (in turn) high CP are quite limited. Defensive stakeholders illustrate the maxim, that one is most vulnerable with one's friends, rather than one's enemies.

Offensive stakeholders can help a great deal in achieving objectives, but pose little relative threat. Perhaps they are already killing the organization on this issue, and their actual behavior could not be any worse. If there is relatively little downside risk, virtually any strategic program is worth a try, and opportunities for gain should be exploited.

Hold stakeholders can be of relatively little extra help or harm. However, we must remember that they may currently be quite vital. CP and

EXHIBIT 5.5   *Generic Stakeholder Strategies*

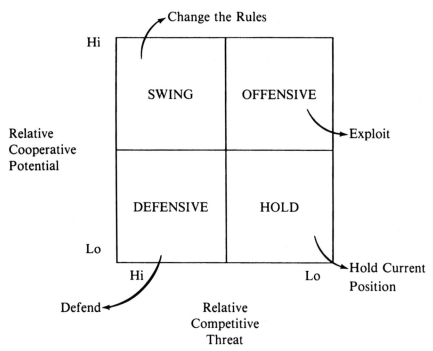

CT measure changes in behavior, since we are looking at how to formulate new strategic programs or programs which are supportive of current activity. With groups who are unlikely to move, existing strategic programs should be sufficient.

Several propositions are suggested by this analysis:

> *1. The relative power of stakeholders, in terms of potential for changes in current actions, affects the success of particular strategic programs of a firm.*
>
> *2. If a set of stakeholders in a firm has relatively high cooperative potential and relatively low competitive threat, the firm should adopt an offensive strategy to try and bring about the cooperative potential of this set of stakeholders.*
>
> *3. If a set of stakeholders in a firm has relatively high competitive threat and relatively low cooperative potential, then the firm should adopt a defensive strategy to prevent competitive threat on the part of these stakeholders.*

> *4. If a set of stakeholders has relatively high cooperative potential and competitive threat, the firm should adopt a strategy which seeks to change or influence the rules of the game which govern firm-stakeholder interactions.*
>
> *5. If a set of stakeholders has relatively low cooperative potential and competitive threat, the firm should adopt a strategy which seeks to continue current strategic programs, and holds the current position of these stakeholders in place.*

For example, the Congress, the Department of Justice, the FCC, competitors, state regulatory commissions all have relatively high cooperative potential and competitive threats for companies in the telecommunications industry who are trying to enter the computer industry. Thus, for example, AT&T must adopt a version of proposition 4 as a generic strategy with these stakeholders on this issue, and seek to influence changes in the rules of the game. (Whether it should adopt such a strategy at the enterprise level is another less obvious question.) When Firestone finally voluntarily recalled additional production runs of its radial tire, it obviously was in a position where it couldn't lose more, its stakeholders had high cooperative potential (fresh from a victory in coalition form among government agencies, courts and customer groups). Conversely, when Proctor and Gamble issued an early product recall of its Rely tampon it was obviously adopting a version of proposition 3, a defensive strategy, since it believed that irreparable harm could be done to other products, current and future, if it failed to act quickly.

There are other generic strategies which are possible, some of which involve differing transactions with stakeholders. Joint ventures are an intriguing possibility, and it is not clear when strategic positions of stakeholders require joint ventures. Obviously, joint ventures can be a "change the rules" strategy, but with non-marketplace stakeholders, joint ventures can be seen as ways to do joint problem solving on social issues, and thus be in line with both defensive and offensive positions.

SPECIFIC STAKEHOLDER STRATEGIC PROGRAMS

How can these generic prescriptions be put to work to formulate specific strategic programs for key stakeholder groups? Obviously, the specific actions which are necessary will be a function of the behaviors of the stakeholder group which a manager needs to influence. Each generic strategy, however, yields certain kinds of specific programs which can then be tailor-made to individual stakeholder behavior. The following examples will focus heavily on non-traditional stakeholders, as there is a good deal of literature on strategic programs for customers, suppliers, etc.

EXHIBIT 5.6 *Specific Stakeholder Programs*

Change the Rules Programs

---

1. Formal rules changes through government.
2. Change the decision forum.
3. Change the kinds of decisions that are made.
4. Change the transaction process.

Offensive Programs

---

1. Change the beliefs about the firm.
2. Do something (anything) different.
3. Try to change the stakeholder's objectives.
4. Adopt the stakeholder's position.
5. Link the program to others that the stakeholder views more favorably.
6. Change the transaction process.

Defensive Programs

---

1. Reinforce current beliefs about the firm ("preach to the choir").
2. Maintain existing programs.
3. Link issues to others that stakeholder sees more favorably.
4. Let stakeholder drive the transaction process.

Holding Programs

---

1. Do nothing and monitor existing programs.
2. Reinforce current beliefs about the firm.
3. Guard against changes in the transaction process.

Exhibit 5.6 is a summary of the types of specific programs which can be developed for each generic strategy. While not an inclusive list it does give the range of options available. Following, are examples of each of these types of programs, saving the "change the transaction process" program for the chapter on implementation (chapter Six).

"Change the Rules" Programs

There are at least four kinds of specific programs which can be designed to change the rules under which the firm operates with a particular stakeholder. These four kinds of programs are not mutually exclusive, and can often be used in combination with each other. First, there are formal changes in rules, whereby the firm seeks to change the rules that have been enacted into law, evolved as administrative rules, or are perhaps even enacted in the charters of non-governmental organizations. Second, there can be a change in the decision forum, a change in who makes certain decisions and in where the decisions are made. In government, the issue of "jurisdiction" is an important one and is a strategic variable which should not be overlooked. Third, the firm can change the kinds of decisions that are made, and thus refocus the relationship with a stakeholder around a different set of issues. Finally, the firm can change the process of transaction. Let me explain how these programs can work with a number of key stakeholder groups.

Activist Groups

Several utilities have adopted a change the rules program with groups that have traditionally been intervenors in their rate cases. One such program involves changing the decision forum from the adversarial rate case arena to surroundings more conducive to negotiation and communication, whereby the consumer leaders and the utility managers discuss upcoming rate proposals and try to agree on how to mutually proceed. Often times, the consumer group will still intervene in the rate case, but the company can gain an understanding of the consumer's point of view, and the consumer group does not feel bound to fight the company on every single issue. In fact there are some cases where the consumer group has agreed to certain company proposals, and both have agreed to disagree on others. By changing the forum in which, at least some, decisions are made, a company can begin to break down the adversarial barriers which exist between utility and intervenor. Changing the forum of decisions also begins to change the process by which transactions are undertaken between company and activist.

Environmental groups successfully used a "change the rules strategy" with beverage industry companies in recent battles over "bottle bills." In 1976, proponents of enacting legislation to require deposits on soft drink and beer containers were frustrated by their inability to convince state legislatures of the merits of their point of view. Instead, they adopted a program to change the decision forum, and placed measures requiring deposits on the ballot to be voted on by the voters in Maine, Michigan, Massachusetts and Colorado. Changing the forum caught the industry off-guard, and their response was to argue as if the fight was still in the state legislature — emphasizing jobs and economics rather than litter and a clean environment. The bills passed in Maine and Michigan, and lost narrowly in Massachusetts (and subsequently passed). Opponents of the tobacco industry have adopted a similar program, by collecting signatures for a "no smoking in public" initiative, which has been for the most part unsuccessful.

Government Agencies

Several industries have adopted a program of trying to change the formal rules under which they are regulated, by lobbying for legislation which would substantially reduce the "regulatory burden" on them. The deregulation of petroleum prices is a clear example of changing the formal rules. The Business Roundtable has tried to influence the kinds of decisions that are made with respect to government agencies and business, by sponsoring a study to analyze the costs of regulation. By focusing attention on such costs, regulatory decisions will, hopefully, be more sensitive to the economic impact which they have. AT&T's decision in 1976 to introduce "The Consumer Communications Reform Act," dubbed "The Bell Bill" was an attempt to change the forum of regulatory policy from the FCC who had been distinctly pro-competition, to the Congress. The Bell Bill can also be seen as an attempt to change the formal rules under which the telecommunications industry was regulated. The recent Consent Decree is consistent with that program of changing the rules, in general, for the industry, and in fact changing the very nature of the telecommunications industry.

Employees

Several companies have undertaken to change the rules under which they manage the relationship with their employees by introducing "Quality of Work Life" programs. Basically these programs change the decision forum to "quality circles" and change the kinds of decisions that are made. They also change the transaction process with employees, and can be fragile victims of management style and a history of an adversarial relationship with employees.

Offensive Strategic Programs

There are a number of programs which can be used to bring about cooperative potential with stakeholders. Stakeholders who have high cooperative potential may well have an adversarial relationship with the firm that is so bad that virtually any change will have a positive effect. Thus, there are a wide range of programs which must be carefully analyzed in formulating a strategy to bring about cooperative potential. Included in this range of options are: (1) changing the stakeholder's beliefs about the firm; (2) doing something (anything) different; (3) trying to change a stakeholder's objectives; (4) adopting the stakeholder's position; (5) linking the issue to others that the stakeholder sees more favorably; and (6) changing the transaction process.

There are numerous examples of these types of strategic programs. The simplest type of program to change a stakeholder's beliefs about the firm is a product or service repositioning program. New uses are found for old products, which change the customer's ideas about the product or service. By trying to change a stakeholder's beliefs about the firm, managers are betting on the fact that the stakeholder's behavior is a result of erroneous assumptions about the firm. One company undertook a similar strategy by learning to listen to its critics, and to show the critics that the firm was made up of "reasonable individuals" who in fact were quite concerned about a particular social issue, but who had little idea how to solve the issue.[11]

If a situation with a stakeholder group is already quite negative, and if there is little that group can do to hurt the company further, then virtually any action is worth a try. However, random action or action which goes to reinforce current negative beliefs about the firm can entrench and intensify the current negative behavior. Firms which have long-standing feuds with certain media groups may be in a position to bring about cooperative potential simply by changing a small point of corporate policy. Two examples are scheduling press briefings by executives instead of public relations managers, and by calling the press to alert them to a problem before they find out from other sources, and paint a picture of the firm as "secretive" and "anxious to cover up." The logic of such a strategy is that the hostile media will find out anyway, so why not take this opportunity to try and turn things around.[12]

A program that is more difficult than the two already mentioned, is to try and change the stakeholder group's objectives, that is, to convince that group to want the same things as the firm. Many dollars are spent implementing programs which are aimed at changing stakeholder's objectives. Advocacy advertising campaigns are sometimes aimed at changing groups' objectives with respect to the proper role of government. Campaigns often trumpet the virtues of free enterprise and ridicule the efforts of government to interfere in market processes. These programs should be used with caution as a net result can often be to change a stakeholder group's beliefs about the firm doing the advertising; namely, the stakeholder can come to believe that the ads are self-serving and a waste of stockholder's resources.

On the other end of the perspective, is a strategic program to adopt the objectives of a stakeholder on a particular issue. This is standard operating procedure in the marketplace, or at least it should be, and can be carried over to other arenas as well. Labor-management cooperation can be fostered if union goals are accepted by management, and unionization can even be prevented in cases where management understands and adopts the goals of employees. Such a strategic program is usually undertaken only after a long strike when both company and union are hurting. Of course, there may be inefficiencies to such an approach, but if cooperative potential of a particular stakeholder is truly vital to the survival of the firm, then "giving in" has to be considered.

One effective strategic program is to link the issue under consideration to broader concerns of a particular stakeholder group, and to show that stakeholder group that their support on the issue is consistent with their support on a larger issue. Companies in the oil industry could well have adopted this strategy in trying to show that deregulation was in the interests of groups worried about conservation. Such a program could have been implemented by undertaking a joint research project to show how regulation artificially raises the price of oil. The industry could have volunteered to set aside a certain portion of its profits from deregulation to fund further research on conservation of energy. Instead, the windfall profits tax was passed and everyone was a loser.

Defensive Strategic Programs

Defensive strategic programs are necessary when a stakeholder group holds the keys to failure on a project, but cannot really help achieve its success. A typical situation that calls for defensive programs is a trade organization's executives dealing with its membership. Quite naturally, organizations who belong to trade organizations can veto certain courses of action, and if they do not support the actions of the trade organization's management then the organization is doomed. However, there is little cooperative potential because usually the member organizations are as supportive as possible. Hence, the rational trade organization manager has to guard against "loss of support" from his or her members. The general question is how to prevent the degeneration of actual behavior into competitive threat. There are several analogous situations to offensive strategic programs.

In this case the manager would not necessarily try to change the attitudes of the stakeholder, but rather would try to reinforce current attitudes. In a sense the manager must "preach to the choir" who are already believers. By constantly reinforcing current beliefs the manager protects against changes in beliefs that would yield more negative behavior. Again, trade organizations are instructive, as are professional organizations. Annual meetings are replete with "how much the organization has done for you during the past year."

Stockholders are another case in point, for while there is little cooperative potential for stockholders as a group, there is relatively high competitive threat, if a great number of them try to sell the stock at the same time: hence, the ritual of the annual meeting and the "slickness" of the annual report. Some companies have even begun to conduct "stockholder interviews" to let them know that they are not forgotten.

Another version of a defensive strategic program, is to let the stakeholder group drive the transaction process between the group and the firm. That is, managers are "over responsive" to the concerns of these stakeholder groups. Utilities are over responsive to the concerns of public service commissions, simply because while the commissions cannot guarantee high rates of return and positive rate cases (the intervenors determine such cases along with market conditions, etc.) they can deny the company's position. Thus, their competitive threat is always high, even though on some issues their cooperative potential may be high, as well. By allowing the commission to drive the transaction process and by responding promptly to requests for information and studies, the company tries to insure against the commission's always saying "no." A similar case is the attention paid to requests from legislators, at the state and national level. Lobbyists will respond quickly to requests, and do not (for the most part) try to get too many issues on the agendas of legislators, preferring to let the legislator drive the process.

Holding Programs

Even though some stakeholders have relatively little cooperative potential or competitive threat they may still be important. Programs need to be thought through which maintain current behavior. Obviously some variants of early programs are appropriate, such as reinforcing current beliefs or "preaching to the choir." Current programs which are influencing stakeholder behavior must be monitored, so that the major issue with holding programs is an issue of control rather than program formulation. Holding programs must logically guard against "changes in the rules of the game," and consequently when "change the rules" programs are formulated they must be checked to see if they change the rules for more than one stakeholder group.

INTEGRATED STRATEGIC PROGRAMS FOR STAKEHOLDERS

Even though there are programs for individual stakeholders, the sum of these programs may not add up to the desired direction for the firm on the issues(s) under consideration. Either there may be interactions among stakeholders which cause dysfunctions or there may be inefficiencies in the programs themselves. By making the situation "win-win" for one stakeholder group we may make it "win-lose" for another group. Thus, we must address the issue of how to integrate the strategic programs for multiple stakeholders.

There are two basic ways to tackle this issue. First, we can recognize that there are commonalities in behavior and objectives, and hence, return to the analysis of the earlier section to discern common threads among stakeholder groups. Alternatively, we can search for common threads among the strategic programs developed for individual groups.

For example, in the earlier analysis of the Supersonic Transport Program, a behavioral analysis of McNamara and the PAC revealed a common concern with the economic and technological justification of the program. A similar analysis of the "stakes" of key Congressional leaders and other agencies would have revealed a similar concern. Thus, an integrated strategy to deal with the concerns of all of these stakeholders would be for the industry to allocate some resources to fund a joint panel of experts to lay these issues to rest once and for all. Such a strategy would address the common behavior of asking questions about the feasibility of the program, and build on the common objective of "getting the facts."

AT&T's strategy of going to Congress and getting the rules changed for the telecommunications industry could well be viewed as an integrated strategy to deal with the Congress, the FCC, competitors, the Department of Justice and others. One could argue that in trying to deal with each of these stakeholders separately, AT&T should have noticed that their strategy for each had to include a position about industry structure. Thus, the company had to justify monopoly market positions to the FCC. It had to argue against allegations of unfair competitive practices in its arguments with the Justice Department. It had to answer similar allegations in civil anti-trust actions, etc. Thus, AT&T managers could have noticed that they needed a strategy to pull together these diverse threads to achieve consistency and to change the rules of the game.[13]

Emshoff and Freeman (1981) have shown that the United States Brewers Association had at least two integrated strategic programs with respect to the beverage container issue and, in particular, the legislation requiring deposits on non-returnable containers. Focusing on the common concern with the costs of container legislation, they suggested that the USBA volunteer to set aside a certain amount of money equal to the difference between the "forced costs" of removing the containers as litter as would be required by legislation, and the "free market costs" of removing the litter, that would occur if no deposits were mandated. If free market costs were truly less than the mandated costs then all concerned stakeholders would be winners. Alternatively, Emshoff and Freeman claim that if the USBA developed strategic programs for each stakeholder, they would notice that the key to the success of most of these strategies was the issue of the validity and the credibility of the industry's economic studies. Therefore, the creation of a joint panel of experts to review the studies that had been done and to commission a definitive study which all parties would agree to sign-off on would go a long way towards establishing the credibility of the study. The USBA should be willing to take the risk involved if the economics of the situation were as they believed. Thus, integrated strategic programs for stakeholders are possible, even though the formulation of such programs are a creative managerial act.

SUMMARY

I have shown in this chapter that strategic programs can be developed for each important stakeholder group. These programs will depend on the analysis of stakeholder behavior, and on the ability of managers to clarify their own "theories" and "models" of stakeholder actions. I have indicated how the stakeholder approach to strategic management gives rise to generic strategies for stakeholders, and in particular how the work of Porter (1980) can be extended to include "stakeholders" as one of the forces that shape strategy. I have briefly indicated how strategies for multiple stakeholders can be integrated into comprehensive programs which address many stakeholder concerns at once. There is a great deal of research yet to be done in the area of formulating strategic programs for stakeholders. I have merely indicated how the stakeholder approach fits into this schema which seeks to bridge the gap between strategy formulation and implementation.

NOTES

1. I shall not distinguish between a program and a strategy, as in ordinary usage these two terms are often interchanged. "Strategic programs" are simply organized approaches to dealing with a stakeholder group, that looks beyond the immediate transactions which have to occur.
2. In Lorange's schema strategic programs forge a much needed link between the formulation and implementation tasks. I believe that more research on strategic programming may find that it is more important than formulation.
3. However, I do not assume that the firms under consideration in this chapter, by way of illustration, have undertaken an enterprise analysis or a stakeholder audit. Hence, my discussion of strategic programming is independent, I hope, of what came earlier.
4. Once again, the metaphysical position staked out in chapter Three comes forward. It is behavior that is observed, not attitudes and beliefs (which serve as useful,

even necessary explanatory concepts). Strategies should aim towards changing behavior. Vincent Carroll has been helpful on this point.

5. The rationale for these three categories is described more fully in Emshoff (1980) and Emshoff and Freeman (1981).

6. To constantly attribute irrationality to a stakeholder would be to admit that our theory of that stakeholder's behavior could not account for the observed behavior, and would require revision. "Irrationality" is often a substitute for "I disagree."

7. For an illuminating discussion see Wisdom (1953, pp. 248–282).

8. I am grateful to Professor Mel Horwitch of MIT for many hours of discussion of the SST and the stakeholder concept. While he would not agree with the analysis put forward here, he is responsible for drawing my attention to the rich data that the SST gives us. In addition Horwitch (1982) can also be read methodologically, as purporting an historical approach to better understand the issues and problems in strategic management.

9. Generic strategies are really nothing more than guidelines or frameworks within which a particular strategic plan must be worked out. They should focus attention on implementation, since they do part of the conceptual work of formulation.

10. For instance see Porter (1980, pp. 28–29).

11. See "Abbott Labs: Similac" in Sturdivant and Robinson (1981).

12. See Banks (1978) for an excellent discussion of the business-media relationship.

13. These speculations about AT&T represent my own analysis rather than any "insider knowledge."

Six

IMPLEMENTING AND MONITORING STAKEHOLDER STRATEGIES

INTRODUCTION

In this chapter we discuss how the stakeholder concept can be used in the implementation and monitoring tasks of strategic management. Once again, I do not assume that the programs and strategies to be implemented or monitored are necessarily those developed using the methods in the previous two chapters. Chapter Three shows that the three levels of stakeholder analysis — rational, process and transactional — must achieve some degree of "fit" if an organization is to have a high capability for stakeholder management. This chapter explores the transactional level in more detail, through an analysis of how to implement strategies and programs for stakeholders. In addition, the monitoring task of strategic management can be seen as seeking to ensure that the three levels of analysis fit together in some coherent fashion.

The transactional level of analysis is the bottom line of strategic management, where the organization "engages" the external environment.[1] It is where the organization "does its business." The transactional level is the set of behaviors which an organization undertakes to establish and maintain the relationships that it has with its stakeholders. It asks, "what do we do now," and "how do we engage in the behaviors that our strategies and programs warrant?" Yet another term is "strategy execution," the carrying out of strategic tasks and seeing them through to completion. While the very concept of strategy execution is action-oriented there are several conceptual schemata which can be useful in analyzing an organization's ability to successfully conduct transactions with its stakeholders.

Monitoring or controlling has traditionally been applied only to the operational side of organizations, through analysis of variances from budgets. The old dictum, "we plan in order to control, and we control in order to plan," gives rise to the concept of planning and controlling as continuous and iterative processes. Strategic management yields a more complicated concept of control as monitoring the "degree of fit" between organization and environment, only one part of which is an analysis of variances.[2]

In this chapter I shall analyze the implications of the stakeholder concept for implementation activities and propose a checklist of concepts that can be useful. I will set forth a framework for controlling and monitoring, and suggest that this task can (and should) be used to regularly check the degree of consistency among the rational, process and transactional levels. Finally I shall describe a case study of the implementation and monitoring activities of American Services Inc., a disguised description of a large corporation that began to use the stakeholder concept.

IMPLEMENTATION OF STRATEGIC PROGRAMS

Once strategic programs have been formulated to achieve strategic direction, these programs must be translated into action plans. "Who is to do what" must be answered, and the organization must begin the task of implementing the programs. Effective organizational planning systems do not force managers to reinvent every program at each stage of the planning cycle. Existing programs are reevaluated, but for the most part continue as planned. The operational aspects of the business are slower to change, and for good reason, as they yield the current base of resources for new and support strategic programs. Nonetheless, the new programs and those which support current and new programs must be integrated with the current tasks of the business. Exhibit 6.1 depicts how the sum of the strategic programs gives rise to both departmental budgets and program budgets (Lorange, 1980).[3]

Each program that the company undertakes requires that several organizational units be given resources to execute that program. Thus, by adding up the resources spent by each unit on a particular program we arrive at a program budget, PB1. Similarly, each organizational unit will work on a number of programs, some of which are existing operational programs and some which are new strategic programs. By adding up the resources that a unit spends on all of its programs we can get a total organizational unit budget, OB1. If an organization is "perfectly efficient"

Exhibit 6.1   *Implementation of Strategic Programs*

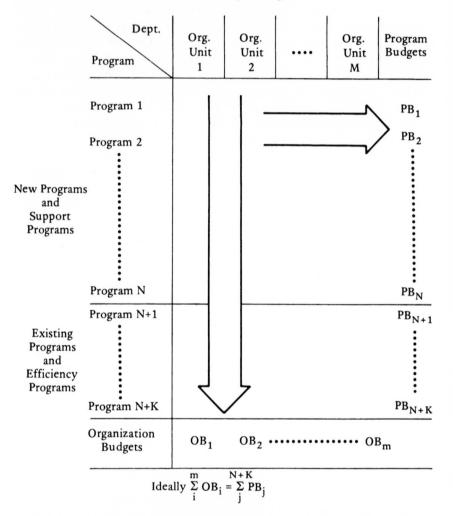

then the sum of its program budgets will equal the sum of its organizational unit budgets, or $\Sigma PB_i = \Sigma OB_i$. While in reality such an equality obtains only by accounting system manipulations, Exhibit 6.1 can be used as a checkpoint for aligning organizational budgets with program budgets. Some such process, a variation of Planned Programmed Budgeting and Zero-Based Budgeting, must be the basis for an organization's budgeting activity if it is to be properly connected to the strategic management activities, i.e., if the strategies are to be executed.

Organizational managers stake out their turf on issues and operations, and tradition plays a role in the territorial struggle for power and influence. Thus, there are traditional divisions of responsibility for dealing with stakeholders which do not necessarily lend themselves to the implementation of integrated strategic programs, whether of the new or support variety.[4] The task of implementation is both to work within the traditions of an organization and to work outside those traditions where they are inappropriate. If the claim of the preceding chapters has any validity, it has suggested that traditional ways of looking at the firm must change to more closely align the firm with reality. Therefore, the implementation task of stakeholder management becomes crucial, not only because it is where "rubber meets the road," but because it implies that organizational change and development are necessary if the changing external environment is to be met with improved company peformance.

Conceptually, the implementation task looks quite simple. Exhibit 6.2

EXHIBIT 6.2   *Implementation Matrix for a Particular Strategic Program*

Organization Units or Departments	Stakeholder		
	Congress	Customers	Employees . . . . .
Public Affairs	Action Step 1, Time t_1 Action Step 2, Time t_2	. . .	
Key Executives	. . .		
Division 1 Managers			
. . . .			

depicts an implementation matrix in which actions by organizational units and members are plotted against stakeholder groups who are intended to be affected. Each strategic program developed can be plotted on such a matrix. However, this matrix merely focuses the strategic programs into action. Suppose that a firm undertakes a change the rules strategic program with a stakeholder such as the Congress. It may set out actions such as:

1. draft model legislation;
2. open dialogue with key representatives on legislation;
3. obtain commitment of representatives to introduce legislation in upcoming Congressional session;
4. develop lobbying effort with members of key committees in the House and Senate;
5. marshall support of stakeholders in coalition; and
6. etc.

Each of these actions should have a time frame, and an organizational unit responsible for meeting the schedule. In addition, support programs may be undertaken by other organizational units. The company may want its marketing representatives to explain the proposed changes to major customers, or have the department responsible for employee communication prepare material for all employees. A series of speeches by executives and board members may be planned. In short, the move from strategic programs to implementation is the move from a carefully laid plan of action towards a flurry of activity. Exhibit 6.2 becomes a tool for creating an overall picture of how the implementation of the strategic program is to proceed.

Within this overall picture of who is responsible for carrying out each action, over the specified length of the strategic program in question, there are several issues for discussion which can determine if Exhibit 6.2 can be used (discussed in order): (1) Allocating resources; (2) Gaining commitment; and (3) Changing the transactional process, or organization development as it applies in this particular context.

Allocating Resources

Most large organizations have formalized budgeting processes which allocate resources to the various organizational units on a yearly basis. The rationale for resource allocation varies by organization and by the kind of budgeting system in use in the organization. On the one hand, historical analyses of past budgets are used to justify yearly increments, while on the other hand, the position of a particular business in the organization's portfolio may be used to give resources to that business or take resources away from less attractive businesses. Capital budgeting models using sophisticated operations research techniques, and "what if" financial planning models have had a tremendous impact on the budgeting processes in most major corporations.

I shall not review these processes, nor argue that they are fundamentally mistaken. However, I do believe that any budgeting process that is to be consistent with the strategic processes of a firm, must address the overall issue of how resources are allocated to deal with various stakeholder groups.

Quite simply, if a particular stakeholder is vital to the future success of a firm, resources must be allocated to deal with that group. If government can affect the future success of a firm, resources must be allocated to deal with government, rather than hoping that government will go away, or bemoaning the fact that the firm is a creature of government. Likewise, consumer goods companies must allocate resources to deal with consumer complaints, that is if repeat buying is necessary to their success. Electric utilities must allocate resources to deal with issues of environmental safety and quality, if intervenors and critics can affect their ability to raise necessary funds. In short, there must be consistency between the effects of stakeholders and the amount of resources that are allocated to deal with them.

Emshoff and Saaty (1978) have recommended a technique called "prioritized hierarchies" to actually quantify the importance of stakeholder groups and to check that resources are allocated in terms roughly equal to the importance of each group, else the system is inherently biased in terms of current allocations. Lorange (1983) has argued that the strategic part of the budget must be separated from the operating part of the budget to give clarity and urgency to strategic programs that are new. Otherwise, Lorange claims, new strategic programs will naturally be overlooked in favor of existing ones. That is, the existence of a current base of operations prevents a completely "rational" allocation of resources. Issues of power and turf within the organization and the simple fact that no manager likes to have resources taken away from him or her, make "rational" resource allocation processes fraught with difficulties.

The criteria for judging the importance of stakeholders, and thus the actual amount of resources allocated to dealing with a particular group, will vary by organization and by the values of its managers. Given the discussion of values in chapter Four, we see that the adoption of a particular enterprise level strategy may well dictate a different allocation of resources, depending on how managers see the mission of their business. Such a broad based definition of "what we stand for" will carry over into the resource allocation process at the level of implementing particular strategies. Generically there are at least two different approaches to determining a workable set of criteria. The first involves senior managers judging which groups are more likely to have an effect on a particular program and must be dealt with on some basis. The second approach actually relies on the expectations of key stakeholder groups around particular programs. Mendelow (1981) developed a method for surveying both senior management and key stakeholders on the question of performance criteria on certain issues. He found that top management and stakeholders had different perceptions of what was expected from the organization. Each used different measuring scales to judge organizational success. If resources are to be properly allocated, for improved organizational performance, then the issue of the development of a set of criteria needs to be addressed.

While a dollar-for-dollar allocation in terms of stakeholder importance cannot be justified, since we know so little about appropriate processes here, I do want to suggest that a rough equivalence needs to be insured. It is simply folly to believe that organizations will, in and of themselves, automatically adapt to changes in the environment by allocating resources to meet these changes. Thus, not only do the new and support strategic programs need to be singled out from the operating budget, à la Lorange (1983), but there must be an explicit process for checking the degree of fit of the strategic budget with the degree of importance of stakeholders.

The underlying reason for this explicit checkpoint in the strategic budget, is that the organizational bias towards the status quo or towards history is really a bias towards a stable environment. Allocating resources based on last year's budget, or even based on a portfolio analysis, assumes that the environmental forces are roughly the same as last year or that the factors that make up market attractiveness are relatively stable. In highly turbulent environments more flexible allocations of resources must be made and, in particular, managers must be willing to depart from the status quo.

It is well known that the budgeting process can become unworkable when it fails to take account of the big picture and hinders the achievement of the firm's major goals. And, budgeting becomes an organizational ritual when it relies too heavily on "the numbers" (Lorange, 1980). An equally disturbing problem occurs when the budgetary process pays too little attention to the external environment. Of course, if strategies are properly formulated the strategic programs themselves will reflect the importance of key stakeholder groups. However, the budget can serve as another checkpoint for insuring that stakeholder concerns are taken into account.

Allocating resources for new and support strategic programs can take several forms. Obviously, existing organizational structures can be changed, and with such changes a reallocation of resources occurs. It is becoming increasingly common, however, to adopt moves which are less drastic than complete reorganizations. Teams and task forces can be put together quickly and human resources can be allocated to a particular project. Allocating dollars is a bit trickier, and depends on the flexibility of the budgeting system. Often, the chairperson or leader is charged with the expenses of the task force until the appropriate transfers can be made.

Alternatively, liaisons can be established with the responsibility to support a particular unit in terms of a stakeholder. For example, ABX utility had a public relations unit charged with consumer affairs. Because of the sophistication of the consumer groups that affected ABX it was unrealistic to expect the consumer affairs group to be the sole spokespersons for the company. They had neither the depth of knowledge, nor the decision making authority that the consumer groups wanted, yet they did have the sensitivity to the consumer issues that the more traditional rate making experts did not have. Hence, liaisons from this unit were assigned to the rate departments and given some resources. Galbraith (1973) describes other organizational forms which can be used to reduce the uncertainty caused by having to implement new strategic programs.

Another method for allocating resources to new strategic programs is the addition of new people and new organizational units. In the early 1970s the Bell System undertook a strategy to beef up its marketing capability to meet shifting environmental concerns. It consciously looked outside the company for expertise in order to reallocate resources towards this expertise. It went to one of its future competitors and hired a number of managers with marketing expertise, and several of these managers were promoted rapidly, giving the proper signals to others in the organization that "marketing expertise" was a way to get ahead. Bell then beefed up the marketing department and eventually reorganized along market segments. Over a period of time insiders began to get the message, and Bell began to be more responsive to competitors and customers. However, only by adding new people and creating fresh organizational units was the strategy successful.

Often, hiring outside the firm is necessary to implement new programs. The obvious problem is the difficulty in integrating the new person and his or her organization into the existing firm. By hiring new expertise to deal with a particular stakeholder we thereby allocate resources, both human and financial, to deal with that stakeholder.

More subtly, as the above example illustrates, changes in values can be used to bring about a reallocation of resources in a firm. By negotiating quality of work life programs into the union contract, one firm insured that its divisions would allocate resources to a change the rules strategic program with its employees. Without such a potential sanction, little effort would probably have been given to such a program in the hustle and bustle to meet production quotas and to increase productivity in the usual ways. The company had done no explicit management development in 25 years and found that it must sensitize its managers at all levels to the new union agreement and the change in managerial style which it required. It undertook a training program which has been continued, even in the face of a reduced bottom line. The value change represented by the QWL program was implemented in a way to insure that resources were allocated. While there is no assurance of success, allocating the proper resources is a necessary condition for even a chance of organizational effectiveness and survival over time.

Gaining Commitment

A second major issue in implementing strategic programs for stakeholders is how to insure commitment to the program from the organizational units involved, and the managers responsible for carrying out the program.[5] Obviously a necessary, but not sufficient, condition for gaining commitment is to allocate resources in a fashion that at least makes implementation possible. There are at least three other concepts that are important in understanding the issue of gaining commitment: (1) participation; (2) incentives; and (3) shared values.

Participation

Perhaps the most important advantage of strategic management systems is the opportunity that they afford for participation in understanding and running the affairs of the corporation. A number of research studies have shown that participation and commitment are related, however, the logic is much older and simply says that alienation occurs when one no longer has a sense of creating or participating in the final product. Therefore, the more participation in the creation of strategic programs for stakeholders, the more likely the commitment to implementing the programs. Corporate policies which dictate what organizational units can and cannot do with respect to certain stakeholder groups are sure to fail to establish successful transactions with that stakeholder, no matter how well intentioned the policy.

Incentives

A second variable which must be understood and managed properly to gain commitment for the implementation of strategic programs is the use of incentives. Kerr (1976) has claimed that it is "folly to hope for A and to reward B." Thus, it is pointless to hope that managers carefully take stakeholder concerns into account when implementing strategies, and reward them on another basis altogether. Retail stores that want to be known for their customer service and policies of taking merchandise back if the customer is dissatisfied, regardless of the reason, would do well not to penalize department managers for taking back merchandise.

Reward systems are not confined to monetary rewards, but include who gets promoted, patted on the back and the choicest assignments. The complete set of rewards and incentives within an organization is quite complicated as Herzberg (1966) has shown, yet again there must be a rough equivalence between the rewards and punishments that are meted out and the importance of stakeholders. Companies who reward managers for making a certain number on a measurement index, must realize that it will be the exception rather than the rule when non-index behavior is found. If strategic programs call for new products, then those managers who work for new product introduction must be promoted, regardless of where they fit on other criteria. If strategic programs call for taking the offensive with a stakeholder group which has been critical of company activities, then managers who undertake to turn around the relationship need to be rewarded, or at least not punished, even if they are not successful.

Shared Values

Each strategic program will involve certain types of behaviors which may, or may not, fit into the current system of rewards in the organization. Hence, each new strategic program must be checked to see if it requires behaviors which will run counter to the accepted "winning behaviors" in the organization. Executives in company ABC simply could not understand why division managers did not allocate the capital over which they had control to achieve a company wide investment program. Unfortunately, the division managers' yearly bonus rested heavily on meeting their profit commitments, and dollars spent on upgrading facilities made the profit index look bad. Companies which are committed to a quarter by quarter increase in Earnings Per Share (EPS) should for the most part forget about making strategic investments, and hence should forget about new strategic programs, unless they have an operational base which is extremely healthy and projects unlimited growth and opportunities. To do otherwise is simply to force managers to act in bad faith. It is hard to make tradeoffs between short term returns and long term viability. Incentive systems which exacerbate this difficulty run the risk of reinforcing the search for excuses rather than reinforcing the creative drive to use current resources in the most productive manner.

A related issue is the distinction between the real and the visible costs and benefits of action. Simply put, the real costs and benefits of action are in terms of the contribution of the action to the achievement of the organization's mission or even its enterprise strategy. The visible costs and benefits of action are in terms of what others in the organization see as a result of the action. Real costs and benefits may at times be invisible, such as actions which prevent a disaster, or actions which prevent a stakeholder from exercising competitive threat. When organizational reward systems take only visible costs and benefits into account managers soon get the message that a risky action must be assessed in terms of one's "exposure" to senior management and to others who influence promotion, etc. Actions which try to anticipate the effects of the environment and to lessen the effects are seldom rewarded in an organization that rewards visibility. It can easily be accepted practice to blame the environment, just as it has become standard business wisdom to blame the economy. We need to remember that creative business leadership outpaces the economy and the external environment in general. We cannot hope to implement new strategic programs for stakeholders when the organizational incentive systems run counter to success.

Changing the Transaction Processes

If an organization is going to do what its strategy requires then it must carefully assess its interactions with stakeholders. There are several different ways that organizations interact with stakeholders. (Here again, I am going to focus on non-traditional stakeholders though most of this applies equally well to customers and suppliers. Marketing and operations management are well worked out disciplines which are concerned with proper customer and supplier interactions.) Exhibit 6.3 lists some of the more typical ways that organizations interact with their stakeholders: Ignore; The PR Approach; Implicit Negotiation; and Explicit Negotiation. Let's see how each works and focus on the range of negotiation-like processes that are available to manage these processes more effectively.

Ignore The Stakeholders

Trivial as it may sound, some organizations simply do not interact with those groups and individuals who can affect or are affected by them. Perhaps such inaction is a form of "denial," or perhaps it is simply a breakdown of organizational processes such as environmental scanning which, after all, are not infallible. Or, perhaps ignoring certain stakeholder

EXHIBIT 6.3   *Transaction Processes for Stakeholders*

Ignore the Stakeholder
_____

- Do nothing
- Allocate no resources

The Public Relations Approach
_____

- Tell the company story
- Opinion leader communication
- Image-building

Implicit Negotiation
_____

- Best estimate of stakeholder position

Explicit Negotiation
_____

- Two-way communications
- Informal negotiations
- Setting and turf
- Proposal-response-compromise cycle
- Unilateral action
- Win-win solutions

groups is a result of using the old framework of customer-supplier-owner-employee, in a world where it is no longer appropriate. Regardless of the underlying reasons, organizations which ignore their stakeholders are in for big trouble, sooner or later.

Company KSD found that they ignored a particular stakeholder group which knew how to use the political process to affect KSD. The group got a state legislature to sponsor a bill that would affect KSD's operations in the state. By the time that KSD managers organized to try and defeat the bill it already had enough sponsors to pass. KSD had to forego a large sum of potential profits in that state because of the restrictive legislation.

The consequences of ignoring competitors from Japan and Germany are all too familiar to a number of managers in industries who are experiencing layoffs, lost profits and an inability to compete. Many companies are paying the price of ignoring non-domestic competition in terms of whopping investments needed to quickly modernize facilities, structuring new relationships with the work force and calling for government help in industries such as steel, automobiles and consumer electronics.

The example of Major Oil in chapter Four illustrates graphically the price that the oil industry paid in ignoring or virtually ignoring OPEC until it had gained almost total control of the production of oil. When OPEC was initially formed in 1960 it was a "weak signal" to oil company planners. In the words of one executive, "we knew OPEC was around, we thought it was some kind of joke." No longer is OPEC a joking matter for the industry, or for the rest of the industrial world.

Sethi and Post (1982) have categorized the response patterns of several firms in the infant formula industry, and inaction is initially the favored response. When inaction occurs, a stakeholder can take its needs to another firm to be satisfied; it can exit. More likely, it will begin to use its political power, in terms of voice, to try and force a response from the firm. Once the initial use of coercive power is made, the conflict can escalate, and the firm must play "catch up."

A variant of the ignore the stakeholder strategy occurs when no resources are allocated to deal with a stakeholder, or to deal with possible future stakeholders. The firm may as well be ignoring the stakeholder, for the absence of resources sends the same signals. The lack of any organized effort means that the firm will not participate in the initial phase of issue identification, where it is crucial to influence the discussion and the definition of the issue.

One obvious way for organizations to interact with stakeholders more effectively is simply not to ignore them. Some organizational process or some manager must be responsible for continually surfacing the transactions that are, and are not, made with the organization's stakeholders.

The Public Relations Approach

Most large organizations have public relations departments whose task is to communicate with the "public." While I shall analyze the PR function later (chapter Eight), it is worth mentioning that many organizations depend heavily on the PR department to interact with many of their key stakeholders. Most PR people are trained as communications experts in schools of journalism. Typical stakeholder interactions revolve around "communications" programs, where the PR people tell the stakeholders or "publics" or worse still, "audiences," about the company's plans and how the plans affect the stakeholder. Often this approach simply incites a stakeholder group to action.

Alternatively, PR people undertake "speaker programs" and "community leader luncheons," whereby so-called "opinion leaders" are informed as to the company's plans. The common thread of the PR approach is that any communication is one-way. PR people "tell our story," sometimes with the help of PR consulting firms who put together catchy campaigns to please executives. The focus of such campaigns is "image" and while the image of the firm is not to be overlooked it does not automatically follow that a firm with a "good image" is very well off in terms of meeting stakeholder needs.[6]

Implicit Negotiation

A third method of interaction is for the firm to take stakeholder concerns into account in the formulation of strategic programs, and then to implement those programs using the normal organizational units of the firm. Because the firm has tried to take stakeholder concerns into account before a strategy was implemented, it can often mitigate any objections that a group may have. Several utilities have begun to try and anticipate stakeholder objections to rate proposals, and to design rate structures which answer those objections.

The problem with implicit negotiation is that it is only as good as the attribution of positions to stakeholders that goes on in the planning stages. If implicit negotiation is to be effective there must be a conscious decision to rely on secondary source data, rather than asking the stakeholders themselves. The need to validate information necessary for implicit negotiation leads naturally to a more direct process of explicit negotiation.

Explicit Negotiation

It was hypothesized in chapter Three that organizations that have high stakeholder management capability (i.e., fit together the rational, process and transactional levels in a consistent and effective manner) use explicit negotiation processes with stakeholders. Effective explicit negotiation processes require the understanding and management of several key variables as depicted by Exhibit 6.3.[7]

Communication processes with stakeholders must be two-way, if the results are to be meaningful. If managers cannot understand stakeholders' positions and if stakeholders cannot understand the positions of the firm, then a meaningful communication program must be undertaken. Communication is quite complicated. Each party brings a set of biases to the communication, and the possibilities for misunderstanding are numerous. The further apart an organization is from its stakeholders in terms of shared values, the harder truly two-way communication will be. Managers must learn to "like getting yelled at."

The story of Abbott Labs as chronicled by Sturdivant and Robinson (1981) is a case in point. Mr. Cox, the CEO of one of Abbott's divisions responsible for infant formula undertook a lengthy communication process with the critics who wanted a total ban on infant formula in third-world countries. As a result of this process, Abbott has begun to be differentiated from others in the industry who have adopted a different strategy. Thus, while Nestle's has suffered the consequences of a product boycott, Abbott has been singled out as an exemplary company in the industry, leading to increases in sales and profits.

The key to successful communication is perhaps the credibility of the communicating parties, and credibility is "party-relative." The Watergate incident illustrates the role of credibility in government, but has important lessons for executives as well (Muzzio, 1982). When credibility is lost, true communication is impossible. Each side distrusts the other and a great deal of effort must be put forth in trying to restore the credibility of the communicating parties.

Other lessons from the public sector include the scrupulous attention paid to credible communications in times of international crises. Only by managing the communications process did Kennedy avoid nuclear war over Cuba in 1962. A "hot-line" sits in the White House as a reminder of the importance of maintaining open channels of communications, regardless of whether they are often used. Jordan (1982) recounts the difficulties that President Carter found in communicating with the government of Iran during the hostage crisis. Meeting in secret, and in disguise, with two intermediaries with no obvious relationship to the hostage crisis compounded the difficulty of settling a sticky and dangerous international situation.

"Informal negotiations" refers to negotiations which take place outside the formal arenas of government hearings, or judicial proceedings, or other organized forums where there is a set of formal rules by which all parties must abide. The advantages of informal negotiations are obvious. There are no restrictions on communications, and positions do not have to be taken "for the record." Formal proceedings are not conducive to creative solutions, and experimentation is not encouraged. When methods of informal negotiation are used to their fullest, the formal proceedings, if they exist, can become ritualistic and virtually unnecessary. "Formality" is a relative term. A simple meeting with a stakeholder group with whom the company has had no previous contact can be a formal proceeding, while meeting among groups with longstanding relationships can be informal. Effective transaction processes make use of informal negotiations.

A related issue is where negotiations take place and what is the setting of the talks. One consumer leader runs a joint panel for members of industry and consumer leaders at a resort to try and remove both groups from the day-to-day battles and to foster real communication. Another activist complains that business leaders do not understand that most of the members of his group are volunteers and hence cannot come to daytime meetings simply because they all have jobs. He appreciates the well-meaning managers who try to involve group members in corporate decisions, but the setting is all wrong. Setting and turf can be intimidating if used incorrectly, and they can be destructive of meaningful negotiation. They are variables which must be thought through when planning explicit negotiations with stakeholder groups.

One interpretation of my claim that managers need to understand and communicate with stakeholders is that they should communicate for the sake of communication, or to improve the image of the firm. Again, while image may be important, I am more concerned with action. Actions demand that managers be prepared to make proposals, to respond to proposals from stakeholder groups and that they be willing to compromise. Managers who are not experienced "traders" will often experience difficulty in their stakeholder transactions, just as they will experience difficulty in their dealings with their peers. The central idea of negotiation is "compromising," which involves giving up certain things to get other things.

Company XAC has tailor-made a stakeholder process to surface "bargaining chips," those positions on issues on which the company can compromise. The process forces managers who interact with stakeholders to explicitly recognize where the interests of the company and key stakeholders overlap. These managers go to stakeholders with a careful understanding of what they need to give up to get stakeholder support or action on an issue. The process is not infallible but it does force these managers to think about exchange and compromise as the primary media of transaction. There are times when managers must take risks and commit themselves to positions which run counter to "company policy." If managers are not willing to do so, then real negotiation cannot take place, since the limits of the transaction can never be reached.

A favorite method of interacting with stakeholders deserves careful scrutiny; namely, the use of unilateral action. Unilateral action involves taking actions alone, without any communication beforehand. Companies which ignore their stakeholders perform unilateral action, but many who communicate regularly and negotiate with their stakeholders do so as well. The paradigm of unilateral action comes to us from foreign policy: "we'll put the missiles in Cuba and see what Kennedy does," or, "we'll take the hostages in Iran and see how Carter responds." In each case an action is taken and a response is provoked. Unilateral action increases the risk of conflict escalation. Each side has a tendency to overreact, because it is not certain, to use the vernacular "where the other is coming from." Its theory about the stakeholder is put to the test. Companies which unilaterally announce a plant closing escalate any possible conflict with their employees at the plant that is affected and at all other plants as well. Internally, managers who take unilateral actions with respect to their subordinates are feared and often undermined. Bad news is not easy to tell, and conflict is difficult to manage, but the use of unilateral action makes it worse. The conflict or bad news will not go away, and we will be called to account for the unilateral action itself.

The key to successful transactions with stakeholders is for managers to think in terms of "win-win" solutions. How can the many parties that are affected by a particular program come out as winners. There are few situations in the real-world, where there are only winners and losers. Even in strictly competitive markets, one must realize that if the game is truly won and major competition is eliminated, there is no more fun to be had, and an anti-trust suit to be fought. Where there is conflict, interests are partially opposed, but because there is a conflict of some interests among parties, it does not follow that there is a total and complete conflict of interest. It does not pay to lose sight of those areas where interests coincide. Managers responsible for interactions with stakeholders must constantly think in terms of how can the other party win. What are the currencies in which the stakeholder is paid? Perhaps it is "exposure" or "media attention," or maybe it is in "forcing the company to change." Can we give something in terms of these currencies? If so, the chances for successful transactions are increased. The stakeholder theories developed in formulating strategic programs are invaluable in trying to formulate proposals and responses that are mutually satisfying. The natural bias of managers to translate their own payoffs, usually in terms of economics, to stakeholders, must be avoided.

Changing the transaction processes with stakeholders involves managing a number of variables. The list depicted by Exhibit 6.3 is not meant to be very comprehensive, but rather provocative, so that we can begin to understand our own transactional styles. More generally, the organization must pay attention to the skills and the values of those managers who are engaging different stakeholder groups. The skills that yield success in dealing with stockholders and suppliers may not be successful in dealing with activists and government, or even employees and customers. We must explicitly undertake a process of matching managers with the stakeholders for which they are responsible.

Changing the transaction processes in an organization is a program of organizational development. An inventory of skills must be taken and training and development programs must be initiated to build skills. Support programs for managers who are acting as change agents must be started, and the temperature of the effort must be taken regularly. The literature on Organization Development is voluminous and I shall not review it here. However I believe that some ideas can be oriented towards helping the organization change its transaction processes with stakeholders. These concepts must deal with the reality of how an organization is currently transacting business with its stakeholders, and hence must deal with a number of forms of negotiation. Without such change, all of the strategic management in the world will not be implemented, and the road to decline will be paved with the carefully laid plans.[8]

MONITORING PROGRESS WITH STAKEHOLDERS

Yet another task of strategic management is to constantly evaluate and monitor progress with respect to the strategies that have been developed. The concept of "control" is not new, but it has usually been restricted to the relatively short term task of finding variances from budgets. More recently, strategic management theorists have begun to apply the control concept to the longer-term issues of whether the corporation is achieving its strategic plans. "Strategic Control" checks to see if the portfolio is still balanced, if programs are on track and if the general direction of the business is still appropriate. Controlling strategy is equally important as formulating and implementing strategy. The pilot must not only set the course for the ship, but must constantly keep watch to see that it is on course, and that the original course is still an appropriate direction for all concerned.

Exhibit 6.4 depicts four basic concepts that can be used in controlling organizational performance: (1) implementation control, (2) control of strategic programs, (3) control of strategic direction, and (4) control of "what we stand for." Lorange (1980, 1983) has identified the first three levels of control and explained how they can work. I will enrich Lorange's analysis by adding an explicit concern with stakeholders and using the stakeholder concept as a framework for the more abstract tasks of control, namely tasks 2 and 3 as well as add task 4 to explicitly address the need to monitor progress on the basic values of the firm and its managers.

Implementation Control

The easiest, or at least most familiar, application of the control concept is in an analysis of variances from budgets. The questions, "Did we do what we said, are there variances from our original allocation of resources, why or why not" are all common questions to which every manager knows how to prepare the answers. I shall say no more about this relatively well-known area except to point out that if the budget has been separated into actions required under existing programs and actions required under new and sup-

EXHIBIT 6.4   *Monitoring and Controlling Progress*

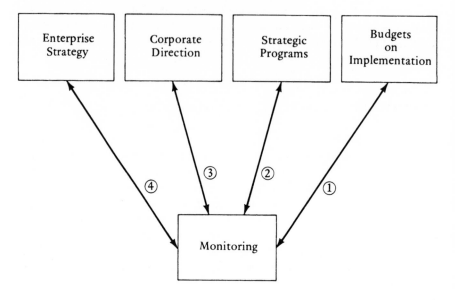

Tasks:
1. Implementation Control
2. Control of Strategic Programs
3. Control of Strategic Direction
4. Control of "What We Stand For"

port programs, then a careful watch must be kept not to underestimate the new programs. While favorable variances are usually welcomed as signs of managerial excellence and financial diligence, in this case, they may well be signs of an inattention to strategic program implementation.

Control of Strategic Programs

The formulation of strategic programs as outlined in chapter Five and the implementation matrices as depicted in Exhibits 6.1 and 6.2 contain a framework for monitoring progress with respect to strategic programs. Each strategic program has two key variables. The first is a set of milestones by which the program will be implemented. When milestones are constantly missed, and when schedules are constantly revised, then we know that the strategic program is in trouble. In our earlier example of trying to change the rules with the Congress, if the milestone of getting a piece of legislation

EXHIBIT 6.5   *Monitoring Progress of Strategic Programs*

		Hi	Keep an Open Mind	"Back Burner"
Certainty of "Theory of Stakeholder Behavior"				Gather Data for Revision
		Lo	Monitor Constantly	

Certainty
of
"Theory of
Stakeholder
Behavior"

Hi — Keep an Open Mind — "Back Burner"

Lo — Monitor Constantly — Gather Data for Revision

Hi   Lo

Importance of
Stakeholder Transactions
to Program Success

introduced is missed over a sufficient span of time, and if little support can be generated in the key committees, perhaps a rethinking of the strategic program is in order. Note, however, that missing milestones is not sufficient to change the generic strategy. Perhaps a change the rules program is still in order, but a different set of action steps may be necessary if it is to work.

A second variable from the strategic program formulation task which bears monitoring is the theory of stakeholder behavior which was created in order to explain actual, cooperative and competitive behavior. Is the theory on which the program is based still accurate and valid? Perhaps our analysis of stakeholders' objectives and beliefs was mistaken, or perhaps they have changed. Exhibit 6.5 depicts four managerial postures with respect to monitoring progress based on the theories or mental models of stakeholder behavior. Constant monitoring of the interactions between organization and stakeholder is called for in those cases where the manager is rather uncertain about the stakeholder and where the stakeholder's support is crucial. Where there is a higher degree of certainty the manager must keep an open mind, and may even initiate research to validate the model that is being used. Thus, it is critical that the control process surfaces hard questions, and forces managers to be introspective in terms of the biases on which their strategic programs are based.

Control of Strategic Direction

The third control task is to check that the strategic programs are taking the corporation in the desired direction. Are we achieving the results that we desire, corporate-wide, and if not why, or if so, why? Are we lucky, or did things go according to plan? Is our business portfolio on track? Once again, the key to successful control at the level of strategic direction is a constant monitoring of the critical assumptions that we are making about the environment, and in particular the assumptions about the future actions of key stakeholders. Most strategic planning systems have some sense of this idea, and they regularly include the assumptions about the future business environment. Usually these assumptions are about the macro-economic situation or are simple quantifications of the political and social risks of doing business in a particular country. (See chapter Three for a critique of environmental scanning processes.) Unfortunately, these assumptions are quite abstract. It is not the macro-economic environment which causes a particular strategy to fail, but rather the actions of stakeholders. Groups and individuals and their actions are real, not macro-economic variables. Now these variables do give rise to a set of expectations on the part of groups and individuals and, hence, are part of the motivating force behind their action. However, we must think critically about how macro-economic variables affect each stakeholder group rather than accepting blanket statements about the economy and inflation. The same critique can be made towards the simple quantification of political and social risks.

Controlling strategic direction requires that managers set forth explicitly the critical assumptions about each important stakeholder group, and how changes in the validity of these assumptions would affect the direction of the firm. Failure to do so rests the direction of the firm on abstract concepts and substitutes hope for careful and clear-headed analysis.

Emshoff (1980), Mitroff and Emshoff (1979), Emshoff and Finnel (1979), Mason and Mitroff (1982) have all set forth how assumptional analysis can be used in formulating business strategies. The controversy which this approach has raised in using so-called "dialectical analysis" is beside the point, when one considers the simple logical fact that if we knew the conditions which were necessary and sufficient for the truth of a certain proposition, we would have a procedure for determining the reasonableness of that proposition, namely, by determining the reasonableness of the conditions. By setting forth the assumptions which a particular strategy makes in order for it to be successful, by appeal to simple logic, we have a built-in control mechanism. When the assumptions become unreasonable, the strategy must, ipso facto, become unreasonable. Assumptions serve as another check on strategy formulation, which may well have been undertaken via a different process, contrary to the argument of Mason and Mitroff (1982).

The format of Exhibit 6.6 requires managers to set forth three kinds of assumptions for each category of stakeholders: behavioral, coalitional, and contextual. Behavioral assumptions refer to assumptions about how stakeholders will act. Examples would be the passage or non-passage of major legislation by Congress, the imposition of wage-price controls by the executive branch or the raising or lowering of the posted price of oil by OPEC, etc.

Coalitional assumptions are harder to uncover, and represent those coalitions that must occur or not occur if the corporate direction is to be achieved. Examples might be national labor leaders willing to work with executives from major industries to achieve a greater sensitivity to the need for higher productivity; or that the anti-nuke movement not garner the support of Congress or political candidates.

Contextual assumptions are assumptions about the way that the world works which may be important to the success of a particular program. They

EXHIBIT 6.6   *Key Assumptions About Stakeholders*

Government Stakeholders

1. Behavioral Assumptions
   —
   —
2. Coalitional Assumptions
   —
   —
   —
3. Contextual Assumptions
   —
   —

Activist Stakeholders

1. Behavioral Assumptions
   —
   —
2. Coalitional Assumptions
   —
   —
3. Customer Assumptions
   —

Customer Stakeholders

1. Behavioral Assumptions
   —
   —
2. Coalitional Assumptions
   —
   —
3. Customer Assumptions
   —
   —

Financial Stakeholders

1. Behavioral Assumptions
   —
   —
2. Coalitional Assumptions
   —
   —
3. Contextual Assumptions
   —
   —

Miscellaneous Assumptions

1.
2.
3.

represent the framework or conceptual map of the decision makers (Mc-Caskey, 1982).[9] These assumptions may well be reducible to behavioral and coalitional assumptions, but the reduction may be unknown. Examples may be the economic beliefs of managers that the money supply determines the interest rates, or that a tax cut will stimulate demand for a product, and increase government revenue. Contextual assumptions may also be about how processes work. For instance, many executives get an education when they work in Washington and find out that the government does not work the way that their 7th grade civics books told them (Fenn, 1979). Contextual assumptions are especially important for companies operating in new contexts, in new markets or new countries, where even the most common conventional wisdom does not hold true.

Finally, I have included a category in Exhibit 6.6 called "miscellaneous assumptions" which can be used to catalog stray ideas which seem important, but do not seem to fit any of the categories listed. Creativity is a difficult force to marshall, yet monitoring progress on strategic direction requires an attempt to think critically and creatively.

The control process here is not very sophisticated. It does not necessarily include the use of econometric models, nor does it require an elaborate bureaucratic process and endless tracking of multiple indices. Rather, it depends on the conceptual skills of managers, and their ability to ferret out the key assumptions on which success is based, and to monitor those assumptions in a systematic fashion. Research can, and should, be used here to both validate and uncover the assumptions hidden underneath the strategic direction of the firm. Such research must be focused, and it must be relevant in the sense that it attempts to work out the logic of a particular set of assumptions, and the resulting validity of a strategy when one or several assumptions are no longer valid.

Control of "What We Stand For"

Chapter Four contained a lengthy discussion about the need to explicitly formulate an enterprise level strategy, and the need for executives to carefully analyze their stakeholders, their values and the societal context in which their firm finds itself. If it is a worthwhile activity to formulate such an enterprise strategy, then it is a worthwhile activity to monitor the progress of the organization towards such a lofty goal.

There is no magic potion that gives insights into the appropriateness of a set of values, nor that makes one a fortune teller in terms of the societal issues that will appear during one's lifetime. Rather, the process for controlling what we stand for must be much more flexible. It must be a process of reaffirmation and revival, and a process where dissent is welcomed and encouraged. Obviously, war and revolution count as changing the underlying societal context, yet thinking critically about less obvious changes such as shifts in lifestyles, family composition, two-career marriages, rural poverty, etc. can be equally important—if not insurmountably subtle. More importantly, executives must ask themselves, personally, whether they still share the values of the organization as a whole. Levinson (1978) and others have argued that there are natural points in our lives where we question our values, and where we seek to leave the past behind. These so-called "mid-life crises" are relevant to an executive group trying to understand what they stand for. The rather personal nature of the effects of the organization on its people must not be overlooked, or dismissed as a human weakness, but must be factored into the control process.

Controlling and monitoring must be done at a number of organizational levels. From a traditional analysis of variances to a mushier analysis of the role of mid-life crises in executive effectiveness, monitoring progress in an organization is no easy task. I have tried to merely sketch how such monitoring processes can be undertaken which use the stakeholder concept. However, our discussion of implementation and control raises a more far-reaching issue which needs some resolution, or at least a greater degree of understanding.

KEEPING SCORE WITH STAKEHOLDERS

An underlying theme in our discussion of monitoring and controlling is that managers know how to evaluate their performance vis-à-vis stakeholders. In short, I have assumed that it is possible to "keep score" with stakeholders and that the categories on the scorecard are well known. Measuring corporate performance with stakeholders is far from a trivial issue, and there is a great deal of research that needs to be done. Post (1978) and others have summarized the corporate performance literature, and claimed that measures of "social responsiveness" need to be added to traditional measures of profitability and market value of the firm.[10] Bauer and Fenn (1972) have proposed a corporate social audit and argued for the construction of a "social balance sheet and income statement." Sturdivant and Ginter (1977) have tried to link social and economic performance by analyzing a sample of "the best and worst" social performers. Overall, the literature on corporate performance is in an embryonic stage and, as such, is inconclusive in terms of yielding prescriptions to guide managerial behavior, as well as in yielding a comprehensive explanatory model to guide further research.

The issue of how to keep score with stakeholders is at once trivial and impossibly difficult. It is trivial in the sense that "score will be kept" by the stakeholder group, and the results will be demonstrated by the group's actions. Thus, an analysis of behavior, as outlined in chapter Five, will begin the process of understanding how a stakeholder group evaluates the performance of the firm. However, keeping score is difficult in the sense that we need generalizable measurements that can serve as yardsticks of performance. We need to compare the performance of one firm with another, and we need to compare intrafirm performance over time.

Keeping score with stakeholders boils down into two related problems: (1) how do we measure our performance with each stakeholder and (2) how do we measure our performance with our entire set of stakeholders? Thus, we need to determine one or more simple measures with each individual stakeholder, and we need to have some idea of the interaction effects of these measures. That is, we need to be able to measure "performance as a whole." Mendelow (1981) has written that one process for determining performance measures is to survey stakeholder groups and elicit a set of criteria by which they judge the firm, and to survey top management to surface what they believe these criteria are. From these two data sets, Mendelow argues, one can begin to construct a consistent set of measurements. However, this set of measures, and the ones that could be based on the behavioral analysis in chapter Five, have only internal validity. Perhaps, given enough cases of different firms, one could inductively determine a set of measurements with some validity that goes beyond the particular firm or set of behaviors in question.

Alternatively, one could hasten this inductive process by setting forth, a priori, a set of possible measurements, and seeing if meaningful cross-company comparisons can be made. Exhibit 6.7 is an example of a scorecard that has not been tested, even though some of the measures for each stakeholder have been subjected to rigorous scrutiny. We might also develop a scorecard for stakeholders on a particular issue. Ideally, the sum of the scores of these issue-scorecards would equal the score determined by Exhibit 6.7. By measuring the performance of different firms on the same issue we can more easily determine differences in managing stakeholders. However, such an issue-scorecard must address real strategic issues and not just so-called "social responsibility" issues. For instance, it would be interesting to develop such an issue-scorecard on the companies in the auto industry on the issue of their response to foreign competition.

As an example, let us look at the proposed measures for measuring performance with customers, which is a well-studied phenomenon in marketing. Some well-established measures are sales measured in number of units sold and the real dollar volume of these sales. (Inflation should fool no one.) More difficult measures include the number of new customers, and the

EXHIBIT 6.7   *A Sample Scorecard for "Keeping Score with Stakeholders"*

Stakeholder Category	Possible Near Term Measures	Possible Long Term Measures
Customers	Sales ($ and volume) New customers Number of New Customer needs met ("Tries")	Growth in sales Turnover of customer base Ability to control price

Suppliers	Cost of raw material
	Delivery time
	Inventory
	Availability of raw material
		Growth rates of
		  Raw material costs
		  Delivery time
		  Inventory
		New ideas from suppliers

Financial Community	EPS Stock price Number of "buy" lists ROE etc.	Ability to convince Wall Street of strategy Growth in ROE etc.
Employees	Number of suggestions Productivity Number of grievances	Number of internal promotions Turnover
Congress	Number of new pieces of legislation that affect the firm Access to key members and staff	Number of new regulations that affect industry Ratio of "cooperative" vs. "competitive" encounters
Consumer Advocate	Number of meetings Number of "hostile" encounters Number of times coalitions formed Number of legal actions	Number of changes in policy due to C.A. Number of C.A. initiated "calls for help"
Environmentalists	Number of meetings Number of hostile encounters Number of times coalitions formed Number of EPA complaints Number of legal actions	Number of changes in policy due to environmentalists Number of environmentalist "calls for help"

number of new needs of customers that are met. The idea behind these measures of performance is that the purpose of selling products to customers is to meet the customers' needs. The more new needs that are met, the better managers understand what makes the customer tick, and hence, the better the company can serve the customer. Peters (1981) has argued that successful companies overspend on customers, and that they try to meet many customer needs. Some companies pride themselves on working out new technological applications with the customer. The dollar volume of sales per dollar of selling expense can be a useful measure, but its potential for abuse is substantial, given the managerial talent for reducing expenses. Another measure which comes logically from the Peters study, is "number of tries," i.e., how many times did the company try to meet a new customer need. The idea behind this measure is that success is related to the number of attempts, especially when these attempts are made in conjunction with the customer. Longer-term measures are extensions of these near-term measures, with the addition of a "turnover" measure, which would indicate the long-term satisfaction of a particular customer segment, and a measure of the company's ability to control the price of its products and services, indicating the value as perceived by customers. Different measures may be appropriate for different customer segments and will depend on product, industry, etc. The point of the measures in Exhibit 6.7 is to give a menu, rather than a prescription; and a range of measures, rather than a comprehensive list.

Performance with Congress might be measured in the short term by the number of pieces of legislation that are passed that affect the company. Over the long haul, however, that relationship might be measured by the success of the company's "regulatory philosophy." We might believe that deregulation is a desired philosophy for all business-government relations, and thus measure our success by the number of regulations that affect all business. Or, we might believe that regulated competition is a viable philosophy for business-government relations, and we would thus measure our success in terms of how well we work within the regulatory process, or by how many regulations and pieces of legislation we get which help and protect our industry. Or alternatively, the longer term might be measured by the ratio of cooperative to competitive encounters with the government, with the belief that regardless of philosophy, a cooperative business-government relationship is necessary. It is obviously difficult to specify a cooperative and a competitive encounter, yet rough guidelines can be drawn if such measures are deemed to be worthy of study.

Integrative measures are harder to discern. The beauty of the economic model of the firm is that it yields simple measurable results, which are for the most part absent in the political and social arena. However, these results can be misleading when political and social forces are at work, as they are in the current business environment. The only integrative measures that make sense are those which are related to the overall direction of the corporation, and especially its enterprise strategy. This is not to collapse integrative measures into internal measures of consistency, but rather to show that if we can understand the range of enterprise strategies, as outlined in chapter Four, we have a method of comparison. Stockholder E-strategy firms must be compared with stockholder E-strategy firms, and Rawlsian E-strategy firms must be compared with Rawlsian E-strategy firms. To do otherwise is to compare meters with liters, at least in the present state of the stakeholder theory of the firm. If the enterprise strategy of the firm has truly achieved a fit among stakeholders, values and societal issues, then the only measure is among firms which are trying to achieve a similar fit. Cross-strategy performance is possible, but it will be similar to applying the criteria for single product firms to firms that are diversified conglomerates. The diversified conglomerates do not measure up to the standards set by the single product firms, but who should expect them to? What we see will be the differential effects of diversification. Similarly, by comparing firms with different E-strategies we can find the differential effects of these strategies. We have a long road ahead of us in this area of integrative performance measures. The stakeholder notion gives us only a start.

AMERICAN SERVICES INTERNATIONAL: A CASE STUDY OF IMPLEMENTATION AND MONITORING PROGRESS WITH STAKEHOLDERS

American Services International is a disguised name of a real very large organization.[11] A number of facts about ASI have been changed, but I have tried to leave the clinical facts untouched. In any case, the ASI story should not be read as validating any claim made in this or earlier chapters, but rather as illustrative of how the stakeholder concept can be applied, and thus, how a stakeholder theory of strategic management can be constructed. The purpose of clinical data is to construct theories, not to "prove them" or even to offer any evidence for the truth of their claims. ASI is illustrative of the strengths and the pitfalls of strategic management undertaken in a stakeholder approach, and tells us where more and less theory is needed.

ASI is quite a complicated organization. It has sales of over $15 billion world-wide, with a substantial portion of those sales in the U.S. I will focus on the U.S. operations of ASI, and in particular on the attempt by some ASI managers to deal with an incredibly complex issue.

ASI is highly regulated because of the industries in which it competes and due to some historical facts about the way that regulation has evolved in the U.S. ASI's operations are in virtually every state in the U.S. and the company must deal with state regulators as well as several federal agencies, the Congress, a host of courts, etc. Consequently, ASI is organized by product and function and decentralized geographically. Each geographical unit has several thousand employees, and there are many thousand employees at corporate headquarters in Chicago.

Exhibit 6.8 gives a rough organizational chart for ASI and, in particular, one of its product lines in a single geography. There were lots of dotted line relationships between product lines within geographies, between geographies and to corporate staff functions, making the actual operations of the company a multi-dimensional matrix. Responsibility for dealing with cross-geographical groups, especially national groups, resided at the corporate level with the close cooperation of the geographical level. Guidelines for products, and for dealing with certain stakeholders, especially government agencies, were formulated at the corporate level, and were interpreted to meet local conditions and implemented at the geographical level. There was some tension between corporate and geographical staff resulting from these guidelines, and their resulting interpretations.

Exhibit 6.9 charts the division of responsibility for important stakeholder groups at the geographical level, and Exhibit 6.10 shows the corporate level. Potentially, a high degree of interaction among the stakeholders could cause massive coordination problems and slowness of response, due to the number of functions involved. Within each function, responsibility was further subdivided so that one group in PR handled the media, one group handled employee communications, one group handled community relations, etc.

"Basic Product" accounted for almost one half of ASI's sales in the U.S. Due to the fact that Basic is used by virtually everyone, the superior nature of ASI's technology and regulatory precedent, ASI has a rather high market share. Managers at ASI, however, noticed a number of changes in the external environment that could all focus on Basic and erode the position of ASI in the marketplace in the future. Briefly, ASI managers believed that changes in technology, new competitive pressures, changes in regulation, social changes and changes in the values of ASI managers, all pointed towards a need to reposition Basic Product. The repositioning of Basic needed to be complete, that is, it needed to be repackaged, the market needed to be resegmented, Basic needed to be repriced and there needed to be new applications of the technology which was basic to Basic. Previously, Basic had been sold primarily as a commodity, but technological changes implied lots of niches, and diverse means of product differentiation. Corporate level managers formulated a repositioning program and began the arduous task of implementation, which was expected to take at least five–seven

EXHIBIT 6.8 *Partial Organization Chart for American Services International*

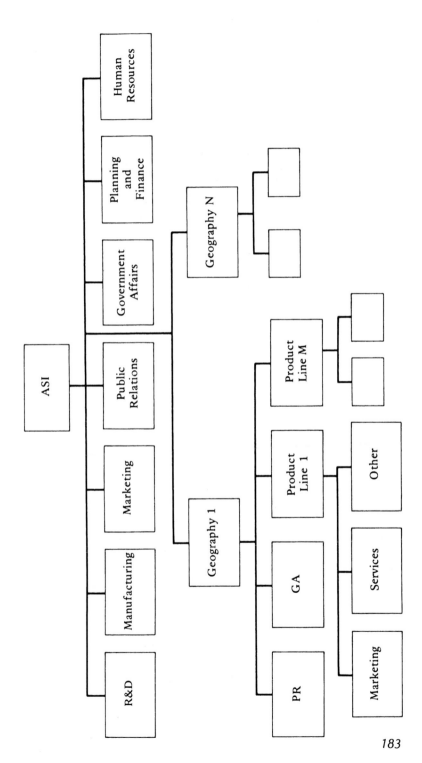

Exhibit 6.9 *Partial Responsibility Chart for Key Stakeholders in an ASI Geography*

	Product Line 1 Customers	Critics	Community Groups	Employees	Media	State Legislature	State Regulatory Agency
Marketing Product Line 1	X						
Service Product Line 1	X						
Public Relations	X	X	X	X	X		
Government Affairs						X	X
Labor Relations				X			
. . .							

Exhibit 6.10   *Partial Responsibility Chart for Stakeholders at ASI — Corporate*

Stakeholder / Organizational Unit	Congress	Trade Assoc.	National Customer Accounts	Investment Community	Stockholders	Public	Corporate Employees	Unions	National Media	National Critics	National Regulatory Agencies
Marketing		X	X								
Public Relations				X	X	X	X		X	X	
Govt. Affairs	X										X
Human Resources							X	X			
Planning & Fin.				X							

. . .

years. In many cases regulatory approval was needed for some of the necessary changes. In the beginning, no explicit programs for stakeholders were formulated, rather, the functional expertise of the existing ASI organization was to be relied upon.

A geography was selected as a test site for the repositioning of Basic, and ASI suffered a defeat in the initial attempt. A coalition of customers, consumer advocates, non-profit groups and community leaders brought an action against ASI to prevent the changes in Basic and convinced a regulatory agency to forbid, at least for the time being, any changes in Basic. State legislators took up the cudgels and introduced legislation that would drastically affect ASI's operations in the state, and only by some last minute compromises, did ASI escape further damage. Consequently, ASI decided to try a different approach to implementation, that included formulating explicit strategies for stakeholder groups, and involved an organizational change process.

Phase I of the ASI change process was to sensitize managers to the need to think in stakeholder terms, and to consider the consequences of managerial action on stakeholder groups. The test case of Basic repositioning was used to illustrate how all functions relying on their own expertise did not necessarily add up to success in a world of complex stakeholder interactions and coalitions. Techniques of analyzing stakeholder behavior and formulating strategic programs were explained and applied retrospectively to the case study. Key ASI managers participated in a 36-hour role playing session where the managers took on the roles of different stakeholder groups, such as regulators, employees, consumer advocates, customers, local officials, etc. Actual representatives of these groups were brought in to help train ASI managers to be more sensitive to their needs, and to help ASI managers "think like their stakeholders." A secondary benefit of this exercise was that ASI got the opportunity to give their story about the need for Basic repositioning to these stakeholder representatives. Stakeholder representatives trained teams, consisting of 4–6 ASI managers, to play that stakeholder's role in the subsequent 24 hours. These stakeholder teams then role-played an implementation of Basic repositioning. This "simulation" of the problem gave the managers an opportunity to try new strategies and transactions with "stakeholders" with little risk, and helped them to better understand the stakeholder positions that were possible. Videotapes of comments of each actual stakeholder were viewed, and the seminar ended by drawing some conclusions and discussing action plans. In addition, ASI undertook a strategic study of Basic repositioning, and produced a guidebook for constructing strategic programs for stakeholders in the geographical regions.

Phase II of this change process consisted of a conscious effort on the part of ASI corporate headquarters to "monitor progress" on the implementation of the Basic repositioning strategy. Managers set out to answer a set of questions at both the geographical and corporate levels. The set of questions is depicted in Exhibit 6.11. ASI undertook a study to carefully determine whether there was an explicit strategy for each stakeholder group. Over 50 stakeholders were identified at the corporate level, and several hundred were identified at the geographical level. Interviews with those managers deemed responsible for a particular group were conducted, with mixed results. Often, the responsibility for a particular stakeholder group was diffuse, or existed in another product line or another functional department, where the repositioning of Basic did not have the same high priority as it did with the managers engaged in the implementation. After all, ASI is a large firm, with many different projects ongoing at the same time, and its managers have multiple agendas. Once holes were found, strategies were formulated and implementation begun, often with ad hoc organizations.

This flurry of activity in Phase II led to another phase of the Basic repositioning project; namely, ASI managers needed to grapple with how the organizational structure and processes could be tailor-made to reduce some of the complexity. Thus, Phase III of the project consisted of the formation of more coordination mechanisms, and formalizing the coordination mechanisms that existed. At the Corporate level a manager was appointed "Stakeholder Management Coordinator" (SC) and given the task of expediting the Basic repositioning. Members from key departments were members of the "National Stakeholder Coordination Team" and served as liaisons with their functional departments. Each department contributed towards the budget of the team. The national SC team had the dual responsibility of insuring implementation at the geographical level and dealing with the cross-geographical stakeholders. Each geography formed mirror images of the national SC team, and another seminar was begun to share

EXHIBIT 6.11   *Questions for a Monitoring Process at ASI*

1. Do we know how each stakeholder will be affected by the Basic repositioning?
2. Do we know how each stakeholder can help us and hurt us?
3. Can we articulate a strategic program for each key stakeholder?
4. Who is responsible for implementation?
5. What assumptions are necessary for the strategies to be successful?
6. Are these assumptions realistic and valid?
7. What new strategies are needed?
8. Is the goal of repositioning Basic still realistic?
9. What could cause us to fail?

local strategies. Again, outside stakeholder representatives were brought in to share their "perspectives" on Basic repositioning. The national SC team spent a great deal of time on the road with the local teams, helping them to raise questions about tradeoffs with other issues and tradeoffs among the concerns of conflicting stakeholder groups. The national team acted as coach, advising and pushing the local teams to try new ideas and to carefully consider all the alternatives. In addition, the national team conducted strategic reviews where the local teams were called upon to review their progress, and specifically to answer some of the questions posed by Exhibit 6.11.

The repositioning of Basic at ASI is still an ongoing project, yet the managers at ASI believe that it will be successful. They have a way of coping with the complexity posed by their own organization and the external environment. There are successes, where Basic has been repositioned, and there are failures where stakeholder groups have prevented the repositioning. There are cases of ASI completely turning around the behavior of a stakeholder group to its cooperative potential, and of course, cases where competitive threat has been a result, hopefully an unintentional one, of ASI action. The inability to act has been overcome, and the narrow vision of the functional organization has been broadened. The jury is still out on ASI's strategy to reposition Basic, yet it is still a profitable company and looks to remain so for the future. More importantly ASI managers have begun to deal with the complexity of their situation in a positive manner, and have begun to develop and apply new managerial processes.

SOME PITFALLS OF USING THE STAKEHOLDER CONCEPT

ASI and others have learned the hard way, by trying to use a concept and seeing where it can and cannot be useful. Several managerial lessons can be gathered from the experiences of managers at ASI and other companies. I state these lessons in the form of some pitfalls to avoid when employing the stakeholder concept. The five pitfalls discussed below by no means form a comprehensive list. The stakeholder approach to strategic management is equally susceptible to other pitfalls of strategic management as per Lorange (1980).

Openness of the System

Use of the stakeholder approach to strategic management assumes that the organization wants to surface difficult issues, which may or may not have workable answers. It assumes the flexibility of process, whether or not organizational change is a result. Often times the mere asking of questions is enough to get a particular manager into trouble. A stakeholder approach is likely to uncover "sacred cows," and managers who do the uncovering are not always the winners. The openness of the system is not always a positive attribute. Closed systems and the rules that govern them often work well, and work quite efficiently. If the environment of an organization truly has not changed, then a stakeholder approach is probably not appropriate. Managers at ASI constantly butted their heads up against others who simply refused to believe that a repositioning of Basic was necessary, and that business as usual was the order of the day. The attempt to change Basic Product was seen as an effort to "stir things up" and to "make a reputation" for certain managers. Thus, openness of the system must be addressed in any change process, as ASI did quite dramatically by putting key managers through the 36-hour role play, and as the ASI SC teams did by sheer persistence.

Involvement of Top Management

It should go without saying that top management support and involvement is necessary for the success of any strategic management system. However, this is especially critical to the success of a stakeholder approach. By surfacing tradeoffs that the company faces with its external environment and raising the issue of whether there are adequate resources to deal with these stakeholders, these processes must have the attention of senior managers. ASI faced some classic dilemmas, such as when the managers of another much smaller product line undertook a similar repositioning, that had the potential of undermining the strategy of Basic in a particular geography. Once the right and left hands got in touch with each other, it was still far from trivial to resolve the problem, and the conflict cost ASI a great deal in terms of lost time and effort, not to mention lost sales. Finally, the dispute reached the appropriate managerial levels and was resolved. However, a more intelligent process for the continual involvement of top management in implementation activities could have avoided the delay and the crisis.

Involvement of Lower Levels of Management

While top management support and involvement in implementation is necessary, so is lower level involvement in strategy formulation. Without this, middle and lower level managers will be asked to carry out programs which they do not necessarily believe in. Countless times at ASI, the same meeting was held over and over, essentially to get managers to recommit to, or reinvent a strategic program that had been handed down as a corporate guideline, literally years before. On the one hand, we might argue that it is the tasks of the lower managerial ranks to be implementers and doers, not thinkers. Yet, if it is important for transactions with stakeholders to fit with the organizational processes, then there must be some involvement in the processes themselves. The classic dilemma of the boundary spanner who is told to go out and "take care of that stakeholder," without any input into the strategic management process was replayed a number of times at ASI and at other corporations.

Analysis Paralysis

The stakeholder approach to strategic management lends itself to a great deal of in-depth analysis of managerial issues. The stakeholder maps (with multi-colored circles and arrows), stakes chart, behavioral analysis and all of the analytical devices set forth in the preceding pages can essentially paralyze an organization. It can be prevented from acting because of the sheer weight of the complexity which it uncovers. One manager at ASI constantly hounded the SC team to "let's do something," and managed to keep the team from falling into this trap. Some of the local SC teams were not so fortunate. They produced beautiful analyses which made wonderful presentations, yet no action resulted. Transactions with stakeholders are the bottom line. Individuals and groups can affect the corporation, not categories of groups, and not graphs and charts on which groups are named. Peters (1981) has claimed that U.S. managers need to adopt a "try it, fix it, do it" mentality, and that must be carried over to the stakeholder approach. The academic's penchant for analysis and the manager's penchant for action must meet in carefully reasoned, but incisive action.

The Snail Darter Fallacy

Closely related to analysis paralysis is the fact that drawing stakeholder maps and analyzing minute behaviors is fun.[12] It can occupy hours of managerial time. But, the distinction between important and non-important stakeholders must be drawn somewhere. As a corporation narrows down its strategic options, so must it narrow down its list of stakeholders. It must leave those who are too small and too insignificant to worry about to others. However, the lessons from the real "snail darter" story must not be lost. We must be careful in making these assessments, for it is just these "snail darter" stakeholders that can at times hold the balance of power on an issue.

SUMMARY

Implementation and monitoring are important strategic management tasks given the stakeholder approach, and I have tried to raise several questions about how they are to proceed successfully. Unfortunately, there is little empirical research on which to rely for guidance. I have used some clinical data from ASI to illustrate how the rather abstract analyses and processes from chapters One to Five can, in fact, be used to manage an organization in a strategic fashion. I have indicated some known pitfalls that should be taken as illustrative of the difficulty of exacting real change from an organization.

Throughout the preceding three chapters my goal has been to indicate how the stakeholder approach to strategic management can actually be used by managers in organizations. The tests of the assertions, hypotheses and bald statements are incomplete, to say the least. Yet by implementing some such processes and by undertaking similar kinds of transactions, it is my hope that organizations can become more responsive to stakeholder needs.

NOTES

1. The notion that an organization "engages" its external environmental sounds more "phenomenological" than it really is. I have used the term to denote an active process of formulating and implementing transactions with stakeholders. Perhaps there are theoretical problems, as per Burrell and Morgan (1979).
2. Lorange (1983) lays out a framework for strategic control on which this chapter draws heavily.
3. See Lorange (1980) for how budgets are constructed from strategic programs.
4. See Lawrence and Lorsch (1967) for the classic study in this area.
5. There is a great deal of literature here. Cummings (1981), Nystrom (1981), Hulin and Triandis (1981), Seashore (1981), Joyce (1981), Mohr (1982) and Argyris (1982) are quite recent essays which review the literature in addition to proposing some new constructs.
6. See chapter Eight below for more on the concept of public relations.
7. There is a vast literature on negotiation, summarized by Bacharach and Lawler (1981) and Schellenberg (1982).
8. See, for instance, Kotter (1978), Beckhard (1969), Beckhard and Harris (1977) and other books in the Addison-Wesley organizational development series, for a sample of the methods and research results.

9. I argued in chapter One that the contextual assumptions of most managers need to be changed.
10. Preston (1982) is the fourth volume of essays in a series on corporate performance.
11. I am grateful to the many managers of ASI whom I have gotten to know over the past few years. Their willingness to share their problems, and their ability to take the stakeholder approach and try to implement it is sincerely appreciated. ASI is thoroughly disguised, however, I have tried not to disguise any essential information.
12. I am grateful to Jim Webber for this point.

Part III

IMPLICATIONS FOR
THEORY AND PRACTICE

The purpose of Part III is to develop some of the implications of the stakeholder approach to strategic management for the corporation as we know it today. I showed in Part I that a stakeholder approach to strategic management was one way to make the corporation more responsive to its external environment, and I set out a basic framework for analyzing the stakeholders in the corporation. In Part II I explained how the stakeholder concept could be used to construct processes for strategic management, and in particular, I showed how direction setting, strategic programming and implementation and control can be enriched by adding a sensitivity to stakeholders. Part III examines more structural issues, insofar as structural issues are those which relate to managerial work at the strategic level. The stakeholder approach dictates some changes for the traditional functions and roles of managers, and hence, for the traditional ways of coordinating the work of the corporation.

Chapter 7, "Conflict at the Board Level," examines some of the conflicts which arise within the board of directors. The work of the board must be rethought on two levels. The first level involves dealing with a host of new stakeholders, and the second involves rethinking how the board deals with stockholders and groups of stockholders. Thus, regardless of the enterprise strategy of the firm, the stakeholder approach can be used to better manage the traditional relationship with owners.

Chapter 8, "The Functional Disciplines of Management," examines the roles of the functions which have traditionally dealt with a number of stakeholder groups. Public relations, marketing, finance, etc. must change given a stakeholder approach, and I suggest some hypotheses for how these disciplines can embrace the stakeholder approach.

Chapter Nine, "The Role of the Executive," examines what it takes to lead today's corporation forward in the face of the external turbulence which most organizations face. The role of the executive as "balancer of stakeholder interests," as "public and private manager" and as "leader of persons" is developed. This chapter also contains a brief summary and points to several areas of future research.

Seven

CONFLICT AT THE BOARD LEVEL

INTRODUCTION

The next two chapters focus on the implications of the stakeholder concept for some selected issues in organization structure and design. In particular I point out how a stakeholder approach can be used when coordinating the work of the board of directors. There has been much recent debate on this issue, but it has occurred in the absence of the literature on strategy and structure, and such debate has centered around a number of proposals for "structural reform" of the board and its processes. I will not directly address all of the sticky issues surrounding "corporate governance." Such issues include: whether the board should bear a fiduciary relationship to its stakeholders, what is the proper role of government in regulating board behavior and many others. I will focus on board behavior and see how the concepts and processes developed in the previous chapters can lead to more effective board behavior.[1]

I believe that a stakeholder approach to understanding effective board behavior can go far in sorting out conflicts which arise at the board level. The ideas which are explained in this chapter should be taken as the results of a preliminary investigation into these topics, and supplementary to rather than contradictory to the volume of research on corporate governance.[2]

THE ROLE OF THE BOARD OF DIRECTORS

What is the role of the director? How is the corporation governed? How should the corporation be governed? What is the proper role of the board of directors? Do boards bear a relationship to stockholders similar to that of a fiduciary to his trustor, whereby the interests of the stockholders should be dutifully cared for by management?[3] Must any action taken by boards, or countenanced by boards, be justified by whether or not it furthers the interests of the corporation and its stockholders?

These are but a few of the thorny questions in need of research in the area of board behavior.[4] Many of these issues presuppose an answer to normative public policy questions in corporate governance, in which there has been a great deal of recent interest (Huizinga, 1983). In particular, the concept of corporate democracy has recently gained good currency. Proposals have been put forth to make the corporation more democratic, and to encourage shareholder participation and management responsiveness to shareholder needs. Others have proposed to make corporations more responsive to a broad range of stakeholder needs and, hence, to encourage the participation of stakeholders in the process of governing the corporation. Reforms from cumulative voting to audit committees have been implemented, and reforms from the Corporate Democracy Act to only one insider on the board have been suggested.[5]

"Corporate democracy" has come to have at least four meanings over the years. The first implies that corporations should be made more "democratic" by increasing the role of government, either as a watchdog or by having public officials on boards of directors. The second meaning implies that corporations should be made more "democratic" in the sense of "citizen" or "public interest" participation in managing its affairs via public interest directors and the like. The third meaning implies that corporations should be made more "democratic" by encouraging or mandating the active participation of all, or many, of its shareholders. Finally, corporate democracy has come to mean employee participation, through employee ownership or through employee participation such as "Mitbestimmung" in West Germany where management and employees each elect directors of the firm, or through more employee participation in work decisions through worker councils or quality circles, etc. The stakeholder approach has implications for each of these levels of the democratization of the corporation and the role of the board in "managing the affairs of the corporation."

The stakeholder approach developed in the preceding chapters advocates that we have a thorough understanding of our stakeholders and calls for the recognition that there are times when stakeholders must participate in the decision-making processes of the firm. One interpretation of the processes developed in chapters Four to Six is that they yield a method for determining the timing and degree of such participation.

At the absolute minimum, this implies that boards of directors must be aware of the impacts of their decisions on key stakeholder groups. As stakeholders have begun to exercise more political power and as marketplace decisions become politicized, the need for such "board awareness" to grow into "board responsiveness" has become apparent. While it is not the proper role of the board to be involved in the implementation of strategic programs, and even some direction setting decisions, it does set the overall direction for the firm (and should be involved in determining the enterprise strategy of the firm if such a determination is to be made). Perhaps more importantly, it sets the "tone" or "style" for how the company deals with stakeholders, both traditional marketplace stakeholders and those which have political power. The board must decide not only whether management is managing the affairs of the corporation, but indeed, what is to count as "the affairs of the corporation."

If this task of stakeholder management is done properly, much of the air is let out of critics who argue that the corporation must be democratized in terms of more citizen participation and an increased adversarial role of government. Issues which involve both economic and political stakes and power bases must be addressed in an integrated fashion. No longer can public affairs, public relations and corporate philanthropy serve as effective management tools for dealing with stakeholder concerns. The penalties for only "doing good" and "having a positive image" are enormous in the wake of OPEC, Love Canal and OSHA. The sophistication of interest groups who are beginning to use formal power mechanisms, such as proxy fights, annual meetings and the corporate charter, to focus the attention of management on what they believe to be the affairs of the corporation, has increased. Responsive boards will seize these opportunities to learn more about those stakeholders which have chosen the option of voice over the Wall Street Rule and exiting to sell the stock. As boards direct management to respond to these concerns, to negotiate with critics, to trade-off certain policies in return for positive support, the pressure for mandated citizen participation will subside.

In addition to the implications of the stakeholder concept for proposed policy changes in corporate democracy, and the context which a stakeholder approach sets for the role of the board, the stakeholder approach has implications for some of the issues that must be addressed in the board room.

The implications of stakeholder analysis for the practical affairs of the corporation and corporation's advisors can perhaps best be illustrated by exploring examples of conflict within the ownership groups of corporations. Stakeholder analysis can be as valuable in addressing these conflicts as in dealing with groups external to the corporation who are seeking an increased voice in its operations. Thus, it can help us determine the proper "division of labor" at the board level and methods of coordination of these tasks.

Given the significance of the voting machinery within the corporation, it is not surprising that many of these internal corporate conflicts take the form of the traditional proxy fight. Over the past two decades, however, a number of techniques have been developed in contests for corporate control. These tactics include direct appeal to shareholder economic interests through tender offers, issuance of blocks of shares to employees, Employee Stock Ownership Plans (ESOPs) or other "friendly" holders, "secondary" boycotts of organizations represented on a corporation's board and "freezing out" certain board members from crucial decisions.[6] Though these tactics span a broad area of the law and are not usually lumped together, from the perspective of the stakeholder approach to the affairs of the corporation, they share the common aspect of a conflict within the ownership group of the corporation.

The ownership group is not always of one mind regarding who is to manage the affairs of the corporation. Battles for ownership of the firm often are fought by directors who do not own the firm, but do in some sense control the management of its affairs. Determining who or what is "the real ownership group" is the key question that often precedes determining the wishes or interests of that group.

Such conflict raises fundamental questions of "the affairs of the corporation" and more fundamentally of the "identity of the corporation," and as will be discussed below, presents especially difficult issues for the board of directors, its advisors and counselors. I shall explore the variety of these conflicts through a set of illustrative examples taken from recent corporate history; and some possible techniques which can be used to handle these conflicts will be analyzed to show their strengths and weaknesses. I will examine three types of conflict: (1) conflicts within the board of directors; (2) outside attacks on the board of directors; and (3) conflicts within the ownership group.

Conflicts Within the Board of Directors

Over the past few years a number of examples of disputes on boards of directors have been serious enough to erupt into the press. One of the most notorious of these disputes occurred at Beatrice Foods, Inc., a huge Chicago-based food conglomerate, in the context of a transition of chief executives.[7]

Beatrice Foods had been rather slow over the years in reorganizing its board of directors away from the insider dominated board of the past. A company that grew largely by acquisitions, first under William G. Karnes and then under Wallace N. Rasmussen, Beatrice owed much of its success to the strength and character of its chief executives and presented them with hand-picked boards to do their bidding. In 1978, faced with an SEC investigation into kickbacks to dairy customers and the impending retirement of Rasmussen, the Beatrice board began to consider how to restructure itself from 11 insiders and 8 outsiders to 10 outsiders and 6 insiders. A committee of the board, composed of Rasmussen and 3 outside directors, took responsibility for the reorganization and for picking Rasmussen's successor. For his own reasons Rasmussen objected to the choice of successor (preferring his own protege to the outside directors' choice) and objected to the new board structure. He managed to rally the insiders around his position and the reorganization proposal and the nominated chief executive were defeated.

As a postscript to the story, Rasmussen's protege, James L. Dutt, has quietly dismantled Rasmussen's influence and has reinstated the board reorganization proposal with generally favorable results. In addition, Dutt seems to have reversed Rasmussen policies on divestitures and other strategic moves, further reducing the former chairman's influence.

The Beatrice Foods story raises interesting questions of board behavior and corporate control. Beatrice's shareholders returned the Rasmussen insider-dominated board to power even while the disputes over reorganization of the board spread through the press; and in bottom line terms the decision to support Rasmussen was quite successful. Yet Rasmussen's activities on the board were sufficiently distasteful that two of the outside directors resigned in response to his maneuvers.

The Beatrice Foods case brings into sharp focus the arguments for and against insider domination of the board. Insiders consistently maintain that their intimate knowledge of the organization, its personnel and culture are the critical elements in sound policy decisions. Outsiders argue that insiders work without direct consideration for the needs of the shareholders (and, possibly, the other corporate stakeholders) and therefore use tactics which are unacceptable. In short, there are arguments on both sides with respect to director performance. However, the issue may ultimately have to be settled by an appeal to public policy considerations of accountability.[8]

Regardless of how suitable goals are ultimately achieved, from a management perspective one should ask, "what sorts of factual information would be helpful in resolving this debate," and "could such factual background be accumulated?" The manifest difficulties in accumulating this empirical support (or even in designing a proper research program to obtain it) indicate that focusing attention on mandating outside directors may be misplaced. The interests of corporate governance may well be better served by efforts to improve the functioning of boards rather than in mandating mechanical structural changes with little, or no, reason to expect that such changes will make a significant difference.

By seeking to improve the functioning of boards, perhaps we can gain insights into and prevent future "messes." For instance, the Bendix-Allied-Martin Marietta-United Technologies case, called "the corporate pac-man" by some, where enormous resources were expended to form a jury-rigged combination of three large corporations. It is difficult to understand the "compelling logic" which led the directors of these firms to act as they did.

The Chrysler-UAW case is another example of where we need to better understand the process of board functioning. A union director, Mr. Douglas Fraser and his successors, will be liable to "manage the affairs of the corporation" while in some sense "representing" union issues and concerns.

Suppose that we accept, as a matter of public policy, the controversial claims that: (1) any two corporations can merge if such a merger does not violate anti-trust laws; and (2) within the bounds of the law, anyone may be elected to serve on boards, including "special interest directors." It does not automatically follow that the results of such a policy will be acceptable from the standpoint of the public interest, the interests of the stakeholders in the firm, or even the interests of the directors and executives of the firm. Independent of public policy questions, we need to address the issue of how the board itself can function more effectively.

An excellent example for analysis is Fairchild Industries' attempt to acquire Bunker-Ramo. The acquisition took an unusual turn due to Bunker-Ramo's decision not to be acquired.[9] Having purchased 20.6 percent of Bunker-Ramo's stock from Martin Marietta Corporation, Fairchild was able to elect its chairman and another director to the Bunker-Ramo board under Bunker-Ramo's cumulative voting rules. Animosity between Fairchild's chairman, Edward Uhl, and Bunker-Ramo's chief executive, George Trimble, led to an attempted "freeze-out" of the Fairchild directors. Stating that he was protecting his company from conflicts-of-interest and potential misuse of "inside information," Trimble insisted that the Fairchild directors be limited in their access to information concerning Bunker-Ramo's business.

The postscript to this story is also happy. Trimble and Uhl, who had been friends for years prior to the episode, have reestablished their ties. The Fairchild directors have been given significant committee assignments on the Bunker-Ramo board and further acquisition talk has been started. Bunker-Ramo has expanded its board to accommodate the two directors replaced by Uhl and his fellow Fairchild director.

As in the Beatrice case, provocative issues of board behavior are raised by the Bunker-Ramo story. There was a limited acceptance of the notion during the height of the battle that, at least de facto, the majority of the board could "freeze-out" the minority. Do directors in some sense have a "right" to information about their company? What are the limits of such a "right"? What is a plausible position for a director on such a board who is affiliated with neither of the contesting parties? Should the fact that this dispute resolved itself be taken as a significant indication of the strength of the current system? Or was this a classic example of behind-the-scenes in-fighting without consideration for the needs of outside shareholders? Due to the nature of board research we do not know why these stories have happy endings (Levy, 1982). However, let's take the Bunker-Ramo case and hypothetically put ourselves into the situation faced by the outside directors.

I will make the assumption for the sake of illustration, and it is not necessarily factual, that Bunker-Ramo's board was split into seven inside, four outside and two Fairchild directors. Consider the position of one of the hypothetical outside directors who is informed by an insider of the plan to freeze-out the Fairchild representatives. What are his options?

To begin his analysis, our fictional director must establish a focal organization and specify its objectives (recall the methods of chapters Four and Five). While there is great flexibility in selecting this focus (the group might range in size from our fictional director himself to the entire corporation) the key requirement is that it be sufficiently coherent to have statable, achievable objectives. In our hypothetical case we assume that our director contacts his fellow outsiders on the board and that all agree in expressing substantial concern over the situation. An informal meeting is arranged at which strategies are to be laid out.

The first step at this meeting is to set forth the objectives of this group. Realistically, it is likely that only a rather general set of objectives can be agreed upon. As the strategies are elaborated, the differences in objectives can more easily be explicated. Exhibit 7.1 diagrams the situation and lists the potential stakeholders.

The strategy generation process begins by seeking valuable partners in coalition; the choice of partners will reflect the objectives of the group. If the outsiders find themselves in agreement that their task is to protect the small shareholders (and perhaps themselves) from the machinations of insiders, they will seek to ally themselves with the management side or the Fairchild side depending on which, in their estimation, is willing to provide a better "deal" for the public shareholders. If their objective is simply to protect themselves from potential legal liability or from unpleasant economic repercussions, they will try to back the side that is the stronger or will provide them with the most secure position. If their objective is to stop the bickering as quickly as possible regardless of who wins or loses, they will seek to formulate a deal that will satisfy the warring parties, perhaps at the expense of the public shareholders. Exhibit 7.2 depicts these choices and attaches labels to each of the generic strategies. Of course, in a real case, more than one of the above objectives may be involved. It is critical that some

E xhibit 7.1   *Stakeholders in Fictionalized Bunker-Ramo Case*

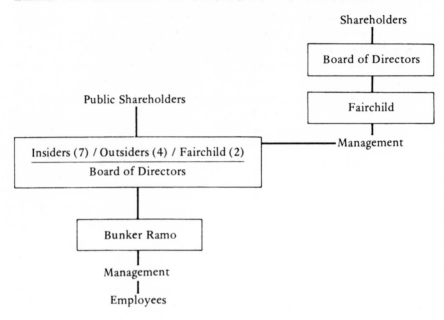

E xhibit 7.2   *Generic Strategies for Outside Directors in Fictionalized Bunker-Ramo Case*

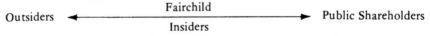

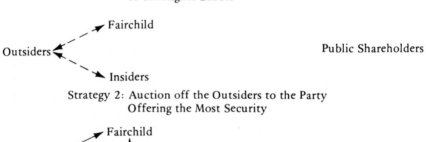

agreement be reached as to the relative importance of the multiple objectives so that intelligent trade-offs can be accomplished.

To achieve these strategies it will be necessary to take other stakeholders into account in devising the appropriate transactions in order to make the rather complex mechanisms involved, responsive. Groups such as Bunker-Ramo employees, Fairchild's other directors and stockholders are available as allies. However, it is not necessary, except perhaps in a logical sense, to take all of these groups into account.

This may all seem rather cold-blooded, but such a strategy formulation process offers hope for a rational formulation of ends and means relationships and at least offers board members an active role in influencing the resolution of the conflict. No judgement is passed on any of these strategies or tactics, nor is it assumed that all would withstand a legal challenge as a breach of fiduciary duty. Rather, the argument is that a stakeholder approach, especially at the process level, can be used by directors and their advisors as a means to begin to make sense of highly complex situations, and to begin to address the issue of board structure in terms of coordinating the work which must be done.

Directors cannot simply assume that such questions will not arise, for if the preceding argument has any validity, it is only a matter of time before the issues get completely out of control. At that time, severe and simplistic structural reform may do the corporate mechanism irreparable harm. As a further caveat it must be understood that, in actual practice, a far more detailed process must be undertaken, similar to that described in chapter Five, whereby the motivations are more subtly evaluated and the interactions of multiple objectives and stakeholders are carefully considered. The above suggestions are therefore highly schematic and simplified.

Outside Attacks on the Board of Directors

In contrast to a struggle between members of boards of directors, perhaps representing splits within the shareholder group, recent years have also seen attacks on boards designed to further the interests of parties outside the boardroom. Such issues are more typical of groups who are trying to make the corporation responsive to social issues of some sort. Vogel (1978) analyzes these attempts and concludes that they have been quite ineffective in general. However, where shareholder groups have been able to marshall coalitional support from government and other groups, some change has occurred. Issues range from "Campaign GM" waged by "The Committee to Make General Motors Responsible" to church groups petitioning Nestle's, Abbott Labs, etc. over the infant formula controversy. It may seem obvious that stakeholder analysis as developed in the previous chapters is useful here, however recent shifts in tactics make the analysis more difficult.

One of the most notable of these fights was the attempt by the Amalgamated Clothing & Textile Workers' Union (ACTWU) to effectively isolate J.P. Stevens & Company within the business community. There are other instances of this type of conflict, mostly arising in the labor-relations context, which raise interesting questions for board behavior.[10]

The initial conflict between J.P. Stevens and the ACTWU goes back many years and has continued through disputed union election proceedings, before the National Labor Relations Board and in the Courts.[11] Frustrated by their inability to defeat J.P. Stevens with the legal tools available, ACTWU has sought to apply pressure to J.P. Stevens' board of directors to alter corporate labor relations policies. The union has used its financial leverage in threatening to direct its pension funds out of Manufacturers Hanover Trust where James Finley (J.P. Stevens' ex-chairman) was elected a director. The Union has also threatened to run its own candidate for the board of directors of Metropolitan Life Insurance Company (a major lender to J.P. Stevens). Recently, as a result of the pressure on Metropolitan Life and indirectly on J.P. Stevens, Stevens has acquiesced and signed its first collective bargaining agreement with the ACTWU.

The implications of the J.P. Stevens case are, as yet, dimly perceived. The mere threat by the union to contest the election of directors at Metropolitan Life seems to have been sufficient to catalyze this major insurance company (who held over 35 percent of J.P. Stevens' debt) into action. Furthermore, the threat required merely 25 signatures to commence and might have cost Metropolitan Life $5–7 million to fight. On this account, it might seem that the ACTWU has found a huge lever to apply against a firm. On the other hand, many knowledgeable observers trace the turning point of the 17-year fight to the single election victory by the union in 1974, when union organizers were able to make much of the fact that the low stock market values of that time had eaten away at the profit-sharing and E.S.O.P. benefits which J.P. Stevens had granted its employees.

The union turned to use of leverage in the board of directors of J.P. Stevens and on the boards of "allied" corporations as, more or less, a last resort. It is likely that most unions and union members prefer an adversarial position vis-à-vis their employer. The pluses and minuses of union-management cooperation have been bandied about a great deal in recent years, particularly in connection with the government bail-out of the Chrysler Corporation, in which the union was guaranteed a seat on Chrysler's board. Management must become aware, however, that when the union does pressure the board of directors and uses the machinery of corporate governance, they will not ask permission to do so or request that views be heard. Such power, if acquired by the unions, will exercise control over management. Furthermore, it is doubtful that there are legal tools available to prevent such activities by unions or others without thoroughly stifling corporate democracy. Management and boards will have to learn to negotiate in a new environment.

Although the type of situation posed by the J.P. Stevens affair may seem broad enough in itself to cover many corporations and labor-management disputes, in fact it represents only a small fraction of the potential for external attacks on the board. To see the potential extent of this problem, one need only note the increasing demands that the beneficial owners of voting securities be empowered to control the voting of their securities. An examination of the J.P. Stevens affair shows how that issue extends beyond mere voting policies, since Metropolitan Life's holdings of J.P. Stevens securities were mostly non-voting. For tax and other reasons (a great deal of the capital flowing to corporations in the U.S. comes from intermediaries) it is almost inevitable that the trustees of these funds will come under pressure to use the voting power or sheer economic clout that they represent to do the beneficiaries' bidding.[12] In certain cases this is mandated by law, such as in E.S.O.P.'s of closely held companies, but there is no need for a legal grant of power where substantial economic strength is manifested. In this broader view, the problem extends beyond private firms and corporate governance to the indisputable effect that public employee pension fund purchases of state and local government obligation will have on the governance of these political bodies.[13]

It is probably safe to say that the beneficiaries of a pension fund would not desire that the investment policies of the fund be modified unless a truly unusual situation developed.[14] On the other hand, employees truly polarized by management might indeed take such steps. Much of the necessary power is already in their hands; additional legislation will merely strengthen their position. In these cases, once again there will be no requests to management or the board for "voice" or "representation," and the scenario described in chapter 1 will be replayed at the board level.

Berle and Means' distinction between "ownership and control" may have to be rethought here. If ownership is construed in a sufficiently broad manner to include "those who have some claim on the assets of the firm," then it is possible through the office of institutional investors, pension fund managers, etc., for "owners" to demand much more control of the firm. If, on the other hand, we interpret control, in the sense of "those groups and individuals who can affect the firm," then control may be fragmented due to the emergence of multiple stakeholders. The potential gap is enormous, and the problems of the director and senior management caught in the middle reinforce the need for a clear understanding of stakeholders and the issue of stakeholder legitimacy. Unless "effective control" is to pass into the hands of others, managers and directors must address the claims of numerous forms of "owners."

Conflicts Within the Ownership Group

A more confusing issue still is that of conflicts within the ownership group itself. This final category of conflicts encompasses the other two, since the board primarily represents the interests and views of the shareholder-owners. Here the phrase "conflicts within the ownership group" will be viewed narrowly to mean "conflicts between shareholders, as shareholders for control of the corporation or voice in its management." This is the classic proxy-fight context, which has seen new significant developments in the past few years.

Two rather distinct purposes of a proxy fight can be distinguished at this point in the development of the "art." The first type attempts to wrest control of the business to significantly alter managerial policies or change managerial personnel. This is perhaps the most classic form of the institution. More recently, the proxy fight has been used to affect the decision to sell the business. This latter type of conflict frequently arises when management succeeds in keeping offers to purchase shares away from the shareholders through legal maneuvering or threats of a contested takeover. In these cases shareholders may not agree with management's appraisal of the offer and may wish to have a more active voice in the decision as to whether the firm should be sold. These two types of proxy fights are well illustrated by the recent SCM proxy battle and the conflicts between Orion Capital corporation shareholders and its managers.

The SCM proxy battle was notable for the quality of the dissident slate of directors proposed by Willard F. Rockwell, ex-chairman of Rockwell International. Rockwell initiated the fight due to his professed unhappiness with managerial policies of Charles P. Elicker, SCM's president. Rockwell charged that those policies were responsible for the current low share price of SCM and that divestiture of some of SCM's "losing" businesses was necessary to regain proper profitability. Elicker countered Rockwell's attacks on management policy and proceeded by personally attacking some of the members of Rockwell's proposed slate, as well as Rockwell himself. Although a number of Rockwell's proposed board members chose to abandon the effort, the battle continued through published letters to the shareholders and into the annual shareholders meeting where management turned back the dissident slate.

A very interesting turn of events developed briefly when Royal Little,

ex-chairman of Textron, Inc. announced that he had lined up a potential ac-
quirer for SCM shares at a favorable price should Rockwell's slate of directors be successful. Soon afterwards, however, this announcement was
repudiated. The no-holds-barred and take-no-prisoners nature of the SCM
fight is typical of many proxy battles. The antagonists see (or claim to see)
no place for compromise and the battle is conducted on a winner-take-all
basis.

It seems correct that shareholder voting be conducted, for the most
part, on an all-or-nothing basis in which very few individual decisions are
left to shareholders and management is given relatively free reign to carry
out its policies. There is little reason or hope to expect deeper shareholder
involvement in corporate policy issues. This all-or-nothing structure seems
to have misled managers into thinking that the correct method to conduct a
proxy battle is a sustained refusal to negotiate. Just the opposite is true. The
very existence of a substantial proxy battle should demonstrate to managers
that there is some need to broaden its horizons and seek to encompass the
dissident group within the corporate organization once again. A negotiation
strategy which examines the potential opportunities and threats posed by
each combatant is perhaps the only sensible approach. Ultimately there may
be a "win-lose" fight. However, if alternatives to win-lose fights are not explored, then opportunities may be foregone. It may be possible to win a proxy
fight and not further the interests of anyone connected with the corporation. By applying the techniques and processes developed in chapters Three
to Six, a more thorough understanding of the issues and stakes of the interested parties can be gained. Armed with these tools, board members will
be able to function more effectively.

The most difficult problems posed by this type of conflict are left for
the board of directors—the corporation's formal set of advisors, and the
lawyers, bankers and other counselors who advise managers more informally.
When the ownership group is badly split, what are "the affairs of the corporation" that corporate law obliges the board to oversee?[15] A point of view
is required which is independent of the perspectives of the warring parties.
The search for a compromise position, with a clear-headed appraisal of the
strengths and weaknesses of the opposing parties is the key element in finding this needed perspective. Corporations and their counselors must become
more adept at this negotiation process; and in this regard, the process of
dealing with stockholders and internal stakeholders may not be so different
from the process of managing the corporation's relationships with other
stakeholders. The newer type of proxy battle is nicely illustrated by the
disputes between the shareholders and managers of Orion Capital Corporation.

Orion Capital is the successor corporation to the infamous Equity Funding Co. Its activities include life insurance and an investment company operation.[16] Over the past few years, Orion Capital has rebuffed attempts by Shearson, Loeb, Rhoades, a large brokerage house (now owned by American Express) and U.S. Life Corp. to purchase part or all of its assets. A group of shareholders has publicly requested the board of directors to consider such offers more favorably and to consider that management owns only a small percentage of the company, and this does not reflect the shareholders interests. The president of Orion Capital, Alan Gruber, has consistently stated that the board of directors is fully aware of its duties toward its shareholders and has taken these factors into account in considering the offers. Although a final resolution of this conflict has not, as yet, appeared, it seems likely that the dissident shareholders will not succeed with their strategy.

To those familiar with the "take-over market," the Orion Capital situation is not unusual. Questions as to the role shareholders could and should play in responding to unsolicited offers are among the most hotly contested issues in corporation law. Furthermore, dissatisfied shareholders have attempted to use the courts to obtain redress against directors who have aided management in fighting off prospective purchasers. As yet, none of these court actions have succeeded, but there is some evidence that the "business judgement rule" and other protections for corporate directors may be cracking. The business judgement rule is applied by the court to determine whether a director used "sound business judgement" when a derivative action is brought against management and directors.

While much attention in this area has, naturally, been focused on the precise definition of the duties of directors and the rights of shareholders and the legal procedures by which these duties are enforced and rights vindicated, insufficient attention has been given to the strategies that the board and its advisors may adopt in efforts to locate a resolution of these disputes. As long as managers have firm control over their decisions, there is little need to compromise (although, of course, their positions may not be entirely correct), but if and when managers' prerogatives in this area are eroded by the courts or the legislatures or when it faces an economically powerful adversary, negotiation may be in order. Note, for example, the narrow defeat of Carl Icahn in his attempt to gain a seat on the board of Hammermill, Inc. for the purpose of locating a prospective purchaser for the corporation.

The board and its advisors will be faced with the problem of identifying "the affairs of the corporation" in a situation where the identity of the corporation is called into question. Defining and practicing consistent and coherent approaches to this type of problem is as necessary, if not in fact more necessary, in addressing this area of corporate governance than is additional specification or modification of legal substance and procedure in these cases. The tasks of the board are multi-faceted here, and a simple analysis of the formal proceedings that are appropriate will not be sufficient.

IMPLICATIONS FOR THE BOARD AND ITS ADVISORS

Up to this point I have claimed that the lay of the land in the area of board behavior has changed in recent years with shifts in the stakes held and the power wielded by various corporate stakeholders. Furthermore, some of the most successful and problematic of these shifts have come to rest within the ownership group of the corporation, as well as the more highly publicized structural changes via government and special interest participation. Examples of the conflicts thus generated have been presented to bring some of the issues into focus. The parallels thus demonstrated between conflicts which arise in the stakeholder confrontation, and the more classic stockholder confrontation, require that the analytical techniques developed in chapters Three to Six to deal with the former case be applied to the latter. Three issues are brought into focus by taking a stakeholder approach to the effective functioning of the board: (1) defining the focal organization; (2) the responsibility of the advisors of the firm; and (3) the evaluation of proposals for reform.

The Focal Organization

Stakeholder management applies not only to the typical "we-they" confrontation with labor or environmentalists, but also to the cases in which it is much harder to see "we" and "they." The starting point of any stakeholder analysis is the determination of point of view, or stakeholder-in-which-organization. It is by virtue of a relationship to a focal point that stakes are established. Throughout the previous chapters it has been clear that the focal point has been "the corporation" or more precisely, "the managers in a corporation." Because of the nature of some of the tasks facing the board, the structure of the focal organization raises more complex issues. Indeed, there is no single right answer to the choice of focal organization.

In the usual case of the corporation versus kibbitzer groups, management or the board easily views itself as the focal organization and analyzes the problem from the viewpoint of the corporation's objectives, and develops strategic programs for action with that group. If, as in the Beatrice Foods or Bunker-Ramo cases, the board is split badly enough, it may not be practical to choose the board of directors or the corporation as the focal organization. In other cases, such as the J.P. Stevens situation, sufficient coherence may be obtained at the board level to justify it as a choice of focus. On the other hand, if the split in the board is severe enough, a smaller group, such as the group of outside directors, may be the appropriate focal organization. The inherent "relativism" of this position on focal organizations squares with a similar position in chapter Four on enterprise level strategy.

I have shown that the stakeholder approach offers no concrete, unarguable prescriptions for what a corporation should stand for. Rather, it tries to make available the variety of flavors which are available for choice, by surfacing the possible combinations of stakeholders, values, and societal issues. Thus, while the stakeholder approach to strategic management is put forth here as a normative theory, it is not normative in the sense that it prescribes particular positions of moral worth to the actions of managers. Instead, it presents a framework for discussing a host of differing moral views. Likewise, I shall not claim that a particular point of view must be taken in doing a stakeholder analysis of the tasks of the board, but rather, that some point of view or other must be taken, and that given a point of view, the logic of the stakeholder approach lays out a menu of alternatives.

The Advisors of the Firm

The problems are dramatically illustrated by considering the perspective of an outside advisor to the corporation who is trying to decide just who the client, or focal organization, really is.

With sweeping language the American Bar Association's (ABA) Code of Professional Responsibility defines the responsibilities of a lawyer who is counsel to a corporation:

> A lawyer employed or retained by a corporation . . . owes his allegiance to the entity and not to a stockholder, director, officer, employee, representative or other person connected with the entity. In advising the entity, a lawyer should keep paramount its interests . . .[17]

While the general thrust of this admonition may be clear to some, it certainly provides no guidance when competing interests represent, or colorably claim to represent the "entity." Nor does it help a lawyer advising a corporation where conflicting interests of the entity are proposed. And such an admonition would be of even less help to a board member attempting to resolve an internal conflict within his or her corporation.

In fact, when courts have been presented with cases where the status of the corporation as client was raised, they have gone far beyond the "entity" philosophy of the Code of Professional Responsibility. In *Garner* v. *Wolfinberger*[18] the court was called upon to rule on the right of the corporation (i.e., management) to claim attorney-client privilege in a derivative action (it should perhaps be noted that the ABA, as amicus, argued extensively in favor of granting absolute privilege). The courts, although stating that corporations, in general, have the power to establish attorney-client privilege, also held that they do not have an absolute right to do so, and stated that "conceptualistic phrases describing the corporation as an entity separate from the stockholders are not useful tools of analysis." Management does not manage for itself. The court went on to hold that given the particular relationship between the corporation and its shareholders and the nature of the derivative action in question (that the corporation acted inimically to the stockholders' interests), the absolute attorney-client privilege could not obtain.

In *Garner* v. *Wolfinberger* the court embarked on a search for the focal organization in assessing the relationship between attorney-corporation-shareholder. It should be noted that the court's analysis took specific cognizance of the type of conflict between corporation and shareholder. This type of analysis will produce different results under different types of circumstances, and this is as it should be. Similarly, members of the board and their advisors must take a pragmatic approach in searching for a focal organization in situations of conflict. The strategy generation process outlined in the discussion of the hypothetical Bunker-Ramo-Fairchild case is one method to begin such a pragmatic approach.

Evaluation of Proposals for Reform

I have stopped considerably short of endorsing structural reforms to the board of directors, and in doing so, I have ignored many of the so-called "complications" of the corporate governance debate. The preceding analysis has addressed some of the implications of the stakeholder approach for this debate, but the focus of attention has been on the board of directors in its current circumstances, given the regulatory, economic and political climate in which it finds itself. I have again relied on a philosophy of voluntarism that I believe is consistent with the stakeholder approach, and have tried to counter-balance the great weight of attention expended upon changing the (perceived) status quo and mandating certain types of board structure or behavior with attention placed on a realistic appraisal of the current situation and a sensitive elaboration of the potential lines of action currently available. Thus, while the stakeholder approach tries to set a realistic context for the analysis and development of policy alternatives, and thus the division of labor and coordination thereof by the board, it stops short of lending support for a number of proposals recently explicated. Perhaps a conception of the corporation can be worked out, whereby the directors of the firm have a fiduciary obligation to stakeholders. But, such a revision of managerial capitalism is beyond the scope of the present analysis.[19]

To those who advocate one of the many types of reform in the name of corporate democracy, there is a caveat. The possible combinations of voting power, economic power and political power as outlined in chapter Three above, which are available under the status quo to the "interested stakeholders" in the corporate governance debate have barely been explored, as the J.P. Stevens case should indicate. It is important that in the rush to make improvements in the corporate governance process, the full impact of each change be thoroughly understood. Conversely, it is equally important that corporate directors and their advisors understand the current environment and act accordingly. Too often, directors opt for a convenient "low profile" position which, in its passivity, ignores strategies which are available and which may result in benefits to all the parties concerned—those with equity, economic and political stakes and power bases.

Legislation to modify the structure of corporate governance acts, in the terms used here, effectively mandates certain alliances and coalitions and thereby eliminates some paths of action from the director's repertoire. In so doing, such legislation in effect performs an elaborate balancing act, weighing and ranking the interests of the participants in these conflicts. A more sensitive analysis of these cases frequently reveals a situation in which there are competing legitimate ownership interests within the corporation which have the effect of, at least temporarily, dissolving the corporation as an effective entity. In these circumstances it is extraordinarily difficult to weigh and balance the interests in a particular case, let alone in the whole corporate economy. The motivation behind the legislation, however, is clear. In too many cases corporate boards have structured their work ineffectively, either through lack of tools and techniques, or through lack of courage and stamina, and have taken passive attitudes and allowed management to strike its own bargains, to the detriment of the corporation and its stakeholders.

The processes of strategic management developed in the preceding six chapters can, and should, be used at the level of the board of directors. I believe that by doing so, directors and managers can achieve the goals of reformers voluntarily while keeping a substantial amount of control over their own future. To conceive of board structure in other than these process terms, is to run the risk of legislating "mechanical structures" which will do far more harm than good in terms of ensuring the responsiveness of the corporation to its stakeholders.

NOTES

1. The stakeholder concept has a number of implications for the broader question of corporate governance. See Freeman and Reed (1983) and Evan (1975).
2. I am grateful to David Reed for collaborating on the research and writing of the ideas of this chapter. His professional training as a lawyer has led to more ideas and a more comprehensive approach than I could possibly have managed alone.
3. See Berle and Means (1932, pp. 220–221). For a discussion of the implications for corporate governance see Evan (1976, pp. 89–107).
4. See Levy (1981; 1982) for an analysis of the problems and issues in doing research on boards.
5. For a sample of the issues see Dill (1978), Bradshaw and Vogel (1981), Ferrara and Goldfus (1979), and Huizinga (1983).
6. For the use of issuance of stock to ESOPs see *Klaus* v. *Hi-Shear Corp.,* 528 F. 2d 225 (9th Cir. 1975); for the issuance of stock to friendly holders, see *Care Co.* v. *Treadway Corp.,* 490 F. Supp. 669 (2d Cir. 1980). The other techniques are described below in detail.
7. The Beatrice Foods story was widely chronicled in the business press. See *Wall Street Journal,* May 7, 1980, p. 22:1; July 21, 1980, p. 1:6; *Business Week,* April 9, 1979, p. 36; September 10, 1979, p. 76; *Barrons,* January 14, 1980, p. 48.
8. However, such a discussion would take us too far afield.
9. The Bunker-Ramo story is chronicled in *Wall Street Journal,* March 31, 1980, p. 12:2; April 23, 1980, p. 12:2; May 5, 1980, p. 21:3; June 11, 1980, p. 37:6.
10. Since unions are external to the firm, they count as stakeholders.
11. A complete history of this struggle would require another book. For useful surveys see Buzzard (1978), and Kovachs (1978). The Union's victory is chronicled in *Wall Street Journal,* October 20, 1980, p. 1:1.
12. For private firms, the Employee Retirement Investment Security Act (ERISA), 29 U.S.C. Sections 1001–1381 (1976) governs the investment of these funds. See H.R. 14138, 95th Congress, 2d Session, for a public employee version of ERISA.
13. See, e.g., *Witheres* v. *Teachers Retirement Sys. of N.Y.,* 447 F. Supp. 1248 (S.D.N.Y. 1978) aff'd, 575 F. 2d 1210 (2d Cir. 1979), in which the teachers' retirement system investment in New York City's obligation was upheld against a challenge of imprudence.
14. See, e.g., "Sacramento Unions Blast 'Social Concept,'" *Pensions and Investments,* November 5, 1979, p. 1.
15. Del. Gen. Corp. Law section 141(a); M.B.C.A. section 35.
16. The Orion Capital story is summarized in *Wall Street Journal,* October 15, 1980, p. 35:6.
17. EC 5–18, Code of Professional Responsibility. The Code has been recently revised and I have been told by a colleague that the issue is addressed but not completely solved, as indeed it cannot be.
18. 430 F. 2d 1093 (5th Cir. 1970).
19. Such an analysis is the subject of a current research project with W.M. Evan.

Eight

THE FUNCTIONAL DISCIPLINES
OF MANAGEMENT

INTRODUCTION

The purpose of this chapter is to discuss the implications of the stakeholder approach to strategic management for the traditional functional disciplines of management. Much has happened in the way that managers think about their disciplines and organizational structure, in general. "Organization structure" calls to mind the organization chart and associated job descriptions, at least to most of us. We think of structure in "structured" terms.

Mintzberg (1979a), Galbraith (1973) and others have enriched our concept of organization structure in forcing us to look beneath the naive intuitions that we have. Galbraith focuses on the role of "information processing" and the strategies necessary to increase the ability of the organization to process information (or to decrease the need to process information), by concentrating on "task uncertainty." Such uncertainty does not appear in the organization chart, nor the job descriptions of most corporations. Mintzberg's encyclopedic review of the literature defines "structure" quite simply as, "the sum total of the ways in which it [the organization] divides its labor into distinct tasks and then achieves coordination among them."[1] Structure must somehow reflect the tasks that organization members perform and the ways that such tasks fit together into the output of the organization. Such a concept of structure need not show up on an organization chart nor be ensconced in job descriptions.

Evidence for the change in organization structure abounds in most major corporations. Classical centralized functional structures have given way to decentralized "business unit" structures. In some cases traditional functional disciplines have been merged with project or business unit organizations into a matrix structure (Galbraith, 1973). Vancil (1979) conducted a comprehensive study of the business unit organizations of a number of firms and the degree of decentralization that exists, and the PIMS studies of performance at the strategic business unit level are further evidence that the strategy-structure linkage as defined by Chandler (1962) has become more complicated.[2] As the external environment of business has changed, structural remedies have been sought to cope with those changes.

Responsibility for managing stakeholder relationships, even in the sense of recognizing only employees, customers, stockholders and suppliers, has traditonally been the arena of functional managers.[3] With the move to SBU-like organization structures functional expertise has been decentralized, and the role of the general manager has emerged as integrator of multiple functions at a relatively low level in the organization (Kotter, 1982). In short, the responsibility for managing broad categories of stakeholders has been diffused as organizations have decentralized their corporate functions and reduced the centralized staffs. The resulting gap in terms of a corporate functional strategy that addresses the broad needs of categories of stakeholders, is theoretically bridged by having each business unit develop strategic programs for its own set of specific stakeholders, as per chapter Five and Lorange (1980).

However, the functional disciplines themselves still exist and dominate the thinking in most major corporations, even though they have been dispersed in many cases. The stakeholder approach has implications at the "micro-level" in terms of how these functional disciplines operate in the SBU-environment and in the corporate-wide environment. Each functional discipline is responsible for either giving inputs to the development of strategic programs for stakeholders, or as in the case of public relations in many firms, for the management of a number of stakeholder relationships. How are these functional managers to conceive of their roles in the world described in the previous chapters? In the following sections I will examine the roles of public relations, marketing, finance, personnel, manufacturing and strategic planning as some of the functional disciplines which must be coordinated to manage old and new stakeholder relationships.[4] The processes developed in chapters Four to Six can be viewed as important components of the work which these functional managers must perform. In particular, the stakeholder concept applied "internally" to the corporate structure as it may currently exist in a particular organization yields analyses similar to those in chapter Seven.

"INTERNAL STAKEHOLDERS"

Organizations are complex phenomena and to analyze them as "black boxes" à la Exhibit 1.2, with the organization in the middle of a complex world of external forces and pressures, does not do justice to the subtlety of the flavors of organizational life. In a seminar on the stakeholder concept some years ago, executives quickly pointed out that the corporation could be replaced in a stakeholder map with a particular department or even a particular manager, and that many of the "stakeholders" of a department or a manager would be internal. I rejected that notion for some time, yet it appeared again and again in seminars and discussions on the stakeholder concept. I do not fully understand the reason, but I believe that it has to do with some of the issues discussed above. That is, the modern corporation has become so complex in terms of its structure, that organizing concepts which differentiate the stakes of internal members and seek to coordinate or integrate their contributions are needed. Kotter (1978) has argued that the notion of "power" seeks to capture part of this complexity. Also Tushman (1977) and more recently Pfeffer (1981) have argued that organizational behavior must be rethought in terms of power and politics, rather than span of control, legitimate authority and the like. And, there is a sense in which the stakeholder approach is consistent with this emerging literature.[5]

There is a sense of "stakeholder" in which groups and individuals that affect a particular manager can be said to be "stakeholders" of that manager, even though these groups and individuals are internal members of the corporation. I shall use "internal stakeholders" to refer to those internal groups who may appear to a particular manager to be much more troublesome than external groups. However, the notion of "internal stakeholder" is a troublesome one.

The point of a stakeholder approach to organizations is to force organizational managers to be more responsive to the external environment. Part of the management problem that pervades U.S. corporations is an inattention to the environment, and the narrow focus on traditional stakeholder groups. By applying the stakeholder approach internally within the corporation, there is a danger that the force of the argument is lost. The stakeholder approach becomes just another "trendy technique" to get other managers to do what they don't want to do, and hence, the problem of externally focusing the corporation is ignored.

Recognizing this danger, perhaps the executives who immediately applied the concept to internal problems had another issue in mind. The manager responsible for carrying out a series of transactions with stakeholders does not, and should not, always actually carry out the transactions alone. Other organizational members and units sometimes have the responsibility for a particular group and must be convinced of the need to go ahead with the program in question. Public relations must convince marketing that a program of image advertising is appropriate, so that the advertising experts in marketing can actually manage the implementation of the campaign with the ad agencies, media, etc. Service representatives must convince sales persons that a new policy is in the customers' interests. R&D managers must convince manufacturing that materials can be bought from multiple sources to go ahead with new product plans. Planners must convince almost everyone that planning is important, and hence that the forms should be completed. Thus, as Kotter (1978) puts it, there are multiple dependencies inherent in the managerial job, for most managers. Since these dependencies exist over time to form lasting relationships, or the need for lasting relationships, the "environment" of a particular manager begins to look like that of the corporation as a whole, giving rise to the notion of "internal stakeholders."[6]

In an effort to get some empirical test for this notion of "internal stakeholders," a job analysis study for one managerial position was conducted recently for ABC Company. A first level managerial job, call it Job A, was chosen and diagnostic interviews with managers currently in the job were conducted in order to identify "those groups and individuals who could affect or be affected by their behavior." No distinction was made between internal and external groups. The result of the interviews was a listing of 33 separate groups who could be called "stakeholders in Job A." Six of these groups were external to ABC Company and 27 of them were internal groups (See Exhibit 8.1). A questionnaire was then distributed to the set of all managers who currently held Job A (N = 900), to determine if they could meaningfully discriminate among stakeholders in terms of their importance to the successful execution of Job A, and in terms of their helpfulness to the managers in Job A. Clear and distinct "clusters" emerged, and statistically significant discriminations at the .05 level were made. The clusters varied depending on several sets of characteristics of the managers, but in general the respondents were able to clearly differentiate among the 33 groups in terms of their helpfulness and their importance. The null hypothesis that managers could not differentiate among their "stakeholders" in terms of helpfulness and importance, or that the pattern of their responses could be explained equally well by a random number generator, was disconfirmed. While there is more to be said about this study and its methodology, replicability, and formal results, it gives some, albeit limited, validity to the notion of "internal stakeholders."[7]

It is still important, however, to square this notion with the central

EXHIBIT 8.1   *"Internal Stakeholders" in a Managerial Job*

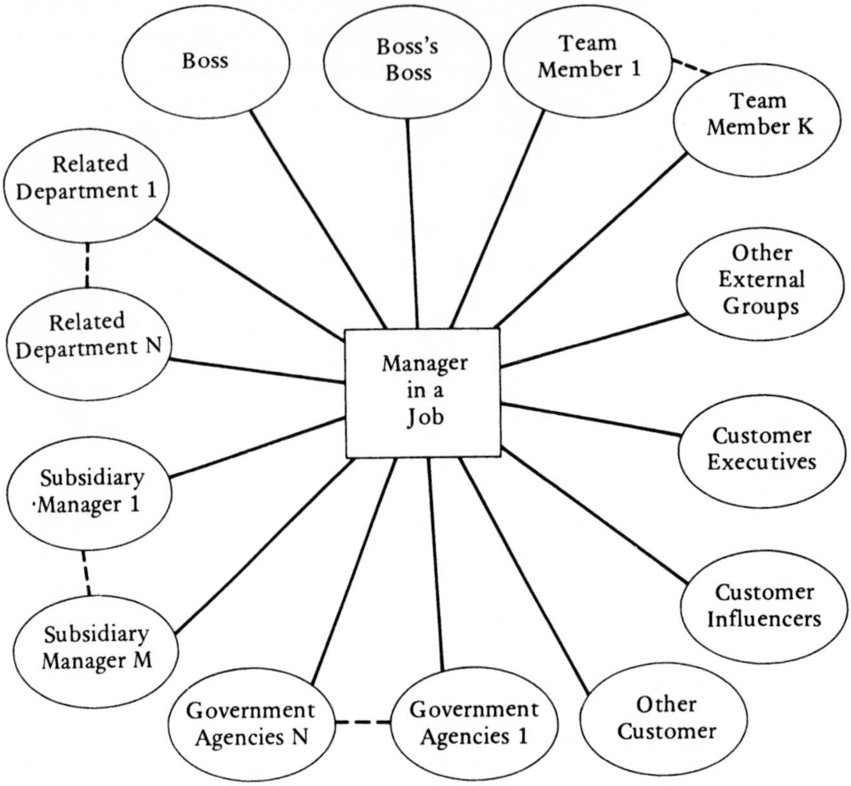

argument of this book, namely, that the stakeholder approach focuses the corporation externally. Quite simply, internal stakeholders must be seen as the conduit through which managers can reach other external stakeholders. (They may also be an impediment, but even so, they remain the major available channel open to a stakeholder.) In Job A the 27 internal stakeholders were important to satisfying a smaller number of external stakeholders. Public relations managers use marketing as a conduit to the customer and the public. Oftentimes, the only way that a manager has of reaching another stakeholder group is through the actions or inactions of another organizational member. Such internal stakeholders become the channel through which the manager reaches out to the external stakeholder.

In order to fully appreciate the implications of the stakeholder approach to strategic management for the traditional disciplines, this notion of "internal stakeholders as a conduit to external stakeholders" can be helpful. To implement cross-functional strategic programs à la American Services International in chapter Six, the available channels to stakeholders must be realistically assessed. This implies that internal groups which control a channel to a stakeholder must themselves be considered in the planning process. This notion can be applied to the traditional functional disciplines, and how programs for change can be undertaken.

EXTERNAL AFFAIRS: A NEW ROLE FOR
PUBLIC RELATIONS AND PUBLIC AFFAIRS

Public Relations News defines Public Relations as follows:

> Public Relations is the management function which evaluates public attitudes, identifies the policies and procedures of an individual or an organization with the public interest, and plans and executes a program of action to earn public understanding and acceptance.

Given such a definition, the function of the public relations manager is to be externally oriented, to make the company sensitive to the concerns of the external environment and to convince the external environment (the public) of the worthiness of company positions. The stakeholder approach requires a redefinition of the public relations function which builds on the communications skills of PR professionals, yet is responsive to the real business environment of today.

Over the course of the past several years while conducting the research on which this book is based, I had occasion to talk with several public relations and public affairs executives in a number of organizations, and several who were active in the various PR/PA professional associations. I noticed one overwhelmingly common feeling about "the PR job," and that is frustration. The following quotes from the interviews that I conducted, mostly for other purposes, are but a few of the stated reasons for this frustration:

- No one in the company listens to us. They do things as if we didn't exist, and expect us to handle it.
- Our publics don't listen to us. They want to speak to someone who can make decisions.
- Investigative reporting has gotten out of hand. When the media call I am not sure if I should even talk to them. The press is impossible.
- The marketing people pretend that the public doesn't exist.
- What we have been doing for the past 20 years, and doing well, just isn't enough these days.
- I can't be all things to all people, and it seems that that is what it takes now.

More fundamentally, these comments illustrate an increasing feeling that while PR is more important than ever, in the current business environment the concepts and tools that have evolved for PR managers to use are increasingly ineffective. Exhibit 8.2 depicts the role of the PR person as boundary spanner (Thompson, 1967), having little credibility inside the organization (too identified with external groups) and little credibility outside the organization (too identified with the organization). In short, as Exhibit 8.2 depicts, the PR manager is caught in the middle of all of the environmental change described in chapter One.

EXHIBIT 8.2   *The Role of Public Relations as a Boundary Spanning Activity*

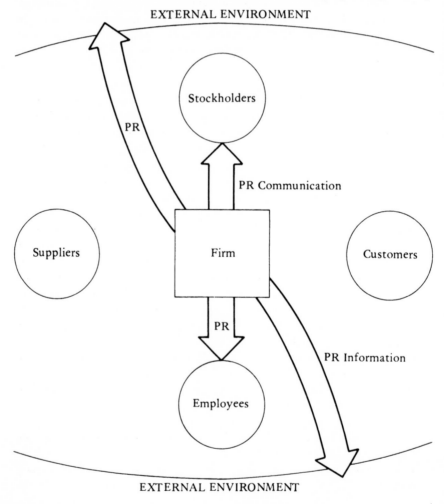

As long as there is a small amount of change, then the PR manager can actually fulfill the role of "defender of the corporation" and "plan and execute a program of action to earn public understanding and acceptance." However, given the external and internal change which has occurred, this role is no longer realistic. Armed with the traditional weapons of the vitriolic press release, the annual report, a slick videotape, corporate philanthropy, etc. today's PR manager is a sacrificial lamb on the altar of multiple stakeholder dissatisfaction with corporate performance.

One analysis of the stakeholder approach is that it spreads the traditional PR role among every manager responsible for formulating strategic programs, where multiple stakeholders must be taken into account. The interactions among stakeholder programs, together with other factors, yield new and emerging issues which will affect the corporation. Thus, if managers merely balance current issues and negotiate with stakeholders, as recommended in chapters Four to Six, new issues and new stakeholder groups will not be managed until they can already have some tangible effect on the organization. It becomes the task of PR to not only participate in the strategic management processes described above, but additionally to scan the environment for new issues and new stakeholders and to bring these to the attention of the business unit managers responsible for unit performance. Ansoff (1979) and others have written of issue management and some firms, such as Allstate Insurance, have instituted issue management programs. The key to success for issue management, however, must be its ability to surface and track real issues that affect the strategic direction of the corporation or business unit that is the "client" of the issues management/PR group. Issue management needs to be integrated with the stakeholder concept to produce realistic assessment of the issues. Stakeholders for all of their trouble, have the virtue of being real, while issues are only useful conceptual abstracts. Actions of stakeholders affect managerial performance directly. Governments pass laws, single issue groups protest and march, customers buy or don't buy products, etc. If managers can integrate issues and stakeholders then a concern with the future as it affects the present can be realistically implemented.

Some companies have begun to differentiate public relations and public affairs quite sharply. In a major study of the public affairs function a group of scholars at Boston University (Mahon, 1981; and Post et al., 1982) found that well over half of the public affairs departments in existence were created in the last ten years and over one third within the last five years. As reported in Post et al. (1982) the Boston University group discovered that 80 percent of the companies surveyed included government relations and community relations as central to the mission of public affairs, and 70 percent included corporate contributions and media relations as part of the public affairs function. The broadening of public relations, and its evolution into "public affairs" has been an interesting response to changes in the business environment. What has evolved is a concept of "external affairs," whereby a group of managers (perhaps PR, or perhaps PA) is given the task of managing particular external groups.

I believe that the stakeholder concept can be useful to these "external affairs" (EA) managers as they try to function effectively in the external world of today. Exhibit 8.3 illustrates a matrix of issues and stakeholders where the EA job is highlighted. The exhibit focuses on five key tasks: (1) identifying new stakeholders, or calling attention to those stakeholders whom other managers have overlooked; (2) beginning the process of explicitly formulating strategies with these stakeholders; (3) helping to integrate the concerns of multiple stakeholders; (4) negotiating with key stakeholders on issues of mutual concern; and (5) searching for new issues, and illuminating new concerns for other managers in the firm. Let me explain how EA managers can begin to accomplish each of these tasks.

EXHIBIT 8.3 *A Stakeholder Approach to "External Affairs" (EA)*

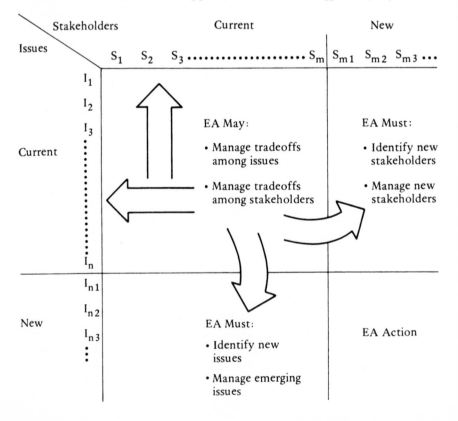

For the most part the task of identifying new stakeholder groups is an overlooked task in the corporation, and the task of creating the stakeholder map of the firm-as-a-whole is never completed. Corporate planners scan the environment for a narrow set of variables, namely, those that affect the corporate plan, which all too often has nothing to do with the majority of the key stakeholders. EA managers are in the best possible position to know who really are the stakeholders in the firm, and to communicate this message *internally* to the general managers who are responsible for developing integrated business strategies.

Operating managers in marketing, production, finance or other functions or profit centers, are often too busy to worry about the effects of current issues on stakeholder groups over time. Therefore, someone needs to explicitly formulate a statement of the organization's objectives or mission in dealing with each stakeholder group. Such a statement becomes a guidepost for managers whose organizational units affect that stakeholder. It helps to make tradeoffs among tough strategic issues that have differentiable effects on one stakeholder. It helps to give the organization and the stakeholder a sense of direction in terms of the overall stakeholder relationship. What is the overall corporate posture with respect to government? Are the actions of multiple organizational units consistent with that posture? What is the overall corporate posture with respect to consumer advocates? Are complaints handled, in every division, consistently with that posture? Is there an organized communication forum for managers and consumer leaders? These are only a few of the necessary questions which must get answered, and which are never asked, in the fragmented, day-to-day managerial world.

Rarely are tradeoffs among multiple stakeholders considered. Managers stick to their functional knitting, and make decisions based on satisfying that external group with which they are most comfortable. EA managers must raise "the bigger picture." How do we formulate policy or practice, while taking multiple stakeholders into account? Their experience with thinking in "big picture" terms can be an invaluable resource to profit center managers caught up in the day-to-day and the here-and-now. It is a task which must be done, else stakeholders will continue to multiply and put pressure on the firm through external means such as government, competitors, etc.

EA managers have communications skills. If Stakeholder Management is taken seriously, then these skills must be turned towards negotiation with stakeholders. Negotiation is a give and take process, a process of compromise, and of establishing "win-win" solutions. It is not identical with communication, but communication skills are a necessary ingredient in successful negotiation. EA managers cannot negotiate, if they cannot make tradeoffs and cannot make decisions. Therefore, this task depends on immersing the manager in the operations of the business. The EA manager must be seen as a valuable resource to the general manager, as a manager of vision and insight who can help the general manager decipher a complex external environment and one who can negotiate with a multiplicity of stakeholder groups.

Finally, the EA manager must think broadly and put together the pieces of Exhibit 8.3 to identify new and emerging issues *and* stakeholders. The EA manager must be able to understand how the issues fit together, and she must be sensitive to the changes in the stakeholder environment. The EA manager in the current business environment must be willing to take risks, and to manage these new issues and stakeholders *before* they are recognized and legitimated within the firm.

The Wellen Company's experience with a construct such as Exhibit 8.3 may be useful to illustrate the role that external affairs managers can play. The Wellen Company is a multi-product and service firm operating primarily in a specific geographical region of the U.S. Several managers in Wellen's PR department were given the task of preparing analyses of future strategic issues that could affect the direction of the company. In particular the issues should currently be "weak environmental signals" but potentially of great operational significance. Thus, these PR managers faced a difficult task: how to cast the net of environmental analysis wide enough not to miss important future issues, and yet narrow enough to sense the impact of issues on the operations of the company. The managers began by identifying several obvious issues which would have near-term and long-term effects such as sexual harassment (Wellen is people intensive), long-term cumulative effects of using one of Wellen's key technologies, the strength of the business community in the geography in which Wellen operated, as well as several other issues. "Issue papers" were constructed and circulated to all executives which set forth the issue and defined possible outcomes. The managers found, however, that there was no sense of how these issues might hang together. After several such issue papers, each of which was highly praised by other executives, the managers decided that they needed some kind of integrative framework. Thus, they constructed a matrix similar to Exhibit 8.3 as a means to understanding more fully what their future environment was to be. They listed their stakeholders, and kept a "quiet list" of the internal stakeholders, and the issues on which papers had been written. The managers then set about to do two things: the first was to identify the impact of each issue on each stakeholder and the second was to look for patterns, possible coalitions and contradictory effects where the Company might take one position on Issue A and a contradictory one on Issue B.

The Wellen Company PR managers have not become fortune-tellers and are not expert environmental forecasters. They have begun to experiment with different methods of organizing their environmental search, and more recently have begun to validate the potential effects on stakeholders by establishing dialogues with important groups. By a gradual process of refining the inputs to Exhibit 8.3, the PR managers can begin to change their role to help the company understand why the external environment affects the company as it does. By using their communications skills as PR professionals with the stakeholders, the Wellen managers will get another reference point on the environment, and enable the business unit managers at Wellen to chart the proper courses.

The Wellen Co. experience need not be unique. PR departments, and even single managers assigned to a particular business, can undertake a change process to make PR more effective, and put it more in line with the stakeholder approach to strategic management. How is PR to move to the forefront of managing the modern corporation?

Let me begin to address this question by looking at the past, and arguing for a different future. In short, the argument to be combatted is, "Why think in terms of stakeholders? Why make such a big deal about a new 'buzzword?' We, as PR/PA people, have been doing this stuff, and thinking this way for ages."

The first response is that the traditional role of PR as serving "the public" or "publics," or "communicating with constituencies" or "audiences," or of PA as "lobbying" and "tracking political issues" has not been horribly successful. Recent surveys show that the level of confidence that these "publics" have in business institutions is abysmal and dropping fast.

The second response is that PR and PA managers must take responsibility for change, and formulate explicit change strategies. These strategies must focus on organizational problems, and not professional elegance. The issue is far deeper and more important than producing another slick videotape, or getting the last 2 percent out of the traditional programs of contributions, press releases, etc.

The third response recognizes the validity of the need for communication; namely, that words make a difference. U.S. management practice needs real change, not cosmetic change, and the words that we use make a difference in how managers see the world. *Managers must see external groups for the stake that they, in fact, have.* In short, using "stakeholder" is important because it yields the connotation of "legitimacy."

The first issue on the agenda for change is that EA managers must face the reality of the problem: change is needed. Starting with a little change, such as using a different word, is easier than starting with a 500 page study of the ills of the corporation, or a white paper expressing outrage at the lack of legitimacy of both stakeholders and ourselves as EA managers. The second item on the agenda is to construct a stakeholder map of the firm. If we and our top management will not take some responsibility for leading a change effort towards becoming more responsive to the external environment, then the future may be bleak indeed. The third item on the agenda is for us to construct a roadmap of how the organization is managing current stakeholder relationships. The final item on the agenda is for PR managers to take on an issue, or set of issues, that is important yet manageable, and demonstrate the ability to *ADD VALUE*. It is only by adding value that credibility can be established. Demonstrating how to add value on an issue is not an easy task. It does not necessarily involve trying to produce a cost/benefit analysis of, for example, giving view-graph machines to grammar schools. We must begin to think about how to add value to the work of operating managers, and this means understanding in detail the work of operating managers, and therefore, understanding the operations and businesses of the company.

MARKETING MANAGERS: LINKS TO THE CUSTOMER

Marketing spans a broad range of managerial activities in the modern corporation.[8] From the stereotype of the enthusiastic salesperson to the egghead in marketing research, the tasks of marketing managers cover the spectrum of the firm's dealings with the customer. Over the past several years the discipline of marketing has undergone radical change, from selling techniques to strategic planning for products. The discovery of the product life cycle and the importance of market share, as well as new quantitative methods for marketing research such as multi-dimensional scaling, means that the marketing manager in today's environment has a broad array of conceptual techniques and tools to bring to bear on the customer.

Exhibit 8.4 is a stakeholder map of a marketing manager (at a relatively high level) in a typical organization. The classical split among sales, service and administration exists and is the cause of a great deal of conflict among the piece-parts of the marketing organization. In addition, other key internal stakeholders are other functional (or business unit) managers in production, R&D, planning and other staff departments. As Exhibit 8.4 shows, marketing is the conduit to both customers and competitors. Marketing has both access to and information about both of these stakeholder groups. Internal stakeholder groups will pressure marketing for each of these commodities, and marketing managers must respond to both the internal and external stakeholders.

In some organizations marketing is much more sensitive to internal stakeholders than the external ones. These organizations have "taken their

EXHIBIT 8.4 *Typical Stakeholder Map for Marketing Managers*

eye off the ball" and become isolated from customers and competitors. Salespersons spend a great deal of time completing internal reports and account planning becomes an end in itself. The service and administrative staffs are swamped with paperwork and procedures. The focus is on visibility within the organization. One might hypothesize that in industries where foreign competition has come in to serve a market, that something is drastically wrong with the marketing function in those organizations within the industries. Automobiles, consumer electronics, and steel come to mind as candidates for testing this hypothesis.

When marketing is not seen as the conduit to the customer and competitor by others in the organization, then two important stakeholder groups miss attention. The organization as a whole takes its eye off the marketplace, and regardless of its managerial talent in other areas, it simply will not survive over time in a competitive global game.

Thus, the stakeholder approach dictates that the marketing manager reinforce the role of marketing and the importance of the customer and competitor. Particular maps for each marketing manager, similar to Exhibit 8.4, must be constructed. Marketing managers must learn to work in the non-hierarchical world depicted by the exhibit, as must public relations and the other functional managers. Also, marketing managers must understand how generalizable their picture is; namely, that each functional manager is a conduit to some stakeholder group or other, or is in a role of "pure support" and has only "internal stakeholders." Each function must be "stakeholder serving" in its approach. Internal groups are means to an end, and not ends in themselves.

FINANCIAL MANAGERS

Financial managers and analysts, including accounting and comptrollers in some firms, have come under increasing attack recently.[9] The argument is quite simply that the degree of sophistication of financial systems has led to "management by the numbers," with an overemphasis on the short term performance of the firm. Inflation, recession, global interdependencies and currency devaluations have all played a role in the need for increasingly sophisticated financial control systems.

The job of the financial analyst or treasurer or V.P. of Finance or whatever title is appropriate, is quite complex. There is more to it than just calculating the earnings per share and assuring that the reports are accurate. Exhibit 8.5 depicts a typical financial manager's job in the modern large corporation. The stereotype of the "man with the green eyeshade" is completely inappropriate here, for the financial manager is a boundary spanner of the first magnitude. He or she must conduct transactions with a host of stakeholder groups from government agencies to competitors, in terms of understanding the relative advantage that the firm has in financial terms.

The complexity of the world economy has made the job even more difficult. The financial manager must understand the financial impact of strategic decisions in multiple economies, and must understand the different sets of rules which exist from economy to economy among Western, Eastern and other countries. Without clear policy guidance from government the financial manager must understand the impact of inflation on the firm, and must make this impact known, else the firm will fail to get accurate performance indicators (Drucker, 1980).

EXHIBIT 8.5   *Typical Stakeholder Map for Financial Managers*

Given the complexity of the task, it is no wonder that pathological cases of "managing by the numbers" have arisen. There is simply no overall framework for managing the influence of multiple stakeholders. Macroeconomic variables are grand generalizations of the concrete behavior of stakeholders which actually influence the firm, and academics and practitioners alike understand precious little about the influence of particular sets of economic expectations on strategic behavior.

It is easy to see how financial managers are driven by short-term measurements. Indeed, in times of inflation, measurements such as Return on Investment (ROI) and Discounted Cash Flow (DCF) distort reality when implemented in a simpleminded fashion that does not take into account the effects of inflation.

The financial manager in Exhibit 8.5 must act as a conduit to those important external stakeholder groups. The potential for an internal focus to the financial manager's job is enormous, and will spell absolute disaster for the corporation. Sophisticated measures will be developed which have little relevance to those groups who have a stake in the organization. The financial manager in Exhibit 8.5 must pay special attention to the validity of the financial information systems, in terms of being barometers of the health of the corporation. The experiences of International Harvester and others, who looked great on the balance sheet and income statement one year and were subjected to severe shocks the next, are too costly to be repeated. We must search for measurements which balance short-run and long-run concerns. We must find criteria for setting proper levels of Earnings Per Share and realistic hurdle rates that allow us to meet the needs of multiple stakeholders.

PERSONNEL

No corporate function is more maligned than personnel, or more modernistically, "human resources management," yet it is more important than ever, simply because it takes a hand in preparing the corporate managers to do their job.[10] The personnel, or human resources, managers of today must be broad thinkers and risk-takers, rather than managers who have been pensioned off early and who are eager to protect their "retirement" status. The story of General Motors and the Lordstown Vega Plant where workers sabotaged the assembly line, should be lessons for all personnel managers about the need to keep in touch with those external stakeholders such as unions, employees, the local community, colleges and universities, etc. which can affect the human resources job. Not only does personnel hire or assist in hiring, as well as set procedures for firing, but it must comply with a host of government regulations, such as EEOC regulations and unemployment compensation, etc., plan the career moves of employees, be sensitive to the more recent issues of two-career marriages, workaholism, etc.

Exhibit 8.6 depicts a typical stakeholder map for a personnel manager. An argument similar to the public relations argument can be constructed here, for the status of the personnel manager in many large corporations is not very high. Thus, the personnel manager needs to embark on a similar change process, involving explicitly creating the particular stakeholder maps from Exhibit 8.6, formulating strategies for each stakeholder group and picking an issue to show how personnel adds value to that issue for the operations manager.

At least part of the critique of U.S. management methods is a direct attack on the effectiveness of the personnel discipline. If personnel is supposed to be concerned with "people" why is the stereotype precisely the opposite, that of an endless string of bureaucrats and paper? Concern with management style and skills must reside in personnel as well as in other places in the

EXHIBIT 8.6   *Typical Stakeholder Map for Personnel Manager*

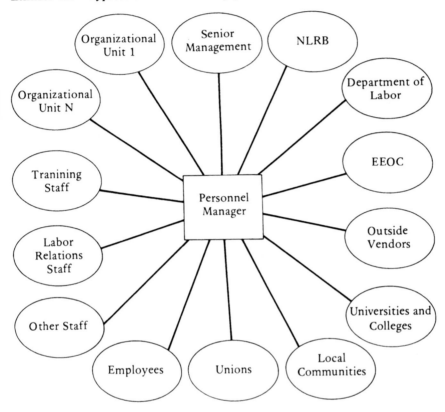

organization. Ouchi (1981) and Pascale and Athos (1981) have argued that Japanese simply "out-people-manage" their U.S. competitors. The personnel function in U.S. corporations needs a reorientation towards serving the stakeholders to whom it is responsible.

MANUFACTURING

Hayes and Abernathy (1980) and others have criticized U.S. management practices for deemphasizing manufacturing, and in particular the manufacturing process.[11] The argument is that, once again, managers have taken their eye off the ball in terms of quality and in terms of innovation in the manufacturing process. High inventories, shoddy quality control, poor employee and labor union relations and a lack of attention to the impact of the plant in a local community are all symptoms of the malaise affecting many manufacturing managers. The examples of West Germany and Japan are constantly thrown in the faces of U.S. manufacturing managers, especially when a firm faces competitors from these countries.

Exhibit 8.7 is a typical stakeholder map for manufacturing managers in the U.S. Two central questions are raised; namely, how can managers enable employees to be more productive, and how can managers serve as a conduit to unions and employees. Age-old tricks such as "the suggestion box" are being used to attack these fundamental problems, yet the problems are not so simple. The relationship between a firm and its employees is multifaceted and involves a complex psychological contract. Expectations are fulfilled or not over long periods of time. Quick fixes simply don't work, unless these expectations are changed. The adversarial nature of U.S. labor-management relations has gone a long way towards contributing to the decline of U.S. industry, and this adversarial relationship must be turned around at the plant level. New ways of thinking about the work that an

EXHIBIT 8.7   *Typical Stakeholder Map of Manufacturing Manager*

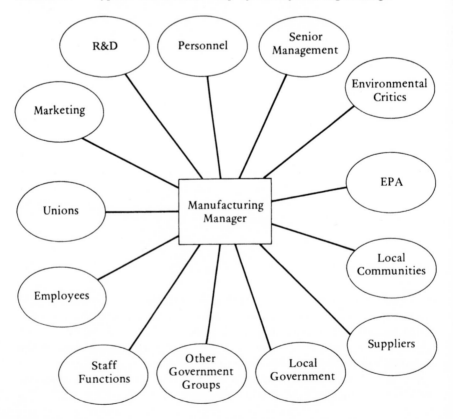

employee does, and new ways of thinking about management must be tried, else the erosion will continue. The responsibility of manufacturing managers in the stakeholder approach is awesome. Not only must these managers think in strategic terms, but they must undertake a change process to gain or regain competitive edge. They must be conduits to the stakeholders which they serve.

A STAKEHOLDER STRUCTURE FOR ORGANIZATIONS

Upon analysis of several key functional disciplines of management it should be apparent that the stakeholder approach can be applied to understanding the work of the corporation in functional terms.[12] Each manager has a certain set of stakeholders to whom he or she is responsible, and a set of "internal stakeholders" who see the manager as a conduit to the external environment. The picture that I have implicitly painted in the preceding pages is one of "radical externalism," whereby every manager's work is either for the benefit of an external stakeholder group or as a conduit to an external stakeholder group. In the functional jobs described above, every manager is a boundary spanner, and the resulting organization is a "stakeholder-serving" organization. I have not prescribed which stakeholders are important, nor which ones should be most important. Such a task is the dominion of the executive in setting strategic direction at the enterprise level.

In the modern complex corporate structure that encompasses multiple SBUs, groups, sectors, divisions, corporate staffs, matrix configurations and the like, it is too easy for the responsibility for stakeholders to become diffused. No one has a handle on the effects of the corporation on a particular category of stakeholders. Responsibility is necessarily decentralized, as work is differentiated. Integration occurs at the business or product level, but not necessarily at the level of summing up the impact of the corporation on a particular stakeholder group. If particular stakeholders have integrative processes of their own, then the possibility for misunderstanding increases. A customer who buys a great computer from IBM and a lousy photocopy machine may not understand what IBM is trying to accomplish with their customers. Likewise, a customer who buys superb local and private network service from AT&T and a lousy PBX may not understand the differences in the organization which result in such product differences. I am not claiming that absolutely everything that an organization does with a stakeholder group has to be consistent with everything else. Only an incredibly unresponsive organization could fulfill that charter. I am arguing, however, for the existence of a manager responsible for bringing the needs of certain stakeholder groups to the constant attention of the other organizational units of the corporation.

By creating a skeletal "stakeholder structure" I believe that an organization can get more closely in touch with the external environment. Such an organization should specialize in bringing stakeholder needs to the foreground, especially those needs that the organization is not currently fulfilling. These "stakeholder managers" would have no formal authority. Rather, they would gain authority through their expertise, and coming to be recognized by line managers as a group who could help. To become known for "adding value" these managers would have to treat the line operation as a client, and seek to serve both stakeholders and internal "clients." One model is that of a lawyer who serves the court and his or her client. The lawyer is an advocate of the court to the client and an advocate of the client to the court. Exhibit 8.8 depicts one possible structure for such an organization. A manager for each important category of stakeholders would be appointed as "Customer Manager," "Environmental Group Manager," "Media Manager," "Government Agency Manager" or whatever, and would

EXHIBIT 8.8   *A Stakeholder Structure for Organizations*

Stake-holder Manager / Org. Unit	Customer	Consumer Advocate Groups	Environ-mental Groups	Government	. . .	S_n
SBU$_1$						
SBU$_2$						
SBU$_3$						
.						
.						
.						
.						
.						
.						
.						
SBU$_m$						

Duties of Stakeholder Manager:
1. Insures responsiveness to stakeholder.
2. Becomes a stakeholder expert.
3. Keeps score.
4. Program integration.
5. Ombudsperson.

be responsible for several key tasks: (1) insuring responsiveness to stakeholder concerns; (2) becoming a stakeholder expert; (3) keeping score between organization and stakeholder; (4) insuring organizational program integration; and (5) serving as ombudsperson between organization and stakeholder. Let me briefly explain each task.

The proposed organization could easily be overlaid onto an SBU-type organization, simply because the "stakeholder managers" would have little formal authority. They would be responsibile for producing a "charter" which would state the goals and objectives of the organization with respect to a particular stakeholder. The goal of the stakeholder manager would be to produce a charter that coincides as closely as possible with the expectations of the stakeholders with respect to the organization, or to have a conscious program in mind to change these expectations. The charter would then serve as a guidepost for SBU managers, not as an ironclad policy. Deviations from the charter would be acceptable and even encouraged, especially when those deviations would better serve a stakeholder's needs. The stakeholder manager would also be responsible for a "transactions audit" for a particular group, to insure (or at least assist in insuring) that the transactions that members of the corporation execute with respect to a particular stakeholder are consistent with the stated strategic direction of the firm.

By carrying out these formal duties, the stakeholder manager would become an expert on his or her particular stakeholder, insuring the organization of a knowledge base for future action. By continuous interaction with a particular stakeholder this base of knowledge would be constantly updated. Data files, newsletters, "stakeholder reviews" and other mechanisms could serve as information dissemination processes to others who would be concerned with that stakeholder.

Stakeholder managers would be assigned the responsibility of formulating and implementing "score-keeping" mechanisms with their stakeholder groups. The scorecard suggested in chapter Six would be adapted for each particular stakeholder group, and measurements would be taken at the appropriate intervals, or original data collected where necessary. This scorekeeping function would not replace, but would supplement, other methods developed by the strategic program implementers in the SBUs. The idea is that two separate measurements can give more useful information than one measurement alone. Personal bias, measurement errors, etc. can be minimized.

Stakeholder managers would also be responsible for achieving some sense of integration across multiple organizational units, and multiple strategic programs within an organizational unit. Formal responsibility for integration would still reside with the SBU manager. However, the stakeholder expert would be called upon to advise on the "interaction effects" of certain strategic programs. Stakeholder experts would ideally operate as a profit center within the corporation, selling their services to SBU managers. Incentives for the stakeholder managers to be knowledgeable, responsive and helpful to corporate strategists at all levels need to be formulated. I am biased towards a "value-added" approach whereby the SBU manager perceives enough value-added to pay for the help that the stakeholder manager provides. The onus would be on the stakeholder expert to convince the SBU manager that he or she had a "stakeholder problem" that the expert could help to solve. Measuring value added would at first be a perception in the eyes of the client and the external stakeholder. However, as more experience is gained, more sophisticated and objective measures could be designed.

Finally, stakeholder managers would become "ombudspersons," or places where stakeholders could go to have disputes listened to, and possibly resolved. The ombudsperson concept has great potential in the corporation, for there is a curious lack of processes which can be used to resolve disputes. Oftentimes, stakeholders who want voice in the affairs of the corporation must petition government at some level, with the result being onerous regulations, or unresponsiveness on the part of government. By cultivating a relationship with particular stakeholders, stakeholder managers could head off potential conflict in the government arena, which is costly to all parties.

While the structure briefly outlined here is quite speculative, some such mechanism needs to be put in place, especially with those stakeholders with whom the firm is currently experiencing negative results. An added feature of the organizational structure proposed here is that stakeholder experts could be pulled together to form a "ready-made" environmental scanning team, full of experts on concrete information about what the stakeholders of the corporation are likely to expect in the future.

SUMMARY

I have claimed that the functional disciplines of management must be rethought in stakeholder terms. Each functional discipline has a set of stakeholders which it serves or should serve, and a set of "internal stakeholders" to which it is a conduit for action with respect to its stakeholders. The changes I have suggested are not drastic ones, but rather represent a "return to basics." I have outlined a change process for each discipline, especially public relations, and shown that a program of making the corporation more responsive to the external environment needs to be undertaken. I have speculated about the organizational structure necessary for such a program and briefly suggested how such an organization could be overlaid on the more traditional SBU organization. Such speculations require a different conception of the managerial job, and the role of the executive.

NOTES

1. Mintzberg (1979a, p. 2).
2. See, for instance, Galbraith and Nathanson (1978), and Miner (1979).
3. Lawrence and Lorsch (1967) showed how the environment could determine the degree of differentiation of tasks and the stakeholder groups to whom a particular functional manager was responsible, as well as the coordination mechanisms which were necessary.
4. Public relations and public affairs have a special role in the stakeholder approach simply because the organization has looked to these functions to do the impossible job of fending off the external changes catalogued in chapter One.
5. To develop this idea would be yet another book. The basic premise is that concepts which view organizations as hierarchical miss the essential nature of what goes on in organizations.
6. I am indebted to Vinnie Carroll for many helpful discussions here, and for making sense of the notion of "internal stakeholders" in a clinical application of the stakeholder concept in project management.
7. Freeman and Carroll (1983) analyze the results of this research in more detail.
8. See Abell and Hammond (1979) for a strategic approach to marketing.
9. See Weston and Brigham (1978) for an introduction to the issues.
10. Schein (1978) discusses some of the current issues.
11. See Hayes (1981) and Wheelwright (1981) for comparisons of U.S. and Japanese manufacturing policies.
12. The organizational structure proposed here should be read as speculative, and able to be tailor-made to particular organizations.

Nine

THE ROLE OF THE EXECUTIVE

INTRODUCTION

The stakeholder approach proposed in the preceding pages dictates a conception of the role of the executive as one who serves a set of stakeholders of the firm and as one who is the guardian of the direction and the values of the enterprise. In this chapter, I will briefly indicate the implications of the stakeholder approach to strategic management for the executives who are responsible for the health of the corporation. I shall begin with the general manager responsible for integrating a number of functional responsibilities and move on to a discussion of the job of the chief executive, who I believe must learn to manage in turbulence. Finally, I shall summarize the main argument of the book and suggest some avenues for further research.

THE GENERAL MANAGER

I began this book with a discussion of the problems of Bob Collingwood, the CEO of the U.S. subsidiary of a large multinational, Woodland International. Within Woodland there are many such managers who are responsible for integrating a number of functional areas. And, even within Bob's subsidiary there are managers responsible for particular businesses, who are in some sense, "CEOs" of their particular businesses. As the modern corporation has decentralized and begun to use strategic management models, the number of general managers and their scope of responsibility has increased. As outlined in chapters Four through Six, strategic management involves a number of managers from all areas of the corporation. It falls to the lot of the general manager to pull these diverse strands of thought and action together.

An examination of enterprise level strategic management immediately raises the question of the role of the executive in setting direction at all levels of the organization: enterprise, corporate, division and business. At the business level the SBU manager's job focuses on defining and bringing to market distinctive business competences in the form of current and new products, new markets, new applications of existing technology and managing the resources of the firm in a productive manner. However, even at the business level stakeholder questions abound. There are unions, suppliers, customer segments, government regulations, local communities, etc. with which the managers in a particular strategic business unit must deal. Division level or business-family level or in some organizations, country-level, managers must deal with the same kinds of issues and stakeholders on a somewhat larger scale. Thus, each general manager at the business or "division" level finds himself/herself caught in a rather large and pervasive network of power and dependence similar to the maps developed in chapter Eight for functional managers. Some stakeholders will be external while others will be internal.

The role of the general manager in large organizations is one of managing within a large network of stakeholders. It is essential that these stakeholders not be viewed as constraints, subject to which, a manager can maximize some objective function, be it profit or market share or even political clout. Rather, the dominant managerial metaphor must be negotiation. The amount of information to be absorbed by the general manager from both external and internal sources is simply too great, and overloads the hierarchical structure. Concepts such as lateral relations, matrix, appropriate strategic information systems and informal negotiations[1] must be combined with careful stakeholder analysis if the general manager is to be successful.

The role of the general manager at the lower corporate levels is more difficult still, when you consider that these managers are being called upon to take risks, to go out and meet with stakeholder groups who might be critics, and who might cause trouble despite the well-intentioned efforts of the general manager. On the other hand, general managers at the lower corporate levels are at critical points in their careers, most probably on an upward path, and simply do not want to be derailed. The reward systems of most large organizations, both formal and informal, are oriented towards short-term results. *For general managers to be proactive and attack problems before they become crises is asking them to often go against the grain of how they are rewarded.* While it is possible to change such reward systems, it is not very likely.

Values can be one control mechanism, and it is here that they are most useful. If the dominant culture in the corporation is a "stakeholder-serving" culture, then regardless of the reward systems, general managers will know that it is their job to go out and communicate and negotiate with key stakeholder groups from customers and suppliers to critics and the media. And, they will know that this external job must be done if the corporation is to succeed. Using values as a control mechanism must aim at the real costs and benefits of action and inaction, as delineated in chapter Six, rather than the visible costs and benefits. The built-in bias for general managers on the way up is in terms of short term, visible costs and benefits, what others in the organization see. Turbulent business environments exact real costs.

THE ROLE OF THE EXECUTIVE INSIDE THE CORPORATION

Exhibit 9.1 is a stakeholder map of the job of the chief executive in a typical large organization. It depicts the harried life of a manager who must serve a number of roles, and who must have multiple skills. Increasingly today, the tenure of CEOs of major corporations is short-lived. When things go badly, as they are for so many organizations, the CEO stands squarely in the middle, shouldering the blame.

In order for the stakeholder approach to strategic management to succeed, the executives of the corporation must be involved in the explicit formulation of an enterprise strategy or a completion of a stakeholder audit. The most important data that are inputs to these processes are the beliefs of the top managers of the corporation. A more rational mapping of stakeholders and stakes (Exhibits 3.1–3.3) does serve as a checkpoint on these judgements, but without an examination of the basic premises on which the executives are running the corporation, rational analysis does no good.

In particular, the CEO must be involved in the stakeholder, values and societal issues analyses that go into the selection of an enterprise level strategy. Chapter Four discussed several cases of self-deception at the level of enterprise strategy. The actions of the management group were inconsistent with the stated strategic direction of the firm. If the CEO leads the process of examining the enterprise strategy, the danger of such a pathological case is minimized, given that the CEO is willing to be candid about his or her own values and their relationship to the corporation. Without such involvement, the development of an enterprise strategy is just another "press release" that looks good in the annual report, but which will fool neither the

EXHIBIT 9.1   *The Role of the Chief Executive*

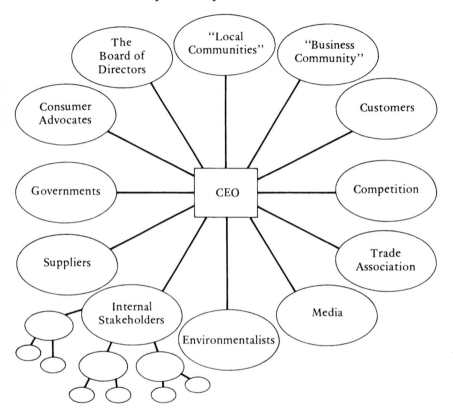

management team of the corporation nor many of the stakeholders, nor improve performance.

Understanding "what we stand for" can cause a great deal of pain, if the process tackles tough issues. In leading the search for corporate values, the CEO has a difficult job. The understanding of an analyst, the business judgement of a CEO and the wisdom of the ancients are almost too much to ask of any one person. Hence, I believe that the effective CEO in large corporations survives and thrives only by creating a genuine sense of "team," with high levels of trust among the team members and relatively little emphasis placed on the formal positions in the hierarchy.

The CEO and the rest of the top management team must take special efforts to communicate the results of the enterprise strategy. If the basic values and attention to stakeholders in the enterprise are not shared at least somewhat down the line, then the enterprise level strategy will go the way of other corporate policies. The essence of the stakeholder approach is that executives can gain commitment throughout the corporation. Research is beginning to show that the culture or shared values in a corporation may well be the most important variable. Deal and Kennedy (1982) and Peters (1981), as well as analyses of cases such as Millipore and Tupperware, have begun to lend credence to the claim that values serve an important control function in the corporation.

In addition, the top executive group must actively involve the board of directors in these direction setting decisions. From a purely egocentric point of view (so as not to be second-guessed), and from the point of view that a board can serve as a resource in the process of analyzing stakeholders and societal issues, the directors must be involved. Some firms have public policy committees on the board which are responsible for part of the task of stakeholder management, but these committees do not always integrate economic and social issues. The days of "tokenism" must be over. The issues outlined in chapter Seven, in managing the "ownership" representatives, are too complex to avoid dealing with them in a genuine manner.

Perhaps the biggest internal role of the CEO and the senior management team is in the control process. In chapter Three I pointed out that strategic reviews were notoriously ineffective, for they easily become "show and tell" rather than meaningful "questions and answers." The CEO can easily remedy this and focus the strategic reviews externally, scheduling "stakeholder reviews" at which the manager under review must present hard evidence about the effects of his or her business strategy on key stakeholder groups. The questions which the CEO asks at these stakeholder review sessions must be in terms of what new and support strategic programs are and have been undertaken to address the stakeholders' concerns, and what ac-

EXHIBIT 9.2   *Sample Questions for "Stakeholder Review"*

1. Who are our stakeholders currently?
2. Who are our potential stakeholders?
3. How does each stakeholder affect us?
4. How do we affect each stakeholder?
5. For each division and business, who are the stakeholders, etc.?
6. What assumptions does our current strategy make about each important stakeholder (at each level)?
7. What are the current "environmental variables" that affect us and our stakeholders [viz., inflation, GNP, prime rate, "confidence in business (from polls), corporate identity, media image," etc.]?
8. How do we measure each of these variables and their impact on us and our stakeholders?
9. How do we keep score with our stakeholders?

tions have been taken, proactively, to avoid future concerns. The validity of the data on stakeholder groups must be questioned to insure that lower level managers have communicated with stakeholders and that the corporate strategy truly addresses the stakeholders' concerns, rather than the corporate strategists' perceptions of the stakeholders' concerns. By engaging in meaningful strategic reviews the top management team can focus the attention of the corporation externally. Exhibit 9.2 is a sample list of review questions which can be used.

Internally, the executive group must act as agents of change, seeking to bring about a responsive corporation that is focused externally. To be a successful change agent the executives must, themselves, understand the external environment in which the corporation finds itself and must take an active role not only in changing the corporation and its internal systems and people, but in the real-time management of certain stakeholder relationships.

THE EXTERNAL ROLE OF THE EXECUTIVE

More and more time is spent by CEOs in dealing with the external environment. Many CEOs spend up to 90 percent of their time dealing with a host of stakeholder concerns, from meetings in Washington to talks with union leaders. The name of the game today, is how to deal effectively with external groups. Hence, in addition to the more traditional managerial role which the CEO and senior management team plays inside the corporation, they must also: (1) serve as spokespersons for the corporation in meetings with key stakeholder groups; (2) serve as participants in the social and political processes; and (3) serve as builders of coalitions.

Many critics of business simply do not want to talk to managers who cannot make decisions, or who cannot commit the corporation to action. There is a need for senior executives to participate directly in stakeholder meetings and negotiations, so that real progress can be made. An obvious example is the recent negotiations which AT&T entered into with the Justice Department to modify the 1957 Consent Decree, and hence drop the pending anti-trust suit. In such a case Charlie Brown, CEO of AT&T had to be intimately involved in the details. No one else would do to represent the interests of the firm. In the subsequent discussions in the Congress around H.R. 5158, again Mr. Brown and top executives had to personally testify and meet with representatives.

However, even in less dramatic situations, the CEO needs to be personally involved. Lee Iaccoca has served Chrysler as spokesperson during the turnaround of that corporation, even making advertisements urging customers to give Chrysler products a try. Other less well-known CEOs spend a great deal of time meeting with governors, leaders of consumer and environmental groups, unions, and other business leaders in trade organizations such as the Business Roundtable.

The ability of the senior managers in a firm to meet with stakeholders and to talk with critics must go far beyond the implementation of strategy and the direct effects on the firm. Executives must take their role as active participants in the social and political process seriously. They must seek to balance the relatively narrow interests of their individual firms with the broader concept of the public interest, especially on issues where "public goods" are involved, such as clean air, water, access to office and power, etc. By going a step beyond lobbying and contributing dollars to campaigns through PACs, executives can encourage the participation and activisim of others. Perhaps if the role of the executive as public servant is taken seriously, as advocated by Lindbloom (1977), the ills cataloged in chapter One of this book would not exist. With executives participating in the political process in a broader way than fighting every piece of legislation that could possibly have negative effects on their firm, the credibility of large organizations will begin to improve. Leading the United Way drive and contributing to the symphony and public television broadcasts are worthy social activities, but they do not hit the mark in terms of leadership in social and political change.[2]

Throughout this analysis I have concentrated on the role of executives in negotiating with groups which may currently be adversaries. However, forming coalitions among "friends" may well be just as difficult. Post (1978) recounts the difficulties of the companies in the infant formula industry in formulating a policy of self-regulation in an attempt to halt a growing controversy. CEOs often believe that their way is the only way. "What the boss says, goes" is still the rule internally, but when the decision-making arena is the external environment it no longer holds. Coalitions formed strictly of like-thinking individuals tend to be inflexible. There is no room, and initially no need, for change. On the other hand, coalitions of a broad range of interests are difficult to hold together, since the interests are so widespread. CEOs must see their role as taking a leadership position in forgoing coalitions on a host of difficult issues. Hardly anyone can disagree with the aims of the United Way, hence, a coalition that supports its activities is quite easy to form and hold together. An issue such as "women's rights in the corporation" is a different story, and is viewed as so "controversial" that few will try to form a coalition committed to equal opportunity for women.

The stakeholder approach implies that executives not avoid controversy, especially where it affects the firm or where it is necessary to confront controversy in order to implement a consistent enterprise strategy. Such an approach, however, requires a different idea of leadership both within the firm, and at a broader external level.

LEADERSHIP TASKS

The literature on leadership in organizations is vast, and encompasses a variety of models and metaphors. From Barnard's (1938) view on the "zone of acceptance" and the need for executives to instill a moral purpose in employees, to the more current and less dramatic pronouncements of "hygiene factors," "expectancies" and "paths and goals," there is a wealth of research which seeks to understand human responses to situations where they are called upon to lead, rather than to follow.[3]

The role of the executive in an organization that takes a stakeholder approach to strategic management is an expanded sense of leadership. The boundaries of the organization are broadened, and given certain enterprise strategies, the executive must lead coalitions of stakeholders. Such leadership will involve the coordination of interests which coincide and the resolution of conflict among interests which do not coincide.

The stakeholder approach provides a context for understanding the other organizational variables. It is within this context that the executive must put together in a coherent fashion the other pieces, such as structure, systems, staff, style, skills and superordinate goal, to borrow Pascale's and Athos' (1981) terminology.[4] Strategic management and organizational structure and processes cannot be managed in isolation from the set of stakeholders which affect, and are affected by, the organization. For example, if the information systems in a firm do not routinely collect and disseminate reports on critics of the firm or on government regulations that affect the firm, then the information systems may well be pulling in the opposite direction of a firm's stakeholders. Alternatively, if the management style and the skills of the managers in a firm are not conducive to negotiating with stakeholders, there is an equal chance for "misfit." The leadership task using a stakeholder approach is simply(!) to understand and take into account the fact that stakeholders provide the setting or the context for managerial decisions. The decisions must integrate a number of managerial tasks, of which strategy is only one.[5]

The basic element of any framework for organizations must include the central building block of the firm, its people. The job of the CEO is to manage this resource in a way that protects and guards, perhaps the most valuable assest of the firm. By spending a great deal of top management time on the selection, training and grooming of people, the CEO makes the leadership role enormously easier. This is especially true in a world of multiple stakeholders, for the firm, now more than ever, lives in a world as visible as a fishbowl. "Fishbowl management" requires skills that are essentially political skills, and which are not necessarily a part of the formal training of managers, either in schools of management or in their preparation to climb the corporate ladder. By encouraging mentor and teaching relationships among different levels of management, and among the managers in an organization and its stakeholders, the CEO can help his or her people gain the insight necessary to manage in turbulence.

SUMMARY AND FUTURE RESEARCH

The stakeholder concept is deceptively simple. It is "simple" because it is easy to identify those groups and individuals who can affect, or are affected by, the achievement of an organization's purpose. It is "deceptive," because once stakeholders are identified, the task of managing the relationships with them is enormous. The variety of "stakes," the necessity of looking at multiple levels of analysis and the need to invent new processes for taking stakeholder concerns into account make a stakeholder approach to strategic management quite complicated.

The major purpose of this book has been to present the "case" that organizations must deal actively with their stakeholders; to develop a means of addressing this idea through the formulation and implementation processes of chapters Four, Five and Six; and to briefly analyze the resulting implications for the traditional structures and functions of the corporation — especially the board (chapter Seven), the functional disciplines of management (chapter Eight) and the role of the executive (chapter Nine). Much more could and needs to be said about each area. Before outlining a future research program, let me briefly recapitulate the major features of this argument for the stakeholder approach as an alternative means of strategic management.

During the past few years the external environment of most business firms has undergone two kinds of change. The first is change within the traditional business framework of converting raw materials into products to be sold to customers, to provide returns to stockholders and jobs for employees. The second is change external to this framework in the form of the emergence of consumer, environmental and other activist groups; an increase in the scope of government; a global marketplace and the resulting strength of foreign competitors; an increasingly hostile media and a general decline in the level of confidence which members of our society place in the business corporation and its managers. Our framework for interpreting external events needs to be revised in order for it to account for the changes that have occurred, and so that managers can begin to respond in a more effective way to the demands that these changes have wrought.

The concept of "stakeholder" has been put forward as one way to revise the conceptual maps of managers. Drawing on research in strategic planning, systems theory, corporate social responsibility and organization theory, the development of this concept can serve as an integrating force to pull together and interpret a broad base of research. The fact that organizations' environments can be interpreted in stakeholder terms, implies that the concept can serve as an umbrella for the development of an approach to strategic management.

Such an approach to strategic management must encompass at least three levels of analysis. It must help managers understand and interpret who the stakeholders in the firm are, what their stakes are and what the bases are for their claims on the firm. It must help managers to formulate processes for routinely addressing the concerns of stakeholders at a number of organizational levels, from grand strategy to product development. The approach must also give guidance in the mapping and execution of transactions with these stakeholder groups, and help to monitor the progress of these transactions as they relate to the purpose of the organization.

The stakeholder approach yields such concrete analytical tools and managerial processes such as "stakeholder maps and stakes," enterprise strategy formulation and values analysis, strategic program formulation and implementation and monitoring systems.

There are a number of implications of the stakeholder approach for managing the affairs of the corporation. Even if a strictly "stockholder" enterprise strategy is formulated, managers can use stakeholder concepts in interpreting and managing the relationship with the board of directors. By carrying forward the notion of "internal stakeholders" as the conduits to external groups, managers can understand their own functional jobs in a nonhierarchical fashion. Finally, the role of the executive as leader in a "stakeholder-serving" organization is one of corporate spokesperson, political and social participant and manager of the human resources of the firm.

My emphasis has been on beginning to construct an approach to management which takes the external environment into account in a systematic and routine way. I have not concentrated on validating the many claims that I have made over the course of the preceding nine chapters, but rather, by explaining the logic of the concept of stakeholders I have tried to set the stage for future research. There are at least four areas of future investigation which need to be undertaken to turn the stakeholder approach into a full-blown "theory of management." Let me comment briefly on each one.

(1) Stakeholder Theory. Much more work needs to be done in terms of linking the stakeholder concept with other concepts in the disciplines relied upon in this study, primarily the discipline of organization theory, and more so, with economics and political science. My formulation of the "stakeholder dilemma" game is but the tip of the iceberg in applying formal decision theory to gain insight into organizational behavior. The generalization of Porter's work, to include non-industry stakeholders, in applying industrial economics to strategic management has been suggestive of future research rather than definitive. The conceptual schemata which I have employed in defining an organization's stakeholder management capability and its array of generic strategy will yield a number of additional hypotheses, which I have not yet formulated. Finally, more work needs to be done in linking the stakeholder concept to other closely related concepts. Chapter Two only touched on the relevant literature.

(2) Empirical Validity. I summarized in chapter Two a growing body of knowledge using the stakeholder concept to measure the responsiveness of organizations to social issues, but much more work needs to be done. In particular the issues of "keeping score with stakeholders" and "formulating enterprise strategies" lend themselves to empirical tests, quite possibly with easily obtainable data. There is much relevant empirical research that currently exists which can be reinterpreted within the stakeholder framework, and such a revisionist task needs to be undertaken. Many of the hypotheses generated in the present study need to be refined and operationalized for testing. In addition, the clinical methods upon which I have relied heavily in formulating the stakeholder approach are not appropriate to further testing. Conceptual and logical rigor must be enhanced by a careful look at the facts of the matter. Organizational experiments (Evan, 1971) need to be undertaken which go beyond specific clincial interventions.

(3) The Role of Values. It is surprising that in a discipline as "normative" as strategic management (especially with its roots in "business policy") very little attention has been paid to the role of values in the strategy process. The predominant view is that values are person-relative and hence not the province of theorists and practitioners of strategy. I believe, as I have indicated in chapter Four, that such an approach is misguided. There are many things to be said about values which are neither "just opinion," nor dry empirical studies of "what someone's values happen to be" or studies of "opinions held." By paying attention to the logic of value con-

cepts, theorists can develop better descriptions and yield more effective prescriptions for managers. Ultimately, the "stakeholder issue" must be resolved in the arena of "distributive justice." The sledding is rough, but the questions cannot be avoided.

(4) The Manager As Fiduciary To Stakeholders. Perhaps the most important area of future research is the issue of whether or not a theory of management can be constructed that uses the stakeholder concept to enrich "managerial capitalism," that is, can the notion that managers bear a fiduciary relationship to stockholders or the owners of the firm, be replaced by a concept of management whereby the manager *must* act in the interests of the stakeholders in the organization? Such a theory will be difficult to formulate. The range of research which must be addressed is broad, from the effects on a market economy and the existence of "collective choice" rules which are in some sense rational to the effects of such a theory on the individual behavior of managers, employees and stakeholders in the firm. However, it is by addressing such alternatives that we begin to understand organizations and their effects on our society and on ourselves.

The business environment of the 1980s and beyond is complex, to say the least. If the corporation is to successfully meet the challenges posed by this environment, it must begin to adopt integrative strategic management processes which focus the attention of management externally as a matter of routine. Organizational researchers can expedite this process and build theories and models which are both logically rigorous and practically relevant to managers. I have tried to indicate how the stakeholder approach to strategic management can be helpful in beginning this process. The stakes are enormous.

NOTES

1. Galbraith (1973), Galbraith and Nathanson (1978) and Galbraith and Joyce (1983) explore these and other relevant concepts.
2. Of course, the role that is played here must be consistent with the enterprise strategy of the firm, given that the executives know what their enterprise strategy is.
3. I believe that an interesting, yet ignored, source of insight into leadership behavior can be found in several recent books on Vietnam, written as historical novels and oral histories of men and women who served in Vietnam. For example see Caputo (1977), Santoli (1981) and Baker (1981). In general, it could be argued that the liberal arts, literature, philosophy, history, etc., offer a great deal of insight into the concept of leadership. "Scientific" attempts to codify and measure these insights are not always convincing.

4. "Stakeholder" could be taken as an 8th "S" in the Pascale and Athos (1981) framework. However, it is probably conceptually more useful to understand the environment in terms of strategy and the setting or context which it provides for the other managerial variables.

5. My use of "strategic management" has been quite broad, encompassing an analysis of the values of the managers and the organization as well as an analysis of the societal issues affecting the firm. "Enterprise strategy" is a different notion than is usually found in the strategy literature, and as such needs much more clarification and research.

BIBLIOGRAPHY

Aaker, D. and G. Day (eds). 1974. *Consumerism: Search for the Consumer Interest.* New York: The Free Press.

Abell, D. 1980. *Defining the Business.* Englewood Cliffs: Prentice Hall, Inc.

Abell, D. and J. Hammond. 1979. *Strategic Market Planning.* Englewood Cliffs: Prentice Hall, Inc.

Abrams, F. 1954. "Management Responsibilities in a Complex World" in T. Carroll (ed.) *Business Education for Competence and Responsibility.* Chapel Hill: U. of N.C. Press.

Ackerman, R. 1973. "How Companies Respond to Social Demands." *Harvard Business Review* 51(4): 88–98.

Ackerman, R. 1975. *The Social Challenge to Business.* Cambridge: Harvard University Press.

Ackerman, R. and R. Bauer. 1976. *Corporate Social Performance: The Modern Dilemma.* Reston: Reston Publishing Co.

Ackoff, R. 1970. *A Concept of Corporate Planning.* New York: John Wiley and Sons.

Ackoff, R. 1974. *Redesigning the Future.* New York: John Wiley and Sons.

Ackoff, R. 1981. *Creating the Corporate Future.* New York: John Wiley and Sons.

Ackoff, R. and C. Churchman. 1947. "An Experimental Definition of Personality." *Philosophy of Science* 14: 304–332.

Aguilar, F. 1967. *Scanning the Business Environment.* New York: Macmillan Co.

Aldrich, H. 1979. *Organizations and Environments.* Englewood Cliffs: Prentice Hall, Inc.

Aldrich, H. and D. Whetten. 1981. "Organization-sets, Action Sets, and Networks: Making the Most of Simplicity." In P. Nystrom and W. Starbuck (eds.). *Handbook of Organizational Design, Volumes 1 and 2:* Vol. 1, 385–408. New York: Oxford University Press.

Allison, G. 1971. *Essence of Decision.* Boston: Little Brown.

Andrews, K. 1965. *The Concept of Corporate Strategy.* Homewood: R.D. Irwin Inc.

Andrews, K. 1980. *The Concept of Corporate Strategy,* Revised Edition. Homewood: R.D. Irwin Inc.

Ansoff, I. 1965. *Corporate Strategy.* New York: McGraw Hill, Inc.

Ansoff, I. 1975. "Managing Strategic Surprise by Response to Weak Signals." *California Management Review* 18(2): 21–33.

Ansoff, I. 1977. "The State of Practice in Planning Systems." *Sloan Management Review* 18(2): 1–28.

Ansoff, I. 1979. *Strategic Management.* New York: John Wiley and Sons.

Ansoff, I. 1979a. "The Changing Shape of the Strategic Problem." In D. Schendel and C. Hofer (eds.). *Strategic Management: A New View of Business Policy and Planning:* 30–44. Boston: Little Brown and Co.

Ansoff, I., Declerk, R. and R. Hayes (eds.). 1976. *From Strategic Planning to Strategic Management.* New York: John Wiley and Sons.

Argyris, C. 1982. *Reasoning, Learning, and Action.* San Francisco: Jossey Bass.

Astley, G. 1981. "Towards an Appreciation of Collective Strategy." Presented at a conference, "Non-traditional Approaches to Business Policy." Los Angeles, 1981.

Austin, J. 1961. *Philosophical Papers.* Oxford: Oxford University Press.

Bacharach, S. and E. Lawler. 1981. *Bargaining.* San Francisco: Jossey-Bass.

Baker, M. 1981. *NAM.* New York: William Morrow and Co.

Banks, L. 1978. "Taking On The Hostile Media." *Harvard Business Review,* Volume 56(2): 123–130.

Barnard, C. 1938. *The Function of the Executive.* Cambridge: Harvard University Press.

Barnes, B. 1982. *T.S. Kuhn and Social Science.* New York: Columbia University Press.

Bauer, R. and D. Fenn. 1972. *The Corporate Social Audit.* New York: The Russell Sage Foundation.

Beauchamp, T. and N. Bowie (eds.). 1979. *Ethical Theory and Business.* Englewood Cliffs: Prentice-Hall, Inc.

Beckhard, R. 1969. *Organizational Development.* Reading: Addison Wesley.

Beckhard, R. and R. Harris. 1977. *Organizational Transitions.* Reading: Addison Wesley.

Berle, A. and G. Means. 1932. *The Modern Corporation and Private Property.* New York: Commerce Clearing House.

Bower, J. and Y. Doz. 1979. "Strategy Formulation: A Social and Political Process." In D. Schendel and C. Hofer (eds.). *Strategic Management: A New View of Business Policy and Planning:* 152–166. Boston: Little, Brown and Co.

Bowie, N. 1981. *Business Ethics.* Englewood Cliffs: Prentice Hall Inc.

Bradshaw, T. and D. Vogel (eds.). 1981. *Corporations and Their Critics.* New York: McGraw Hill and Co.

Brams, S. 1976. *Paradoxes in Politics.* New York: Free Press.

Brams, S. 1981. *Biblical Games.* Cambridge: MIT Press.

Brandt, R. 1979. *A Theory of the Good and the Right.* Oxford: The Clarendon Press.

Braudel, F. 1981. *The Structures of Everyday Life: Civilization and Capitalism 15th–18th Century: Volume 1.* New York: Harper and Row.

Broder, D. 1981. *Changing of the Guard.* New York: Penguin Books.

Buchanan, J. and G. Tullock. 1965. *The Calculus of Consent.* Ann Arbor: University of Michigan Press.

Burnham, J. 1941. *The Managerial Revolution.* New York: The John Day Co.

Burrell, G. and G. Morgan. 1979. *Sociological Paradigms and Organizational Analysis.* London: Heinemann Books.

Business Week. 1980. "The Reindustrialization of America." June 30, 1980.

Buzzard, W. 1978. "How the Union Got the Upper Hand on J.P. Stevens." *Fortune* June 19, 1978: 86.

Buzzell, R. and F. Wiersema. 1981. "Successful Share Building Strategies." *Harvard Business Review* 59(1): 135–144.

Calleo, D. 1982. *The Imperious Economy.* Cambridge: Harvard University Press.

Caputo, P. 1977. *A Rumor of War.* New York: Ballantine Books.

Carroll, A. and G. Beiler. 1977. "Landmarks in the Evolution of the Social Audit" in Carroll, A. (ed.). 1978. *Managing Corporate Social Responsibility.* Boston: Little, Brown and Co.

Carson, R. 1962. *The Silent Spring.* New York: Fawcett World.

Chakravarthy, B. 1981. *Managing Coal.* Albany: SUNY Press.

Chandler, A. 1962. *Strategy and Structure.* Boston: MIT Press.

Chandler, A. 1977. *The Visible Hand.* Cambridge: Harvard University Press.

Channon, D. 1980. "Business Government Planning Agreements — Ideology Versus Practicality." *Strategic Management Journal* 1(1): 85–97.

Channon, D. 1979. "Commentary." In D. Schendel and C. Hofer (eds.). *Strategic Management: A New View of Business Policy and Planning:* 122–144. Boston: Little, Brown and Co.

Charan, R. 1982. "The Strategic Review Process." *The Journal of Business Strategy* 2(4): 50–60.

Charan, R. and E. Freeman. 1979. "Negotiating with Stakeholders." *Management Review* 68(11): 8–13.

Charan, R. and E. Freeman. 1980. "Planning for the Business Environment of the 1980s." *The Journal of Business Strategy* 1(2): 9–19.

Child, J. 1972. "Organizational Structure, Environment and Performance: The Role of Strategic Choice." *Sociology* 6(1): 1–22.

Child, J. 1979. "Commentary." In D. Schendel and C. Hofer (eds.). *Strategic Management: A New View of Business Policy and Planning:* 172–179. Boston: Little, Brown and Co.

Christensen, R., Andrews, K. and J. Bower. 1980. *Business Policy: Text and Cases.* Homewood: R.D. Irwin Inc.

Churchman, C.W. 1968. *The Systems Approach.* New York: Dell Books.

Churchman, C.W. 1971. *The Design of Inquiring Systems.* New York: Basic Books, Inc.

Churchman, C.W. 1979. *The Systems Approach and Its Enemies.* New York: Basic Books, Inc.

Cummings, T. 1981. "Designing Effective Work Groups." In P. Nystrom and W. Starbuck (eds.). *Handbook of Organizational Design, Volumes 1 and 2:* Vol. 2: 250–271. New York: Oxford University Press.

Cyert, R. and J. March. 1963. *A Behavioral Theory of the Firm.* Englewood Cliffs: Prentice Hall Inc.

Daniels, N. (ed.). 1975. *Reading Rawls.* Oxford: Basil Blackwell.

Davis, P. and E. Freeman. 1978. "Technology Assessment and Idealized Design." In Elton, M., W. Lucas and D. Conrath (eds.). *Evaluating New Telecommunications Services:* 325–344. New York: Plenum Press.

De George R. and J. Pichler (eds.). 1978. *Ethics, Free Enterprise, and Public Policy.* New York: Oxford University Press.

Deal, T. and A. Kennedy. 1982. *Corporate Cultures.* Reading: Addison Wesley.

Descartes, R. c.1628. *Philosophical Works.* Two Volumes, 1911 edition translated by E. Haldane and G. Ross from 17th Century manuscripts. Cambridge: Cambridge University Press.

Derkinderen, F. and R. Crum. 1979. *Project Set Strategies.* Boston: Martinus Nijhoff Publishing.

Dill, W. 1958. "Environment as an Influence on Managerial Autonomy." *Administrative Science Quarterly* 2(4): 409–443.

Dill, W. 1975. "Public Participation in Corporate Planning: Strategic Management in a Kibitzer's World." *Long Range Planning* 8(1): 57–63.

Dill, W. 1976. "Strategic Management in a Kibitzer's World." In I. Ansoff, R. Declerk and R. Hayes (eds.). *From Strategic Planning to Strategic Management:* 125–136. New York: John Wiley and Sons.

Dill, W. 1978. *Running the American Corporation.* Englewood Cliffs: Prentice Hall Inc.

Donaldson, T. 1982. *Corporations and Morality.* Englewood Cliffs: Prentice Hall Inc.

Drucker, P. 1980. *Managing in Turbulent Times*. New York: Harper and Row.

Drucker, P. 1981. "Behind Japan's Success." *Harvard Business Review* 59(1): 83–90.

Duncan, R. 1979. "Qualitative Research Methods in Strategic Management." In D. Schendel and C. Hofer (eds.). *Strategic Management: A New View of Business Policy and Planning:* 424–447. Boston: Little, Brown and Co.

Dutta, B. and W. King. 1980. "A Comparative Scenario Modeling System." *Management Science* 26(3): 261–273.

Emery, F. and E. Trist. 1973. *Towards a Social Ecology*. New York: Plenum Publishing Co.

Emery, F. and E. Trist. 1965. "The Causal Texture of Organizational Environments." *Human Relations* 18: 21–31.

Emshoff, J. 1978. "Experience Generalized Decision Models." Philadelphia: Wharton ARC Working Papers.

Emshoff, J. 1980. *Managerial Breakthroughs*. New York: Amacom.

Emshoff, J. and A. Finnel. 1979. "Designing Corporate Strategy." *Sloan Management Review* 21(3): 41–52.

Emshoff, J. and E. Freeman. 1979. "Who's Butting Into Your Business." *The Wharton Magazine* 1: 44–48, 58–59.

Emshoff, J. and E. Freeman. 1981. "Stakeholder Management: A Case Study of the U.S. Brewers and the Container Issue." *Applications of Management Science,* Volume 1, 57–90.

Emshoff, J. and T. Saaty. 1978. "Prioritized Hierarchies as a Vehicle for Long Range Planning." Philadelphia: Wharton ARC Working Papers No. 11–78.

Epstein, E. 1969. *The Corporation in American Politics*. Englewood Cliffs: Prentice Hall.

Epstein, E. 1980. "Business Political Activity: Research Approaches and Analytical Issues." In L. Preston, (ed.). *Research in Corporate Responsibility and Social Policy, Volume 2*. Greenwich: JAI Press.

Epstein, E. and D. Votaw (eds.). 1978. *Rationality, Legitimacy and Responsibility*. Santa Monica: Goodyear Publishing Co. Inc.

Evan, W. 1966. "The Organization Set: Toward a Theory of Inter-Organizational Relations." In Thompson, J. (ed.). 1966. *Approaches to Organizational Design*. Pittsburgh: University of Pittsburgh Press, 175–190; also in W. Evan. 1976. *Organization Theory: Structures, Systems, and Environments*. New York: John Wiley and Sons.

Evan, W. 1971. *Organizational Experiments*. New York: Harper and Row.

Evan, W. 1972. "An Organization Set Model of Interorganizational Relations." In M. Tuite, M. Radnor and R. Chisholm (eds.). 1972. *Inter-

organizational Decision Making, Chicago: Aldine Publishing, 181-200; also in W. Evan. 1976. *Organization Theory: Structures, Systems, and Environments.* New York: John Wiley and Sons.

Evan, W. 1975. "Power, Conflict and Constitutionalism in Organizations." *Social Science Information* 14: 53-80; also in W. Evan. 1976. *Organization Theory: Structures, Systems, and Environments.* New York: John Wiley and Sons.

Evan, W. 1976. *Organization Theory: Structures, Systems, and Environments.* New York: John Wiley and Sons.

Evan, W. (ed.). 1976. *Interorganizational Relations.* Philadelphia: University of Pennsylvania Press.

Fahey, L. and W. King, 1977. "Environmental Scanning for Corporate Planning." *Business Horizons* August 1977: 61-71.

Fahey, L., W. King and V. Narayana. 1981. "Environmental Scanning and Forecasting in Strategic Planning—The State of the Art." *Long Range Planning* 14: 32-39.

Fenn, D. 1979. "Finding Where the Power Lies in Government." *Harvard Business Review* 57(5): 144-153.

Ferrara, R. and M. Goldfus, 1979. *Everything You Ever Wanted to Know About the Future of Federal Influence in Corporate Governance.* Washington, D.C.: Financial, Government and Public Affairs.

Feyerabend, P. 1975. *Against Method.* New York: Shocken Books.

Frankena, W. 1963. *Ethics.* Englewood Cliffs: Prentice Hall Inc.

Freeman, E. 1977. "McClennen, Harsanyi and the General Theory of Games." *Philosophical Studies* 31: 123-131.

Freeman, E. 1983. "Strategic Management: A Stakeholder Approach." in R. Lamb (ed.) *Advances in Strategic Management,* Vol. 1. Greenwich: JAI Press, 31-60.

Freeman, E. 1983a. "Managing the Strategic Challenge in Telecommunications." *Columbia Journal of World Business.* Spring.

Freeman, E., R. Banker and H. Lee. 1981. "A Stakeholder Approach to Health Care Planning." in C. Tilquin (ed.). 1981. *Systems Sciences in Health Care/Science Des Systemes Dans Le Domaine De La Sante.* Toronto: Pergamon Press Ltd, 909-918.

Freeman, E. and V. Carroll. 1983. "A Stakeholder Approach to Job Design." Philadelphia: Wharton ARC Working Papers.

Freeman, E. and P. Lorange. 1983. "A Heuristic for Research in Strategic Management." Presented at the Strategic Management Conference, Montreal, 1982. Philadelphia: The Wharton School, Policy and Strategy Implementation Research Program Working Papers.

Freeman, E. and D. Reed. 1983. "Stockholders and Stakeholders: A New Perspective on Corporate Governance." In C. Huizinga (ed.). 1983.

Corporate Governance: A Definitive Exploration of the Issues. Los Angeles: University Press.

French, P. 1979. "The Corporation As A Moral Person." *American Philosophical Quarterly* 16: 207-17.

French, P. 1982. "Crowds and Corporations." *American Philosophical Quarterly* 19: 271-277.

Freud, S. 1933. *The Complete Introductory Lectures on Psychoanalysis,* translated and edited by J. Strachey. New York: W.W. Norton.

Friedman, M. 1962. *Capitalism and Freedom.* Chicago: University of Chicago Press.

Galbraith, J. 1973. *Designing Complex Organizatons.* Reading: Addison Wesley.

Galbraith, J. and D. Nathanson. 1978. *Strategy Implementation.* St. Paul: West Publishing Co.

Galbraith, J. and W. Joyce. 1983, in press. *Organization Design.* Reading: Addison Wesley.

Gladwin, T. and I. Walter. 1980. "How Multinationals Can Manage Social and Political Forces." *The Journal of Business Strategy* 1(1): 54-68.

Goldman, A. 1980. *The Moral Foundations of Professional Ethics.* Totowa: Rowman and Littlefield.

Goodman, N. 1955. *Fact, Fiction, and Forecast.* New York: Bobbs Merrill Co.

Goodpaster, K. and J. Mathews. 1982. "Can A Corporation Have A Consscience?" *Harvard Business Review* 60(1): 132-141.

Goodpaster, K. and K. Sayre. 1979. *Ethics and Problems of the 21st Century.* Notre Dame: University of Notre Dame Press.

Grant, J. and W. King. 1979. "Strategy Formulation: Analytical and Normative Models." In D. Schendel and C. Hofer (eds.). *Strategic Management: A New View of Business Policy and Planning:* 104-122. Boston: Little, Brown and Co.

Grant, J. and W. King. 1982. *The Logic of Strategic Planning.* Boston: Little, Brown and Co.

Green, M. and R. Massie. 1980. *The Big Business Reader.* New York: The Pilgrim Press.

Gutting, G. (ed.). 1980. *Paradigms and Revolutions.* Notre Dame: University of Notre Dame Press.

Halberstam, D. 1969. *The Best and the Brightest.* Greenwich: Fawcett Publishing.

Hargreaves, J. and J. Dauman. 1975. *Business Survival and Social Change.* New York: John Wiley and Sons.

Haselhoff, F. 1976. "A New Paradigm for the Study of Organizational Goals." In I. Ansoff, R. Declerk and R. Hayes (eds.). *From Strategic*

Planning to Strategic Management: 15-27. New York: John Wiley and Sons.

Hatten, K. 1979. "Quantitative Research Methods in Strategic Management." In D. Schendel and C. Hofer (eds.) *Strategic Management: A New View of Business Policy and Planning:* 488-467. Boston: Little, Brown and Co.

Hay, R., Gray, E., and J. Gates (eds.). 1976. *Business and Society.* Cincinnati: South Western Publishing Co.

Hayes, R. 1981. "Why Japanese Factories Work." *Harvard Business Review* 59(4): 56-66.

Hayes, R. and W. Abernathy. 1980. "Managing Our Way to Economic Decline." *Harvard Business Review* 58(4): 67-77.

Heenan, D. and H. Perlmutter. 1979. *Multinational Organization Development.* Reading: Addison Wesley.

Hefler, D. 1981. "Global Sourcing: Offshore Investment Strategy for the 1980s." *The Journal of Business Strategy* 2(1): 7-12.

Henderson, B. 1979. *Henderson on Corporate Strategy.* Cambridge: Abt Books.

Herzberg, F. 1966. *Work and the Nature of Man.* Cleveland: World Publishing Co.

Hirsch, P. 1972. "An Organization Set Analysis of Cultural Industry Systems." In W. Evan (ed.). *Interorganizational Relations:* 143-160. Philadelphia: University of Pennsylvania Press.

Hirschman, A. 1970. *Exit, Voice and Loyalty.* Cambridge: Harvard University Press.

Hirschman, A. 1981. *Essays in Trespassing.* Cambridge: Cambridge University Press.

Hirschman, A. 1982. *Shifting Involvements: Private Interest and Public Action.* Princeton: Princeton University Press.

Hofer, C. 1975. "Towards a Contingency Theory of Business Strategy." *Academy of Management Journal* 18: 784-810.

Hofer, C. and T. Haller. 1980. "GLOBESCAN: A Way to Better International Risk Assessment." *The Journal of Business Strategy* 1(2): 41-55.

Hofer, C., E. Murray, R. Charan and R. Pitts. 1980. *Strategic Management.* St. Paul: West Publishing Co.

Hofer C. and D. Schendel. 1978. *Strategy Formulation: Analytical Concepts.* St. Paul: West Publishing Co.

Horwitch, M. 1982. *Clipped Wings: The Story of the American SST.* Cambridge: MIT Press.

Huizinga, C. (ed.). 1983, in press. *Corporate Governance: A Definitive Exploration of the Issues.* Los Angeles: University Press.

Hulin, C. and H. Triandis. 1981. "Meanings of Work in Different Organizational Environments." In P. Nystrom and W. Starbuck (eds.). *Hand-*

book of Organizational Design, Volumes 1 and 2: Volume 2, 336–357. New York: Oxford University Press.

Hussey, D. and M. Langham. 1978. *Corporate Planning: The Human Factor.* Oxford: Pergamon Press.

Jauch, L., R. Osborn and W. Gluek. 1980. "Short Term Financial Success in Large Business Organizations: The Environment Strategy Connection." *Strategic Management Journal* 1(1): 49–64.

Jordan, H. 1982. *Crisis.* New York: G.P. Putnam.

Joyce, W. 1981. "The Michigan Quality of Work Life Program: An Analysis of Assumptions and Method." In A. Van de Ven and W. Joyce (eds.). *Perspectives on Organizational Design and Behavior:* 121–134. New York: John Wiley and Sons.

Kant, I. 1787. *Critique of Pure Reason,* N. Smith (trans. 1929) from 1787 edition. New York: St. Martin's Press.

Katz, D. and R. Kahn. 1966. *The Social Psychology of Organizations.* New York: John Wiley and Sons.

Katz, D., R. Kahn and S. Adams (eds.). 1980. *The Study of Organizations.* San Francisco: Jossey-Bass.

Kelley, W. (ed.). 1973. *New Consumerism: Selected Readings.* Columbus: Grid Inc.

Keim, G. 1978. "Corporate Social Responsibility: An Assessment of the Enlightened Self-Interest Model." *Academy of Management Review* January 1978: 32–39.

Keim, G. 1978a. "Managerial Behavior and the Social Responsibility Debate: Goals vs. Constraints." *Academy of Management Journal* 21: 57–68.

Kerr, S. 1975. "On the Folly of Rewarding A While Hoping for B." *Academy of Management Journal* 18: 769–783.

Kidder, T. 1981. *The Soul of a New Machine.* New York: Atlantic Books.

King, W. 1978. "Strategic Planning for Management Information Systems." *MIS Quarterly* March 1978: 27–37.

King, W. 1981a. "The Importance of Strategic Issues." *The Journal of Business Strategy* 1(3): 74–76.

King, W. and D. Cleland. 1978. *Strategic Planning and Policy.* New York: Van Nostrand Reinhold Co.

Klein, H. 1979. "Commentary." In D. Schendel and C. Hofer (eds.). *Strategic Management: A New View of Business Policy and Planning:* 144–151. Boston: Little, Brown and Co.

Kleinfeld, S. 1981. *The Largest Company of Earth.* New York: Harper and Row.

Kotter, J. 1979. *Power in Management.* New York: AMACOM.

Kotter, J. 1978. *Organizational Dynamics.* Reading: Addison Wesley.

Kotter, J. 1982. *The General Managers.* New York: The Free Press.

Kovacks, K. 1978. "How the Union Got the Upper Hand on J.P. Stevens." *Fortune* June 19, 1978: 86.

Kuhn, T. 1970. *The Structure of Scientific Revolutions,* 2nd Edition. Chicago: University of Chicago Press.

Lakatos, I. and A. Musgrave (eds.). 1970. *Criticism and the Growth of Knowledge.* Cambridge: Cambridge University Press.

Lasch, C. 1978. *The Culture of Narcissism.* New York: W.W. Norton Co.

Lawrence, P. and J. Lorsch. 1967. *Organization and Environment.* Homewood: R.D. Irwin.

Lenz, R. 1980. "Environment, Strategy, Organization Structure and Performance." *Strategic Management Journal* 1(3): 209-226.

Levinson, D. 1978. *The Seasons of a Man's Life.* New York: Alfred Knopf.

Levy, L. 1981. "Reforming Board Reform." *Harvard Business Review* 59(1): 166-172.

Levy, L. 1982. "Some Problems in Board Research." Presented to The Academy of Management, New York.

Lindbloom, C. 1977. *Politics and Markets.* New York: Basic Books Inc.

Lorange, P. 1979. "Formal Planning Systems: Their Role in Strategy Formulation and Implementation." In D. Schendel and C. Hofer (eds.). *Strategic Management: A New View of Business Policy and Planning:* 226-241. Boston: Little, Brown and Co.

Lorange, P. 1980. *Corporate Planning: An Executive Viewpoint.* Englewood Cliffs: Prentice Hall, Inc.

Lorange, P. 1983, in press. "Strategic Control." In R. Lamb (ed.). *Latest Advances in Strategic Management.* Englewood Cliffs: Prentice Hall.

Luce, D. and H. Raiffa. 1957. *Games and Decisions.* New York: John Wiley and Sons.

MacIntyre, A. 1981. *After Virtue.* Notre Dame: University of Notre Dame Press.

MacMillan, I. 1978. *Strategy Formulation: Political Concepts.* St. Paul: West Publishing Co.

Mahon, J. 1981. *The Corporate Public Affairs Office: Structure, Process and Impact.* Doctoral dissertation, Boston University.

Mahon, J. 1982. "The Thompson-Page Contribution to Social Issues Research." In L. Preston (ed.). *Research in Corporate Responsibility and Social Policy,* Volume 4: 57-76. Greenwich: JAI Press.

Mason, R. and I. Mitroff, 1982. *Challenge Strategic Planning Assumptions.* New York: John Wiley and Sons.

McCaskey, M. 1982. *The Executive Challenge.* Marshfield: Pitman Publishing Inc.

McDonald, J. 1977. *The Game of Business.* New York: Anchor Press.

McQuaid, K. 1982. *Big Business and Presidential Power.* New York: W. Morrow and Co.

Mendelow, A. 1981. "The Stakeholder Approach to Organizational Effectiveness." Pretoria: School of Business Leadership, University of South Africa.

Merton, R. 1957. *Social Theory and Social Structure*. Glencoe: The Free Press.

Miles, R. 1982. *Coffin Nails and Corporate Strategies*. Englewood Cliffs: Prentice Hall Inc.

Miller, H. and W. Williams (eds.). 1982. *The Limits of Utilitarianism*. Minneapolis: University of Minnesota Press.

Mills, T. 1978. "Europe's Industrial Democracy: An American Response." *Harvard Business Review* 56(6): 143-152.

Miner, J. 1979. "Commentary." In D. Schendel and C. Hofer (eds.). *Strategic Management: A New View of Business Policy and Planning:* 289-296. Boston: Little, Brown and Co.

Mintzberg, H. 1979. "Organizational Power and Goals: A Skeletal Theory." In D. Schendel and C. Hofer (eds.). *Strategic Management: A New View of Business Policy and Planning:* 64-80. Boston: Little, Brown and Co.

Mintzberg, H. 1979a. *The Structuring of Organizations*. Englewood Cliffs: Prentice Hall, Inc.

Mitnick, B. 1980. "The Concept of Constituency." Presented to The Academy of Management, Detroit; University of Pittsburgh, Graduate School of Management, Working Paper WP-376.

Mitroff, I. and J. Emshoff. 1979. "On Strategic Assumption-Making." *Academy of Management Review* 4(1): 1-12.

Mohr, L. 1982. *Explaining Organizational Behavior*. San Francisco: Jossey-Bass.

Murray, E. 1976. "The Social Response Process in Commercial Banks." *Academy of Management Review* 1(3): 5-15.

Muzzio, D. 1982. *Watergate Games*. New York: New York University Press.

Nader, R. 1972. *Unsafe At Any Speed*. New York: Grossman Publishers.

Nash, L. 1981. "Ethics Without the Sermon." *Harvard Business Review* 59(1): 79-90.

Negandhi, A. (ed.). 1975. *Interorganization Theory*. Canton: The Kent State University Press.

Nystrom, P. 1981. "Designing Jobs and Assigning Employees." In P. Nystrom and W. Starbuck (eds.). *Handbook of Organizational Design, Volumes 1 and 2:* Volume 2, 272-301. New York: Oxford University Press.

Nystrom, P. and W. Starbuck (eds.). 1981. *Handbook of Organizational Design, Volumes 1 and 2*. New York: Oxford University Press.

Orwell, G. 1949. *1984*. New York: New American Library.

Ouchi, W. 1981. *Theory Z*. Reading: Addison Wesley.

Pascale, R. and A. Athos. 1981. *The Art of Japanese Management*. New York: Simon and Schuster.

Pennings, J. 1981. "Strategically Interdependent Organizations." In P. Nystrom and W. Starbuck (eds.). *Handbook of Organizational Design, Volumes 1 and 2:* Volume 1, 433–455. New York: Oxford University Press.

Pertschuk, M. 1982. *Revolt Against Regulation*. Berkeley: University of California Press.

Peters, T. 1981. *The Excellent Company Study*. New York: McKinsey and Co.

Peters, T. and R. Waterman. 1982. *In Search of Excellence.* New York: Harper and Row.

Pfeffer, J. 1981. *Power in Organizations*. Marshfield: Pitman Publishing Inc.

Pfeffer, J. and G. Salancik. 1978. *The External Control of Organizations*. New York: Harper and Row.

Pinder, C. and F. Moore (eds.). 1980. *Middle Range Theory and the Study of Organizations*. Boston: Martinus Nijhoff Publishing Co.

Porter, M. 1980. *Competitive Strategy*. New York: Macmillan Publishing Co.

Post, J. 1978. *Corporate Behavior and Social Change*. Reston: Reston Publishing Co.

Post, J. 1981. "Research in Business and Society: Current Issues and Approaches." Presented at AACSB Conference on Business Environment/Public Policy and the Business School of the 1980s, Berkeley, 1981.

Post, J., E. Murray, R. Dickie and J. Mahon. 1982. "The Public Affairs Function in American Corporations: Development and Relations with Corporate Planning." *Long Range Planning* 15(2): 12–21.

Preston, L. 1979. *Research in Corporate Responsibility and Social Policy,* Volume 1. Greenwich: JAI Press.

Preston, L. 1980. *Research in Corporate Responsibility and Social Policy,* Volume 2. Greenwich: JAI Press.

Preston, L. 1981. *Research in Corporate Responsibility and Social Policy,* Volume 3. Greenwich: JAI Press.

Preston, L. 1982. *Research in Corporate Responsibility and Social Policy,* Volume 4. Greenwich: JAI Press.

Quine, W. 1960. *Word and Object*. Cambridge: Harvard University Press.

Rawls, J. 1971. *A Theory of Justice*. Cambridge: Harvard University Press.

Rhenman, E. 1968. *Industrial Democracy and Industrial Management*. London: Tavistock Publications Ltd.

Rhenman, E. 1973. *Organization Theory for Long Range Planning*. New York: John Wiley and Sons.

Rothschild, W. 1976. *Putting It All Together.* New York: AMACOM.

Rowe, A., R. Mason and K. Dickel. 1982. *Strategic Management and Business Policy.* Reading: Addison Wesley.

Rudner, R. 1966. *Philosophy of Social Science.* Englewood Cliffs: Prentice Hall Inc.

Rumelt, R. 1979. "Evaluation of Strategy: Theory and Models." In D. Schendel and C. Hofer (eds.). *Strategic Management: A New View of Business Policy and Planning:* 196-212. Boston: Little, Brown and Co.

Sametz, A. 1981. "Strategic Responses to Today's Turbulent Financial Markets." *The Journal of Business Strategy* 2(1): 39-51.

Sampson, A. 1975. *The Seven Sisters.* New York: Viking Press.

Santoli, A. 1981. *Everything We Had.* New York: Random House.

Sass, S. 1982. *The Pragmatic Imagination: A History of the Wharton School 1881-1981.* Philadelphia: University of Pennsylvania Press.

Schein, E. 1978. *Career Dynamics.* Reading: Addison Wesley.

Schein, E. 1980. *Organizational Psychology.* Englewood Cliffs: Prentice Hall.

Schelling, T. 1960. *The Strategy of Conflict.* Cambridge: Harvard University Press.

Schelling, T. 1978. *Micromotives and Macrobehavior.* New York: W.W. Norton Co.

Schellenberg, J. 1982. *The Science of Conflict.* New York: Oxford University Press.

Schendel, D. and C. Hofer (eds.). 1979. *Strategic Management: A New View of Business Policy and Planning.* Boston: Little, Brown and Co.

Schendel, D. and C. Hofer. 1979a. "Introduction." In D. Schendel and C. Hofer (eds.). *Strategic Management: A New View of Business Policy and Planning:* 1-22. Boston: Little, Brown and Co.

Schlesinger, A. 1965. *A Thousand Days.* New York: Fawcett Books.

Scott, B. 1981. "OPEC, the American Scapegoat." *Harvard Business Review* 59(1): 6-30.

Scott, W. and D. Hart. 1979. *Organizational America.* Boston: Houghton Mifflin Co.

Seashore, S. 1981. "The Michigan Quality of Worklife Program." In A. Van de Ven and W. Joyce (eds.). *Perspectives on Organizational Design and Behavior:* 89-120. New York: John Wiley and Sons.

Sen, A. and B. Williams (eds.). 1982. *Utilitarianism and Beyond.* Cambridge: Cambridge University Press.

Sethi, P. 1970. *Business Corporations and the Black Man.* Scranton: Chandler Publishing Co.

Sethi, P. 1971. *Up Against the Corporate Wall.* Englewood Cliffs: Prentice Hall, Inc.

Sethi, P. and J. Post. 1979. "Public Consequences of Private Actions." *California Management Review* 21(4): 35–48.

Singer, P. 1979. *Practical Ethics*. Cambridge: Cambridge University Press.

Smith, A. 1759. *The Theory of Moral Sentiments*. Indianapolis: Liberty Fund Inc., 1976 edition by E.G. West.

Sonnenfeld, J. 1981. *Corporate Views of the Public Interest*. Boston: Auburn House.

Spender, J. 1979. "Commentary." In D. Schendel and C. Hofer (eds.). *Strategic Management: A New View of Business Policy and Planning:* 394–404. Boston: Little, Brown and Co.

Steckmest, F. 1982. *Corporate Performance*. New York: McGraw Hill.

Steiner, G. 1979. "Contingency Theories of Strategy and Strategic Management." In D. Schendel and C. Hofer (eds.). *Strategic Management: A New View of Business Policy and Planning:* 405–416. Boston: Little, Brown and Co.

Stobaugh, R. and D. Yergin. 1979. *Energy Future*. New York: Random House.

Sturdivant, F. 1981. *Business and Society,* Revised Edition. Homewood: R.D. Irwin Inc.

Sturdivant, F. 1977. *Business and Society*. Homewood: R.D. Irwin Inc.

Sturdivant F. 1979. "Executives and Activists: A Test of Stakeholder Management." *California Management Review* 22(1): 53–59.

Sturdivant, F. and J. Ginter. 1977. "Corporate Social Responsiveness: Management Attitudes and Economic Performance." *California Management Review* 19: 30–39.

Sturdivant, F. and L. Robinson (eds.). 1981. *The Corporate Social Challenge*. Homewood: R.D. Irwin Inc.

Taylor, B. 1971. "The Future Development of Corporate Strategy." *The Journal of Business Policy* 2(2): 22–38.

Taylor, B. 1977. "Managing the Process of Corporate Development." In B. Taylor and J. Sparkes (eds.). *Corporate Strategy and Planning*. New York: John Wiley and Sons.

Terreberry, S. 1968. "The Evolution of Organizational Environments." *Administrative Science Quarterly*. 12(4): 590–613.

Thompson, J. 1967. *Organizations in Action*. New York: McGraw Hill.

Tiffany, P. 1982. "Industrial Policy in American Steel, 1945–1960: A Study in Failure." Philadelphia: The Wharton School, Department of Management, Working Papers.

Trist, E. 1981. "The Socio-Technical Perspective." In A. Van de Ven and W. Joyce (eds.). *Perspectives on Organizational Design and Behavior:* 19–75. New York: John Wiley and Sons.

Tushman, M. 1977. "A Political Approach to Organizations." *Academy of Management Review* 2: 206-216.

Utterback, J. 1979. "Environmental Analysis and Forecasting." In D. Schendel and C. Hofer (eds.). *Strategic Management: A New View of Business Policy and Planning:* 134-144. Boston: Little, Brown and Co.

Van de Ven, A. and G. Astley. 1983, in press. "Central Perspectives and Debates in Organization Theory." *Administrative Science Quarterly* 28(2): 245-273.

Van de Ven, A. and E. Freeman. 1983. "Three R's of Administrative Behavior: Rational, Random and Reasonable." Minneapolis: University of Minnesota, Graduate School of Management, Working Papers.

Van de Ven, A. and W. Joyce (eds.). 1981. *Perspectives on Organizational Design and Behavior.* New York: John Wiley and Sons.

Van de Ven, A., D. Emmett and R. Koenig. 1975. "Frameworks for Interorganizational Analysis." In A. Negandhi. *Interorganization Theory:* 19-38. Canton: The Kent State University Press.

Vancil, R. 1979. *Decentralization.* Homewood: Dow-Jones Irwin Co.

Vernon, R. 1977. *Storm Over the Multinationals.* Cambridge: Harvard University Press.

Vogel, D. 1978. *Lobbying the Corporation.* New York: Basic Books Inc.

Von Neumann, J. and O. Morgenstern. 1946. *The Theory of Games and Economic Behavior,* Second Edition. New York: John Wiley and Sons.

Votaw, D. 1964. *The Six-Legged Dog.* Berkeley: University of California Press.

Votaw, D. and P. Sethi. 1974. *The Corporate Dilemma: Traditional Values Versus Contemporary Problems.* Englewood Cliffs: Prentice Hall Inc.

Watzlawick, P., J. Weakland and R. Fisch. 1974. *Change.* New York: W.W. Norton Co.

Weidenbaum, M. 1980. "Public Policy No Longer A Spectator Sport For Business." *The Journal of Business Strategy* 1(1): 46-53.

Weston, F. and E. Brigham. 1978. *Managerial Finance.* Hinsdale: The Dryden Press.

Wheelwright, S. 1981. "Japan — Where Operations Really Are Strategic," *Harvard Business Review,* 59(4): 67-74.

White, M. 1981. *What is and What Ought to Be Done.* New York: Oxford Press.

White, T. 1982. *America in Search of Itself.* New York: Harper and Row.

Williamson, O. 1964. *The Economics of Discretionary Behavior.* Englewood Cliffs: Prentice Hall Inc.

Williamson, O. 1975. *Markets and Hierarchies.* New York: The Free Press.

Wilson, G. 1981. *Interest Groups in the United States.* New York: Oxford University Press.

Wind, Y. and V. Mahajan. 1981. "Designing Product and Business Portfolios." *Harvard Business Review* 59(1): 155–165.
Wisdom, J. 1953. *Philosophy and Psychoanalysis.* Oxford: Basil Blackwell.
Wittgenstein, L. 1953. *Philosophical Investigations.* London: Macmillan.
Yankelovich, D. 1981. *The New Rules.* New York: Basic Books.
Zentner, R. 1981. "How to Evaluate the Present and Future Corporate Environment." *The Journal of Business Strategy,* 1(4): 42–51.

INDEX

intrinsic, 96, 97, 98, 99, 102, 105
moral, 96
organizational, 97, 98, 99, 110
religious, 96
role of, 248–249
shared, 89, 163–164, 242
social, 96
stakeholder, 99
Vancil, R., 86, 215
Van de Ven, A., 42, 43
Variance analysis, 171
Vertical integration, 35
Visible benefits, 164, 240
Visible costs, 164, 240
Vogel, D., 203
Voice, 19, 60, 62, 197, 206, 207, 236
Voluntarism, 20, 74–80, 211
Votaw, D., 38, 39
Voting, 19, 26, 146

cumulative, 196, 200
policies on, 207
shareholder, 207
Voting power, 61, 207, 212

Wall Street Journal, 9
Wall Street Rule 9, 197
Watch-dog view of government, 13
Watergate, 22, 96, 168
Waterman, R., 10, 77, 89, 103
Weidenbaum, M., 14
Wellen Company, 224
West Germany, 232
Whetten, D., 43
Williamson, O., 108

Zero-based budgeting, 156
"Zone of acceptance," 245